Into English

POEMS,

TRANSLATIONS,

COMMENTARIES

....

Martha Collins
and
Kevin Prufer

EDITORS

GRAYWOLF PRESS

Permission acknowledgments begin on page 193.

This publication is made possible, in part, by the voters of Minnesota
through a Minnesota State Arts Board Operating Support grant, thanks
to a legislative appropriation from the arts and cultural heritage fund,
and a grant from the Wells Fargo Foundation. Significant support has also
been provided by Target, the McKnight Foundation, the Lannan Foundation,
the Amazon Literary Partnership, and other generous contributions
from foundations, corporations, and individuals.
To these organizations and individuals we offer our heartfelt thanks.

Published by Graywolf Press
250 Third Avenue North, Suite 600
Minneapolis, Minnesota 55401

www.graywolfpress.org

Published in the United States of America

ISBN 978-1-55597-792-4

2 4 6 8 10 9 7 5 3

Library of Congress Control Number: 2017930118

Cover design: Kyle G. Hunter
Cover art: iStock

Contents

vii   Introduction by Martha Collins

3   **Sappho** *(Ancient Greek, circa 620–570 BCE)*
TRANSLATIONS BY Anne Carson, Willis Barnstone, Mary Barnard
COMMENTARY BY Karen Emmerich

11   **Virgil** *(Latin, 70–19 BCE)*
TRANSLATIONS BY Kristina Chew, Peter Fallon, Janet Lembke
COMMENTARY BY Carl Phillips

19   **Tao Qian** *(Chinese, 365–427)*
TRANSLATIONS BY James Hightower, Stephen Owen, David Hinton
COMMENTARY BY Arthur Sze

25   **San Juan de la Cruz/St. John of the Cross** *(Spanish, 1542–1591)*
TRANSLATIONS BY Roy Campbell, John Frederick Nims,
Antonio de Nicolás
COMMENTARY BY Willis Barnstone

33   **Bashō** *(Japanese, 1644–1694)*
TRANSLATIONS BY Basil Hall Chamberlain, Harold G. Henderson,
Nobuyuki Yuasa
COMMENTARY BY Hiroaki Sato

41   **Giacomo Leopardi** *(Italian, 1798–1837)*
TRANSLATIONS BY Kenneth Rexroth, Eamon Grennan,
Jonathan Galassi
COMMENTARY BY Susan Stewart

49   **Charles Baudelaire** *(French, 1821–1867)*
TRANSLATIONS BY Rosemary Lloyd, Keith Waldrop, Louise Varèse
COMMENTARY BY Cole Swensen

55   **Stéphane Mallarmé** *(French, 1842–1898)*
TRANSLATIONS BY Roger Fry, Daisy Aldan, Peter Manson
COMMENTARY BY Jennifer Moxley

63   **C. P. Cavafy** *(Greek, 1863–1933)*
TRANSLATIONS BY John Mavrogordato, Daniel Mendelsohn,
Avi Sharon
COMMENTARY BY George Kalogeris

71   **Rainer Maria Rilke** *(German, 1875–1926)*
TRANSLATIONS BY M. D. Herter Norton, J. B. Leishman, Robert Bly
COMMENTARY BY David Young

77   **Yahya Kemal Beyatlı** *(Turkish, 1884–1958)*
TRANSLATIONS BY Roger Finch, Sidney Wade and Yurdanur Salman,
Bernard Lewis
COMMENTARY BY Sidney Wade

83   **Anna Akhmatova** *(Russian, 1889–1966)*
TRANSLATIONS BY Gerard Shelley, Andrey Kneller, Stephen Berg
COMMENTARY BY Joanna Trzeciak Huss

91   **Boris Pasternak** *(Russian, 1890–1960)*
TRANSLATIONS BY Lydia Pasternak Slater, Jon Stallworthy and
Peter France, James E. Falen
COMMENTARY BY J. Kates

99   **César Vallejo** *(Spanish, 1892–1938)*
TRANSLATIONS BY Clayton Eshleman, Rebecca Seiferle, Barry Fogden
COMMENTARY BY Cindy Schuster

107   **Federico García Lorca** *(Spanish, 1898–1936)*
TRANSLATIONS BY W. S. Merwin, Catherine Brown, Michael Smith
COMMENTARY BY Rebecca Seiferle

113   **Xu Zhimo** *(Chinese, 1897–1931)*
TRANSLATIONS BY Kai-yu Hsu, Michelle Yeh, Hugh Grigg
COMMENTARY BY Bonnie S. McDougall

123   **Carlos Drummond de Andrade** *(Portuguese, 1902–1987)*
TRANSLATIONS BY Virginia de Araújo, John Nist, Kay Cosgrove
COMMENTARY BY Ellen Doré Watson

131   **Sophia de Mello Breyner Andresen** *(Portuguese, 1919–2004)*
TRANSLATIONS BY Ruth Fainlight, Richard Zenith, Lisa Sapinkopf
COMMENTARY BY Alexis Levitin

139   **Paul Celan** *(German, 1920–1970)*
TRANSLATIONS BY Michael Hamburger, John Felstiner,
Jerome Rothenberg
COMMENTARY BY Stephen Tapscott

147   **Wisława Szymborska** *(Polish, 1923–2012)*
TRANSLATIONS BY Magnus J. Kryński and Robert A. Maguire,
Stanisław Barańczak and Clare Cavanagh,
Joanna Trzeciak
COMMENTARY BY Alissa Valles

155   **Yehuda Amichai** *(Hebrew, 1924–2000)*
TRANSLATIONS BY Glenda Abramson, Benjamin and Barbara Harshav,
Robert Alter
COMMENTARY BY Chana Bloch

163   **Adonis** *(Arabic, b. 1930)*
TRANSLATIONS BY Samuel Hazo, Adnan Haydar and Michael Beard,
Khaled Mattawa
COMMENTARY BY Kareem James Abu-Zeid

169   **Tomas Tranströmer** *(Swedish, 1931–2015)*
TRANSLATIONS BY Robin Fulton, May Swenson and Leif Sjöberg,
Robin Robertson
COMMENTARY BY Johannes Göransson

177   **Marin Sorescu** *(Romanian, 1936–1996)*
TRANSLATIONS BY John F. Deane, W. D. Snodgrass with Dona Roşu
and Luciana Costea, David Constantine with
Joana Russell-Gebbett
COMMENTARY BY Adam J. Sorkin

185   **Félix Morisseau-Leroy** *(Haitian Creole, 1912–1998)*
TRANSLATIONS BY Mary Birnbaum, David Brooks Andrews,
Molly Lynn Watt, Ruby Poltorak
COMMENTARY BY Danielle Legros Georges

193   Acknowledgments

199   About the Contributors

203   About the Editors

Introduction by Martha Collins

Translating a poem into another language—its content, its form, its tone, its nuances—is, as almost everyone who has done it knows, a difficult business. But it also has enormous rewards: for the translator, for the reader, for poetry itself.

Some years ago, I was asked to teach a workshop about this impossible process. Among other materials, including essays about translation, I gave the participants two side-by-side English translations of a poem by Pablo Neruda, along with the original Spanish. Those translations proved to be the most valuable resource I offered. Seeing what different translators have done with the same poem immediately eliminates easy assumptions that beginning translators often make: that there is a single way, a most correct way, or a best way to translate a poem.

The packet of materials began to grow. Soon I had made several compilations of translations, illustrating different kinds of choices translators invariably make, whether they do so consciously or not. Sometime after that, I began asking the students themselves to compile multiple translations of a single poem for class presentation. Their compilations, added to mine, became our most essential "textbook," and gave us an excellent basis for asking important questions about literary translation.

We might begin by asking where, on a continuum ranging from the most "literal" to the most "free," a particular translation lies. (As Willis Barnstone notes in his commentary in this volume, most translations lie somewhere in between.) Where, on another continuum between most loyal to form and most free of it, does a translation of a formal poem lie? What is gained by attempting to replicate meter and/or rhyme, and what is lost? What about levels of diction? More generally, what is the stylistic "register" of a translation, ranging from formal to colloquial, or is there a mixture of styles? If the latter, does this reflect the original poem, or is it an unfortunate (or deliberate) result of the translation? If the poem isn't contemporary, what is gained and what is lost by moving the poem toward modern and even contemporary English? Beyond style, does a translation substitute contemporary references for original ones? At what point does a translation become (in a term introduced by John Dryden in the seventeenth century and used by Robert Lowell in the twentieth) an "imitation"—or, beyond even that, a poem in its own right that might make reference to the original by inscribing *"after Pablo Neruda"* (or whomever) beneath the title?

In addition to these general "continuum" questions are more-specific ones. An examination of multiple translations will confirm what any dual-language dictionary tells us: there are many ways to translate even single words. This is especially true in English, which has, thanks to its multiple origins, an enormous vocabulary. At the same time, other languages have many words to express what we in English consider to be not only a single word but a single concept; that English, having dispensed with "thee" and "thou," has only one word for "you" is an obvious example.

And then there is syntax, the principles by which words are arranged in sentences, which differs considerably from language to language. A so-called literal translation of a French or Spanish poem would have us saying "the tree bare" instead of "the bare tree"—a distinction that might be especially interesting if a line break occurred between the noun and the adjective, since the Romance language would allow us to perceive the general term before its modification. Does a translation attempt in some way to replicate the order in which the original words appear, or is it more interested in keeping the stylistic simplicity or complexity of the original syntax?

All of this is not to mention the knottier problems that most of the contributors to this volume discuss. A translation may go smoothly for a while, and then come upon a section or line that, for any number of reasons (semantic, syntactic, stylistic, cultural), runs into trouble. The trouble spots are the places where multiple translations are most apt to differ. Looking at them carefully can take us more deeply into the nuances of both the original language and English—and, more generally, challenge our assumptions about how language itself works. More specifically, multiple translations can give us a much better sense of the poem than a single translation can, so that even if we can't read the poem in the original language, we can come closer to that experience.

All these benefits began to suggest that an anthology of multiple translations might be a good idea, even a necessary one. There were, as I discovered, a few related resources. One of them, an invaluable essay by Margaret Sayers Peden that presents nine versions of a sonnet by Sor Juana Inés de la Cruz, appears in a book of essays I was using, John Biguenet and Rainer Schulte's *The Craft of Translation* (1989). Then I found Eliot Weinberger's *19 Ways of Looking at Wang Wei* (1987), a pocket-size anthology of seventeen translations, plus the original and a transliteration into the Roman alphabet, of a four-line Chinese poem, with short commentaries on each. Similarly, an essay by Joshua Cohen, published in *The American Voice* in 1988, includes several translations—a "Choral Rendering," Cohen calls it—of Carlos Oquendo de Amat's poem "Rain," written in Spanish. Still later I would find Hiroaki Sato's *One Hundred Frogs* (1995), with its many translations of a famous haiku by Bashō, and Douglas R. Hofstadter's *Le Ton Beau de Marot: In Praise of the Music of Language* (1997), which includes eighty-eight translations of a sixteenth-century French poem, ranging from close-to-the-original to off-the-charts free. I finally discovered an actual anthology of multiple translations, compiled and edited by the distinguished translator Rainer Schulte. But the book, which was custom published and included no commentary, was so thoroughly unavailable that the only way I could get it was to accept the editor's generous gift of one of his few copies.

Useful as these resources were, they made the need for a new anthology seem even more pressing. And so began a great deal of deliberation, leading to conversations with Kevin Prufer about how multiple translations of several poems might be compiled and presented. Out of that deliberation and those conversations came *Into English*.

Our first step was to ask several translators whose work we knew to choose a poem and three translations of it, and then to write a commentary about what they had chosen. We aimed for a range of languages and periods, but knew from the beginning that several compromises would be necessary. Foremost among them: the book could not claim to be representative of the enormous diversities of people and poetries in the non-English-speaking world, past and present. We would be limited to a tiny sample.

Beyond this, each poem in the book would have to have been translated several times. At a time when the vast majority of established non-English-language poets aren't translated for English-speaking readers at all, we knew we'd be drawing from a very small pool of very well-known poets, mostly poets of previous generations who have achieved renown internationally, whose works have been assessed and reassessed by readers, often over decades and even centuries. While this kind of selection says a great deal about the values and sensibilities of poets, scholars, and translators of the past and present, it also says a great deal about the limitations of our English-speaking literary culture, which has for the most part been as Eurocentric as our general culture. A notable reality is that the book you hold in your hands includes not a single poet from Africa. Readers will also notice that we've included more than one contribution from Chinese, French, German, Portuguese, Russian, and Spanish—languages pursued much more frequently by English and American translators.

For similar reasons, female poets are also underrepresented. Although our contributors include slightly more women than men, a large majority of the poets they chose to discuss are male. This is not surprising. Historically, recognized male poets have, due to educational opportunities as well as cultural biases, far outnumbered female poets. Since it takes time for poets to achieve the kind of recognition that makes translations of a work common, multiple English translations of male poets far outnumber those of female poets, and the contents of this book necessarily reflect that unfortunate fact.

Other limitations have to do with the format and aims of the book. First of all, the translated poems had to be short enough that readers could experience them side by side—preferably on two facing pages. It was also important that the book function not merely as a series of meditations on the art of literary translation, but as an enjoyable volume of excellent literary translation in itself. For this reason, we asked our contributors not to select translations they thought were substandard or seriously flawed. We also asked that, wherever possible, they not select their own translations, although it would be fine to offer their personal insights and solutions to difficult problems, or to include their own translations, or parts thereof, within their commentaries.

We were fortunate in our choice of contributors, all of whom are translators of great skill and experience who have thought deeply about the complex issues surrounding translation and poetics; the majority are poets themselves. We aimed for linguistic diversity in extending invitations, but the choice of poet and even of period was for the most part left to the contributors. And since several of them had translated from more than one language, even the choice of language was occasionally a surprise to us.

But the book, arranged chronologically, ends up reflecting in a very general way a history of literary translation into English, and in the process begins to suggest the importance of that history (as well as its limitations). For without translation, our poetic tradition would be a radically different thing, and a poorer one.

For example, there would have been no literary Renaissance in the sixteenth and seventeenth centuries without the classics, represented here by Virgil's Latin, or the influence of Italian and French poetry. As the mention of Alexander Pope's translation of the *Iliad* in George Kalogeris's commentary implies, the importance of literary translation extended into the eighteenth century, and the early nineteenth century produced one of the most famous poems ever written on the subject. Often cited as a poem about *poetry*, John Keats's "On First Looking into Chapman's Homer" is in fact also a poem about *translation*—for without Chapman, Keats could not have read Homer.

> Much have I travell'd in the realms of gold,
>   And many goodly states and kingdoms seen:
>   Round many western islands have I been
> Which bards in fealty to Apollo hold.
> Oft of one wide expanse had I been told
>   That deep-brow'd Homer ruled as his demesne;
>   Yet did I never breathe its pure serene
> Till I heard Chapman speak out loud and bold:

> Then felt I like some watcher of the skies
>   When a new planet swims into his ken;
> Or like stout Cortez when with eagle eyes
>   He star'd at the Pacific—and all his men
> Look'd at each other with a wild surmise—
>   Silent, upon a peak in Darien.

A new planet, a new-to-European eyes ocean—that's what George Chapman's translation was for Keats.[1]

By the late nineteenth century and into the early twentieth, translations of poems had begun to appear more rapidly, more frequently, and with more attention to accuracy. Particularly important for their influence on what we now call "modern" poetry were the late-nineteenth-century French poets, represented here by Charles Baudelaire and Stéphane Mallarmé. While writers like T. S. Eliot were reading these poets in the original (as many earlier poets had read the classics), translations brought them to a wider audience of poets and readers, and thus extended their influence. In the same early modern period, influenced by the imagist movement, Chinese and Japanese poetry began to be more widely read, often, in the former case, through the medium of Ezra Pound's translations. As their appearance in this anthology suggests, translations from both languages have continued to proliferate and influence a wide range of readers and writers; witness, among other trends, the popularity of Japanese haiku.

In the middle of the twentieth century, many American poets began to read and translate more-recent works from both South America and an expanded Europe. Robert Bly and W. S. Merwin (whose translations appear in this volume) were among the poets who began to translate more widely from Eastern European, Scandinavian, and Spanish-language poetry. New Directions had been publishing translations in their annual anthologies for some time, and Bly's editorship of the magazine and press called *The Fifties* (later *The Sixties* and *The Seventies*) expanded both the readership and the geographical reach of translation; other magazines and presses followed, including *FIELD* magazine and its translation series. Of the poets represented in this volume, César Vallejo and Federico García Lorca in Spanish, Rainer Maria Rilke in German, and Tomas Tranströmer in Swedish are among those who most expanded the horizons of American poetry during this period, encouraging poets to adopt and experiment with new approaches and techniques.

And now we are in another period of expanding literary translation, a kind of literary globalization, which has produced more translations from a wider field of languages, including—as represented in this book—Arabic, modern Hebrew, and a growing number of European languages. These later contributions move us closer to, and even into, our own times, and begin to suggest the wider diversity that translations of the future may offer us. You might want to think of this book as a precursor to a volume that would include multiple translations of poems from African languages, from other Asian languages, from lesser-known European languages, and also one that would include more women poets. Danielle Legros Georges's contribution, focusing on a never-before-translated Haitian Creole poem, suggests that direction.

A few words about the commentaries. Again, the latitude we offered our contributors was wide in terms of both length and content. Invited to discuss both the original poem and the translations, some contributors focused more on the poem, others on the translations. Some attempted a nearly line-by-line discussion, while others discuss only a few points. Some generalized about the cultural or aesthetic biases of the translators; others did not. Most approached the task in a positive way, noting the felicities of each translation, though a few focused mostly on specific problems. In one way or another, all the commentaries remind us of the balancing act that literary translation necessarily is, and of the difficulty of ever getting everything quite right. As Cole Swensen writes in her essay on Baudelaire, "All translations need an absolutely untranslatable moment to remind us that any translation is, in fact, impossible—and thus unlimited."

That translations should even be *trying* to get it right is a bias all our contributors share. *Into English* includes very few radically free translations, and even fewer imitations: the most radical formal departure is a transla-tion of a passage from Virgil; the most free translations of content occur in versions of poems by Anna Akhmatova and Marin Sorescu. We didn't ask our contributors to avoid extremely free translations, or even more radically experimental ones, of which there are a great many these days,[2] but most chose translations that aim for the middle ground of being as true as possible to the original on the one hand and trying to produce genuine poetry on the other.

What we see in essay after essay is the writer struggling to understand both the original poem and the choices the translators made—choices that bring the reader of translations ever closer to the original process of poetic composition itself. Translators can learn from following this process, which is one aim of this anthology: considering the artistic choices that others have made can help all of us who translate poems—and write them!—to think more deliberately about our own work. But readers can become more careful and satisfied readers, too. For translation is above all an exercise in careful reading; it may be true that there is no better way to know a poem than to translate it. But coming close to that may be, as Stephen Tapscott suggests, reading the poem "as the conversion, or convergence, of the original with several translations."

We've placed the Haitian Creole poem last (and out of our usual chronological order) because its translations are the work not of experienced translators but rather of poets creating translations in a workshop setting, some of them for the first time. Along with the translations, Danielle Legros Georges offers a word-by-word "trot"—a tool that is a great classroom accompaniment to multiple translations, giving students a chance to work on the same poem, whether they know the original language or not, and also allowing them to see, from the various possibilities offered, that there is really no such thing as a definitive literal version. This final essay suggests, then, both the kinds of poems we can hope to see multiply translated in the future, and something of the means by which that expansion of literary translation is already occurring.

We invite all the readers of *Into English* to be both readers and users. Whether or not your aim is to translate, you can experience a lot of pleasure by making your own comparisons among the translations of any given poem: the more you look and read, the more you're apt to discover. Whether you are a reader or writer or translator, we welcome you to experience what George Kalogeris, quoting Virgil, describes as a process of "song replying to song replying to song."

Notes

1. As almost every anthology that includes this poem notes, Keats made a mistake: it was Balboa, not Cortez, who "discovered" the Pacific Ocean—which brings up a question that sometimes confronts translators: should one correct errors that occur in the original?

2. For an extended discussion of experimental translation, see Joe Milutis, "Bright Arrogance: A Column on Experiments in Translation," a series of fifteen segments that appeared online in *Jacket2*, March 23–June 25, 2015.

Into
English

Sappho

(Ancient Greek, circa 620–570 BCE)

TRANSLATIONS BY

Anne Carson, Willis Barnstone,

Mary Barnard

·····························

COMMENTARY BY

Karen Emmerich

98

(a) 1   ..].θος· ἀ γάρ μ᾽ ἐγέννα[
            —]
          .].ᾶς ἐπ᾽ ἀλικίας μέγ[
          [κ]όσμον αἴ τις ἔχη[ι] φόβα[ι]ς
     4   πορφύρωι κατελιξαμέ[ν
            —]
          [ἔ]μμεναι μάλα τοῦτο . [
          ἀλλα ξανθοτέρα[ι]ς ἔχη[
     7   τα[ὶ]ς κόμα[ι]ς δάιδος προ[
            —]
          [σ]τεφάνοισιν ἐπαρτία[
          ἀνθέων ἐριθαλέων· [
     10   μ]ιτράναν δ᾽ ἀρτίως κλ[
            —]
          ποικίλαν ἀπὺ Σαρδίω[ν
          …] .αονίας πόλεις [

                    .   .   .

(b)   σοὶ δ᾽ ἔγω, Κλέι, ποικίλαν [
          οὐκ ἔχω πόθεν ἔσσεται [
     3   μιτράν[αν]· ἀλλὰ τῶι Μυτιληνάωι [

                    .   .   .

               ].[
          παι α ειον ἔχην πο [
     6   αικε η ποικίλας κ...[

          ταύτα τᾶς Κλεανακτίδα[
          φύγας + …ις απολις ἔχει+
     9   μνάματ᾽· . ἴδε γὰρ αἶνα διέρρυε[ν]

Sappho

98A

]for my mother

in her youth it was a great
ornament if someone had hair
bound with purple—

a very great ornament indeed
But for the one who has hair yellower
than a pinetorch

crowns
of blooming flowers
and just lately a headbinder

spangled from Sardis
        ]cities

98B

but for you Kleis I have no
spangled—where would I get it?—
headbinder: yet the Mytilinean[

          ][
          ]to hold
          ]spangled

these things of the Kleanaktidai
exile
memories   terribly leaked away

translated by Anne Carson (2012)

Hair Yellower Than Torch Flame

My mother used to say

in her youth
it was a great ornament to wear
a purple ribbon

looped in her hair. But a girl
with hair yellower than torch flame
need wear just

a wreath of blooming
flowers, or lately maybe
a colorful headband

from Sardis
or some Ionian city

From Her Exile

For you Kleis I have no embroidered
headband and no idea
where to find one while the Mytilinian rules

These colorfully embroidered
headbands

these things of the children of the Kleanax
In exile
memories terribly wasted away

translated by Willis Barnstone (2009)

Don't ask me what to wear

I have no embroidered
headband from Sardis to
give you, Cleis, such as
I wore
              and my mother
always said that in her
day a purple ribbon
looped in the hair was thought
to be high style indeed

but we were dark:
              a girl
whose hair is yellower than
torchlight should wear no
headdress but fresh flowers

translated by Mary Barnard (1958)

Commentary by Karen Emmerich

Sappho is one of the most famous poets about whom we know virtually nothing. She is said to have been born in the seventh century BCE in two separate places on Lesvos. She may have died there of old age, or leapt to her death on distant Lefkada. Some say she was a lesbian; others tie themselves into knots arguing that she wasn't. She is also said to have lived in exile in Sicily for some years. What evidence we have for these claims is often culled from the poems themselves: while Greek poetry of Sappho's day was almost always written with a specific, often ceremonial purpose or event in mind, Sappho's work tends to be read as if it were entirely autobiographical, the product of a private, subjective, self-speaking lyric voice.

Sappho has become a continual site of return for those who seek an origin of sorts: the first female poet, the original lesbian, the originator of a poetry in which the self and the word are one. Yet the figure of Sappho (or Psapfo, in a transliteration that does less to sand off the rough edges of her name) is in fact the construct of countless imaginations. Likewise, much of what we know as her poetry is the work of scholarly restoration and conjecture: subjected to the obliterating effects of time, her literary remains have been shaped and reshaped by countless scribes and editors, ancient and modern alike.

Sappho had a wide reputation as a poet in antiquity, and her lyrics are said to have filled six papyrus scrolls at the Library of Alexandria. For nearly two millennia after the destruction of the library during the Roman conquest, all that was known of Sappho's work were the scattered lines and passages quoted by ancient grammarians, in texts that were themselves not immune to the effects of time. Then, in the late nineteenth century, a massive find of papyri in an ancient trash heap in Egypt brought countless new texts to light, including a number of comparatively lengthy fragments thought to be Sappho's. Since then, several nearly complete poems have been added to the existing corpus, thanks to further excavations and additional finds in existing collections.

For most of us, these fragments cannot be taken as they are, but must be made legible by specialists: papyrologists, classicists, scholarly editors, and, of course, translators. Take, for instance, the scraps of writing now known as Fragments 98a and 98b. Committed to papyrus in the third century BCE (which is to say, three hundred years after Sappho's death), they are among the oldest surviving material witnesses to Sappho's work. The text on each is a squat block of capital letters, with no punctuation and no spaces between words. The provenance of these fragments is unclear. They were first published in 1939 and 1941 by Achille Vogliano, who obtained one from a scholar in Copenhagen and the other from a European trader who himself bought it at an antiquities market in Cairo. Neither fragment contains an explicit attribution to Sappho: Vogliano initially considered her as a possible source of fragment 98a on the basis of a single word, and afterward found his supposition confirmed by the language and meter. Likely because the two fragments share a similar theme, in 1955 Edgar Lobel and Denys Page suggested they might belong to the same papyrus column, and indeed to the same poem; they published the fragments in the form in which they are presented here. Apart from occasional differences in the reading of a particular letter or word, this is how these texts have been preserved ever since by the scholarly community.

Yet this Greek text is by no means an objective account (if such a thing were possible) of what appears on those scraps of papyrus. The edited text is, rather, the result of a host of interpretive decisions: to attribute the poem to Sappho; to divide the mass of text into particular words and phrases; that these two scraps belong to the same papyrus and poem; that 98a preceded 98b. Perhaps most interestingly and most tendentiously, Lobel and Page hypothesized that the text of 98b, as it appeared on the papyrus fragment, was improperly ordered: they interpreted the three horizontal lines drawn to the left of the last three verses as markers of a scribal error, an indication that those verses actually belong *before* the verses that precede them on the papyrus itself. Ever since Lobel and Page, these two scraps of papyrus have thus been presented in Greek editions as a single fragment in two pieces, with the twenty extant lines reordered according to this hypothesis. If one traces back the threads, however, one finds little consensus about the relationship between these fragments. Page's own commentary on the poem in his 1955

Sappho and Alcaeus bristles with differences of opinion from other scholars, who make assumptions that are "[not] supported by the words actually preserved" and engage in "the wildest of guesses." Page cautions that even his own ideas are not to be taken as indisputable fact: "The evidence declares that there is nothing . . . incompatible with the hypothesis," he writes of one such claim, but there is also "no proof that this was actually so."

For works like those of Sappho, the instability of anything we might take as an "original" creates particular challenges for its prospective translators. Consider the difference between the three English versions of fragments 98a and 98b presented above, which reflect divergent understandings of how to treat this material. I begin with the most recent of the three, from Anne Carson, who presents Greek texts in red on the verso and her English translations in black on the recto; fragments 98a and 98b are presented on successive spreads, as separate yet consecutive texts (though here they are collapsed into a single quotation).

Carson's translation is spare and simple, divided into three-line stanzas, in keeping with a scholarly understanding of Sappho's metrics. The presence of a fragmentary Greek text on the facing page reminds us of the complicated nature of Carson's so-called source. Carson's English text, meanwhile, exhibits a tension between an acknowledgment of that fragmentariness and an urge toward stabilization or completion. The translation includes brackets indicating absent text (though the Greek contains a far greater number of marked lacunae and interpolations), while Carson breaks the text of 98b further, in a sense, by moving the bulk of the second stanza to the center of the page, leaving a long gap in the final line, and translating only one of three discernible words in the penultimate line of the fragment, letting "exile" stand starkly on its own line. In other words, Carson uses brackets and spacing as *gestures* rather than *markers*. The visual, visible anisomorphism between the Greek and the English implicitly refutes assumptions that translation offers one-to-one correspondents, and may have the effect of heightening the reader's awareness of the vast distance of time, language, worldview, and understanding that separates these two texts nestled so closely on either side of the spread.

By the same token, however, Carson's inclusion of a Greek text, as well as her choice to organize her translation in what we might call, for lack of a better term, a "word-for-word" manner, according to the lineation suggested by the Greek on the facing page, may have the opposite effect, of suggesting to readers that this Greek text is *the* Greek text, and that her translation is as accurate and noninterventionist as one could hope (if one would harbor such a hope). Moreover, while Carson's translation *appears* fragmented, the words can actually be read across the gaps as a series of continuous, unproblematically sense-generating sentences. The opening, enjambed line of 98a—likely the tail end of a prior, effaced stanza—reads initially as a dedication. As the poem unfolds, that line is incorporated grammatically into the whole: for the speaker's mother and others in her day, a purple band was considered a great ornament, as opposed to the flashy, spangled "headbinders'" of the city-dwellers of the speaker's present moment. Carson's version of 98a reads as a simple remembrance of times past, when the pure products of nature—a girl's beauty, for instance—could be adorned by things as slight as ribbons.

Fragment 98b, on the following page, is quite different in nature: it refers to specific political figures, as well as to a "Kleis," who is presumed to be Sappho's daughter (though 98b is in fact one of the "sources" of the biographical information that is then brought to bear on subsequent readings of it). Taken together—if indeed they are to be taken together—these two fragments could be seen as tracing a female genealogy through three generations, and referring also to a larger collectivity of girls. Yet Carson's translation also downplays the *femaleness* of this community: the wearers of the headband and flowers are simply "someone" and "one," gender emphatically unmarked.

Scholars are of many minds regarding the historical logic of 98b. Does it refer to the exile of the Kleanaktides, whose absence signals a change in political leadership on the island and perhaps the closure of certain familiar trade routes? Does it refer to Sappho's own exile to Sicily? Is Sappho speaking from reduced circumstances, traveling with a daughter who will experience a childhood in which even a headband is a luxury beyond reach? To me, reading in the current moment, these irretrievable historical details have been overshadowed by the current reality of Sappho's native island, which has become an entry point into Europe for hundreds of thousands of refugees fleeing war and destruction in lands farther to the east; the sea between Asia Minor and the islands has become the province of smugglers, lifeguards, and border control. For me, the "exile" of the word *figas* in my reading of this fragment has come to resonate with a more modern *prosfigia*, the state of being a refugee. History doesn't only efface a text—it also builds ever-changing scaffolds of meaning around what is left.

Of the three translations I discuss, only Carson's gives the reader a visible indication of the fragmentary nature of the textual evidence. Willis Barnstone's *The Complete Poems of Sappho* takes a very different approach: each poem in his volume seems entirely complete, as the elements in each fragment are pieced together into a comprehensible narrative whole. But what counts as the "poem" in the case of 98a and 98b is an open question, one Barnstone answers differently than Carson: he translates each of the fragments as a separate poem, and presents them in his volume more than fifty pages apart. "Hair Yellower Than Torch Flame," his translation of 98a, is brief, contained, propelled by a series of near-perfect iambs, shot through with rhyme ("wear" and "hair") and oblique rhyme ("lately maybe"). There is nothing partial or disconnected about the content: Barnstone adds interpolated connective tissue to bind the existing bits of the source text into a meaningful whole in English. In the first of the poem's two sentences, the speaker's mother enters as a narrating voice, a figure who used to tell stories about an even more distant past, thus doubling the narrative past of the poem. In the second sentence, the uncertain tense of the modal verb "need" allows it to operate as a hinge between that doubled past and the "lately" of the following phrase; the yellow-haired girl who might need (or have needed) to wear only flowers in her hair could be in the speaker's present, the past of the mother's storytelling or youth, or all of the above. The simplest paraphrase of the poem in Barnstone's version might be: When my mother was a girl, purple ribbons were all the rage—but you, girl with the yellow hair, are a flower to be adorned only with flowers.

The poem is one of praise and celebration, of natural beauty, the girl's and the flowers' both.

Carson's successive translations of 98a and 98b emphasize the distance between a past of bucolic simplicity and a present of need. In Barnstone's version of 98a, the primary distinction is between what the mother (specified as the wearer of the ribbon, in contrast to Carson's genderless "someone") used to wear in her hair and what suits the girl (definitively gendered, unstuck in time, and perhaps generalizable) with "hair yellower than torch flame." Yet Barnstone doesn't downplay the theme of exile. Rather, he saves it for later and perhaps even emphasizes it, titling his translation of 98b "From Her Exile" and incorporating it into a section of his book titled "Weathercocks and Exile." This poem, too, gives no indication of the fragmentary nature of the extant Greek text: while Carson's 98B begins in mid-sentence, Barnstone's opens with a simple lament regarding the embroidered headband that the narrator cannot obtain. Once again, interpolated words or phrases bind together the bits of information gleaned from the papyrus. Barnstone's translation also clearly supports an interpretation of the poem as being *about* Sappho, mother of Kleis; his title invites us to read this poem as Sappho's personal lament for all the things that have become mere memories, and that will remain so as long as "the Mytilinian rules."

The last translation I will discuss is the first of the three to have appeared. Published by Mary Barnard only three years after Lobel and Page's edition, it takes a very different approach to the textual quandaries presented by these two fragments. Barnard is also the most explicit, in her afterword, about the complicated history of her sources, and about her own strategy for dealing with fragmented texts from "tattered papyrus." She has chosen, she writes, "to condense instead of filling in the gaps." The only exception to this policy is her titles, which she sometimes lifts from the fragment and sometimes supplies as "elucidation" or "conjecture" as to "the sense of missing lines." Her translation of Fragments 98a and 98b certainly has a surprisingly playful interpolated title—a mother speaking to a complaining teenage daughter, perhaps—but its greatest intervention might be the rather unusual way it combines the two fragments.

Barnard is certainly not the only translator to bring 98a and 98b together into a single poem. Yet rather than simply tack 98b onto 98a, as editors of the Greek text do, she weaves them together such that the opening phrase of the poem combines a line from 98b with the last (not first) line of 98a. Other translations start with a simple, bucolic past, in which all one really wanted was a purple ribbon, and move forward chronologically to a moment when such items are no longer available, ending with a sense of loss. Barnard follows a more complicated trajectory: she *begins* with lack, with the present absence of an item we subsequently learn the speaker once had. We then take one more step backward in time, moving gently from this lack to the positive remembrance of the bucolic youth of a previous generation. In her final, split stanza, rather than ending with the loss of that bucolic past, Barnard renders the absence of a headband irrelevant: the particular kinds of ornaments that best set off the two older women's darker features would, it seems, not suit the yellow hair of Cleis, on whose head fresh flowers—readily provided by nature—are much more suitable. The last stanza, rather than ending with exile and vanishing memories, blossoms into a celebratory affirmation of the simplicity of beauty itself.

To a contemporary reader (you, for instance) comparing this version to Carson's facing-page edition, Barnard's translation might come as something of a shock. It is a tiny gem of a modernist poem, with stanzas joined (or broken) by hanging indents, heavy on iambs and enjambment, compact and squat and riddled with images. There is no reference to exile, nor any sense of unfinishedness, thematic or textual. Yet the visual makeup of Carson's facing-page translation may also give its readers a false sense of its own accuracy, as if we could depend on it to offer no more and no less than is really there in the supposed original—an impossible demand that betrays a misunderstanding of what it is that translation does. Of the three translators, Barnard seems the most willing to actively imagine the work of the translator as a form of editorial work that is both backward- and forward-looking. A translation, like an edition, is an embodied interpretation not just of what a text means, but of what the work itself *is*. This is true of all works of literature, but particularly prominent in ancient works circulating in fragmentary forms. The three translations I have presented, wildly different in their approach to the Greek source materials, show us the wide range of what a variety of interpretive encounters with an unstable source might yield. The richness of Sappho in English has everything to do with efforts like these, to engage seriously not only with a particular source but also with the ongoing history of its construction.

Virgil

(Latin, 70–19 BCE)

TRANSLATIONS BY

Kristina Chew, Peter Fallon,
Janet Lembke

· ·

COMMENTARY BY

Carl Phillips

The Georgics, Book IV, lines 58–66

hinc ubi iam emissum caueis ad sidera caeli
nare per aestatem liquidam suspexeris agmen
obscuramque trahi uento mirabere nubem,
contemplator: aquas dulcis et frondea semper
tecta petunt. huc tu iussos asperge sapores,
trita melisphylla et cerinthae ignobile gramen,
tinnitusque cie et Matris quate cymbala circum:
ipsae consident medicatis sedibus, ipsae
intima more suo sese cunabula condent.

Virgil (29 BCE)

                          Accordingly
when you will have noticed that
        a line
                  of bees   of the sky
                        is discharged   to the stars
                          from its hive

and is *Swarming*   through the clear   summer air   and you
shall marvel
        that
        the dark   the   wind
            cloud   on   by
              is drawn

Behold.

Sweet waters and leafy homes always
they seek; here sprinkle **Delicacies** as bid:
   Balm of Gilead finely ground
and the humble herb *Bee bread*,
and do you make the *Noise of Rings and Jingles*
and strike the Great Mother's cymbals
all around: Bees will settle in herb-treated sites,
will conceal themselves in the most secret spots.
It is a custom all their own.

translated by Kristina Chew (2002)

Then, when you lift your eyes and see a swarm discharged
to ride the skies, a moving smudge through summer,
and marvel at a darksome cloud trailing down the wind,
keep note of how they make—yes—make a beeline
for fresh water and a leafy shade. Then, in that very spot,
sprinkle tastes prescribed as treats: balm you've crushed,
blades of honeywort and borage; have Cybele's cymbals fill the air.
They'll make themselves at home in this charmed site,
and set up on their own—as is their wont—a cradle for their young in its inner reaches.

translated by Peter Fallon (2004)

Therefore, when you look up and see the swarm, newly released,
mounting through clear summer air and the starry heavens,
and you marvel at the dark cloud streaming in the wind,
take close note: always they seek out sweet waters and leafy
bowers. Here you are to scatter traditional dainties—
rubbed bee balm and honeywort's plant, commonly found; raise
a clangor, too, shaking the Great Mother's cymbals all around.
They themselves will settle in fragrant abodes, they themselves,
after their fashion, will hide in the innermost cradles.

translated by Janet Lembke (2005)

Commentary by Carl Phillips

What matters most to me in a translation is faithfulness to the content, in terms of what is *actually* being said (as opposed to *how* it is being said). If I don't know a language, and if I am coming to a text for the first time, I'm completely at the mercy of the translator, and I want to be able to trust that he or she has made it possible for me to believe I have in fact read *War and Peace*, for example, and not a variation on it (side by side with the reality, though, that every translation is a variation). This accuracy is especially important when it comes to teaching. Watching *West Side Story* is enough for students to get the basic plot of *Romeo and Juliet*, for example, but it has otherwise nothing to do with Shakespeare.

After accuracy to meaning, accuracy to—in no particular order—what? Sound? Sensibility? Time, and if so, whose time, that of the text itself, or the present moment in the name of contemporary relevance?

If it is a variation, then—always—to what effect? And by permission of what in particular, within the text itself?

If the choice is to add content to the original, what makes that content essential?

———

Each of the translators I've chosen accurately conveys the content of the passage from Virgil. *The Georgics* is a didactic poem, meant to give instructions concerning agriculture. Book IV is devoted to beekeeping, and in this particular passage we learn the remedy for swarming: when you see the bees swarming through the air, certain foods and sounds will cause them to settle in the very area where the foods have been placed and the sounds made. What distinguishes each translation, then? What makes each uniquely worthwhile—or not?

Kristina Chew's translation is the most immediately noticeable, for how wildly it diverges from Virgil's lineation. *The Georgics* is written entirely in dactylic hexameter, so the lines are necessarily going to be pretty much the same length. Chew has chosen not only to abandon meter, but to have the lines move all over the page. In her introduction, Chew describes her translation as an "American *Georgics*," without exactly saying what that means. To judge by the passage here, "American" seems to me to refer to a freedom with lineation, as well as with font (plain, italic, bold) and capitalization. To what effect?

For one, we get to see the swarming of the bees taking place before us—the lineation enacts the content without sacrificing accuracy to it: When you look, as you are looking now, at swarming bees, do as follows. There's also a certain muscularity, as the lines dilate and contract, flexing, as it were. The italics organize the information—reminiscent of outlining: for "*Swarming*," you'll need "*Balm of Gilead*," "*Bee bread*," and the "*Noise of Rings and Jingles*"; the information is thrown into relief via orthography. Meanwhile, the balm and the bread come under a special category: **Delicacies**. Hence the boldface?

But there is more than one type of muscularity. In the original, Virgil casts two sentences across nine lines. The first takes up four lines and a small portion of the fifth line, where we're brought to a halt at a strong caesura. From there, we have the second sentence, distinguished by a strong end-stop at the colon. (A colon would not have been approved in the Latin of Virgil's day, since the text would have been unpunctuated, but the occurrence of the line break right at the preposition *circum*, whose object precedes it, gives to the Latin the effect of a colon.) From here, as we move toward summation, Virgil not only gives us a line that employs anaphora (the repeated *ipsae*, meaning "they themselves"), but he places the anaphora so as to have the two words frame the line—so there's both a rhetorical and a visual flourish, in addition to the tension between sentence length and line length, which is what generates muscularity here, at the level of syntax. Janet Lembke's is the translation that most closely retains these aspects of the original. While her lines are longer than Virgil's—unavoidably, since Latin is more compressed than English—she is faithful to Virgil's nine. Rather than two, she has three sentences. The first one, as in Virgil, is cast across four lines, and part of the fifth; she retains Virgil's enjambment and caesura (*tecta petunt*) with "bowers" at the start of the fifth line, followed by a period. After that, instead of a single sentence, she has two sentences across the last four lines, but I would argue that her end-stop of a period after "all around" is pretty close to Virgil's colon. And she has retained the aforementioned flourishes with the repetition of "they themselves," the phrases mirroring the frame of the original. So, in addition to its content, Lembke's translation is faithful to Virgil's artistry, a difficult feat.

While Lembke, like Chew, opts for free verse, she seems in this passage to alternate between a seven-stressed and a five-stressed line (I count seven in the first line, and then in each line as follows: five, five, seven, five, seven, seven, five, and five). To this degree, she attempts to convey, at the least, that there is a patterning to Virgil's lines, though she has eschewed actual meter. Peter Fallon doesn't adhere to a particular meter in his translation, but his is the one that routinely settles into metrical regularity, and then drifts free of it—his is more faithful to Virgil's sense of music, we might say. To give just three instances (the stresses marked in my italics), I note that "*Then* when you *lift* your *eyes* and *see* a *swarm* dis*charged*" is a line of iambic hexameter, a trochaic foot followed by five iambic feet; "to *ride* the *skies*, a *moving smudge* through *summer*" is iambic pentameter, five iambs in a row, with an extra unstressed syllable at the end; "and *set* up *on* their *own*—as *is* their *wont*—a *cradle for* their *young* in its *inner reaches*" consists of eight iambs in a row, before the pattern breaks, though a sense of rhythm is retained.

But while faithful to a sense of music and to content, Fallon has three times here added material that isn't in the original. *[P]er aestatem liquidam . . . agmen* literally means "a line through the liquid (or clear) summer" and, by association, "a line through the clear summer air." Chew and Lembke, respectively, offer "a line of bees . . . through the clear summer air" and "the swarm . . . through clear summer air," both pretty close to the original, though Lembke refers to the line as a "swarm." Fallon opts for "a moving smudge through summer," which actually appeals to me as an image, but it isn't in the original. (Interestingly, Chew's play with the lineation visually suggests a moving smudge.) Likewise, "take close note: always they seek out sweet waters and leafy / bowers" (Lembke) and "Behold. // Sweet waters

and leafy homes always / they seek" both adhere to the original. (Chew's inflected "they seek" recalls the inflection of the Latin but sounds awkward in English, which is not an inflected language.) Fallon goes for a sort of pun at this point: "keep note of how they make—yes—a beeline / for fresh water and a leafy shade." There was indeed a line of bees earlier in the passage, but at this point in the original there isn't one, nor is there the least suggestion of the self-conscious (and folksy) "yes" from Virgil's speaker, and I am not sure that anything essential is added by the worn expression "to make a beeline"; here, in fact, it adds a touch of humor that is inappropriate for a didactic poem and that appears nowhere in *The Georgics*. Finally, *intima . . . sese in cunabula condent* translates as "they will hide themselves in the innermost cradles." Lembke comes closest to this ("will hide in the innermost cradles"); Chew is close enough ("will conceal themselves in the most secret spots"). But Fallon's "set up on their own . . . a cradle for their young in its inner reaches" introduces a *purpose* to the bees' activity, to provide for their young, and it also ignores the action of hiding. None of Fallon's additions direly ruin his translation—we still get the idea—but none of them seem exactly essential, either.

Sometimes exact accuracy isn't the way to go, however. *Ubi . . . suspexeris . . . mirabere* means "when you will have noticed [and] you will marvel," and that is just how Chew translates it. But surely "when you lift your eyes . . . and marvel" (Fallon) and "when you look up and see . . . and you marvel" (Lembke) are both accurate and sound more natural.

On the other hand, *Matris* in the original literally means "Mother." Virgil's reader would have known that in this context the mother being referred to was Cybele, a fertility goddess also called the Great Mother of the Gods. To offer what the original says isn't useful for a contemporary reader, in this instance. Lembke and Chew both offer "the Great Mother," which at least suggests that some mother in particular is being referred to. Fallon gives the actual name of the goddess—so we don't have to guess at the mother's identity, though we now lose the mother reference, unless we happen to know who Cybele is. There would seem to be no ideal solution; either way, a footnote is going to be needed. But I do admire how, in Fallon, the use of the goddess's name becomes an opportunity for a kind of triple alliteration: with "Cybele's cymbals," the beginning of each word gives a double "s" sound, the "l"'s in each word nicely echo each other, and both words end on the sound of "z." Again, Fallon seems especially to want the sense of music.

An underlying theme of the fourth book of *The Georgics* is ethnographical: in examining the behavior of bees, Virgil wants to address human behavior. When he speaks of the rivalry between queen bees, he is also speaking of war and power. When he speaks of queens and workers, he is speaking of class structure. In our passage here, the occasional need to rein in a tendency to roam also has its resonances with human behavior, both societal and personal. In the Latin, Virgil conveys these parallels by using words associated with humans. I mentioned earlier that an *agmen* is a "line." More specifically, it's a line of soldiers in battle formation; so, by extension, it can also mean "troops," "army," etc. Meanwhile, outside of a military context, *agmen* can also mean a "crowd," a "herd," a "procession." This latter sense justifies Fallon's and Lembke's decisions to translate the word as a "swarm." Chew has "a line / of bees." No one captures the military sense of the word, so the ethnographic part of the original is lost. Interestingly, though, Chew does achieve this. *More suo* in the last line of the original means "in their custom." (*More* is from the word *mos*, which means "custom"—it's where we get words like "morality.") Richard Thomas, in his notes to the Cambridge edition of the original Latin, says that, while *more suo* translates as "after their fashion" (his translation), "the reference to their *mos* also has an ethnographical dimension." I would say that Chew best retains this dimension, with "It is a custom all their own." The price paid, however, is the compression of the Latin expression, something that Lembke and Fallon get with, respectively, "after their fashion" and (less so) "as is their wont"; but the societal associations of the phrase disappear.

Maybe this is why I have a passion for reading multiple translations of a given work. Each will have its virtues and its flaws—rather like people. By looking at several translations, I think we get a clearer sense not just of the work, but of the hand—and the sensibility—behind it. I wonder if it's too

much to say that translation has a kind of moral or ethical dimension. Our ignorance of a language means we have to abandon ourselves to—have faith in—the translator's knowledge of that language. We have no choice but to trust. To betray that trust, or not to—therein lies the translator's power. As with sex, love—both—everything hinges on the responsibility with which, having found we hold a dangerous power in our hands, we now deploy it.

Tao Qian

(Chinese, 365–427)

TRANSLATIONS BY

James Hightower, Stephen Owen,
David Hinton

....

COMMENTARY BY

Arthur Sze

久在樊籠裡
雞鳴桑樹顛
曖曖遠人村
草屋八九間
雨荒南野際
一去三十年
少無適俗韻

歸田園居

陶潛

復得返自然
戶庭無塵雜
依依墟里煙
榆柳蔭後簷
守拙歸田園
羈鳥老舊林
性本愛丘山

狗吠深巷中
桃李羅堂前
方宅十餘畝
池魚思故淵
誤落塵網中

虛室有餘閒

Tao Qian (406)

Returning to the Farm to Dwell I

From early days I have been at odds with the world;
My instinctive love is hills and mountains.
By mischance I fell into the dusty net
And was thirteen years away from home.
The migrant bird longs for its native grove.
The fish in the pond recalls the former depths.
Now I have cleared some land to the south of town,
Simplicity intact, I have returned to farm.
The land I own amounts to a couple of acres
The thatched-roof house has four or five rooms.
Elms and willows shade the eaves in back,
Peach and plum stretch out before the hall.
Distant villages are lost in haze,
Above the houses smoke hangs in the air.
A dog is barking somewhere in a hidden lane,
A cock crows from the top of a mulberry tree.
My home remains unsoiled by worldly dust
Within bare rooms I have my peace of mind.
For long I was a prisoner in a cage
And now I have my freedom back again.

translated by James Hightower (1970)

Returning to Dwell in Gardens and Fields I

My youth felt no comfort in common things,
by my nature I clung to the mountains and hills.

I erred and fell in the snares of dust
and was away thirteen years in all.

The caged bird yearns for its former woods,
fish in a pool yearns for long-ago deeps.

Clearing scrub at the edge of the southern moors,
I stay plain by returning to gardens and fields.

My holdings are just more than ten acres,
a thatched cottage of eight or nine rooms.

Elms and willows shade eaves at the back,
peach and plum spread in front of the hall.

The far towns of men are hidden from sight,
a faint blur of smoke comes from village hearths.

A dog is barking deep in the lanes,
a rooster cries out atop a mulberry.

No dust pollutes my doors or yard,
empty space offering ample peace.

For a long time I was kept inside a coop,
now again I return to the natural way.

translated by Stephen Owen (1996)

Home Again among Fields and Gardens I

Nothing like all the others, even as a child,
rooted in such love for hills and mountains,

I stumbled into their net of dust, that one
departure a blunder lasting thirteen years.

But a tethered bird longs for its old forest,
and a pond fish its deep waters—so now,

my southern outlands cleared, I nurture
simplicity among these fields and gardens,

home again. I've got nearly two acres here,
and four or five rooms in our thatch hut,

elms and willows shading the eaves in back,
and in front, peach and plum spread wide.

Villages lost across mist-and-haze distances,
kitchen smoke drifting wide-open country,

dogs bark deep among back roads out here,
and roosters crow from mulberry treetops.

No confusion within these gates, no dust,
my empty home harbors idleness to spare.

After so long caged in that trap, I've come
back again to occurrence appearing of itself.

translated by David Hinton (2008)

Commentary by Arthur Sze

"Returning to the Farm to Dwell" is a landmark poem by Tao Qian (365–427). It is the first in a series of five poems and celebrates a return to a simple life in the countryside. For over a decade, Tao Qian worked as a government official, but he felt constrained and grew increasingly dissatisfied. In 405, Tao Qian retired to the countryside, where he farmed, planted chrysanthemums, drank wine, and wrote poetry. In cultivating his spirit, he became one of the early, great dropouts in the tradition of Chinese poetry.

In the first translation I've selected, James Hightower has chosen to use a line in English for each line of Chinese. The original Chinese consists of five characters to a line, where there is a caesura between the second and third characters. The characters are thus read 1-2/3-4-5. Hightower chooses to remove this caesura, except in line 8, and his translation is notable for its steady rhythmical flow. The primarily end-stopped lines give his translation a sense of measure and quiet authority. Tao Qian's extensive use of parallelism easily comes through: "elms" and "willows" are the first two characters in line 11, while "peach" and "plum" are, correspondingly, the first two characters in line 12. The clarity and pace of this translation are admirable, and the opening and closing couplets are, I think, simply but effectively presented.

In the second translation, Stephen Owen employs couplets, and this strategy helps to highlight the parallelisms. For instance, in the first two characters of lines 15 and 16, the couplets contrast "a dog is barking" with "a rooster cries." Also, the opening and closing couplets frame ideas of nature: line 2 has the phrase "by my nature," while the last line circles back with "I return to the natural way." Indeed, the idea of inner nature expressed in the last two characters of the poem, *ziran*, is crucial to clarifying Tao Qian's meaning. The phrase *ziran* is used five times in the *Dao De Jing*. The two characters can be conceived of as "it-self becoming," and the meaning can be interpreted as "the natural way of everything becoming itself." *Ziran* implies a kind of spontaneity and fulfillment of essential nature. Hightower translates the phrase as "freedom," though his footnote suggests that "naturalness" is closer in meaning.

In the third translation, David Hinton also employs couplets, and he uses "net" and "caged in that trap" to intensify the experience of confinement. He furthers the deep feeling for hills and mountains by rendering it as "rooted in such love." And his elegant use of negations—"nothing like all the others," "no confusion within these gates, no dust"—heightens the experience of emptiness and space that is not mere negation. This empty space allows crucial room for discovery. Here, *ziran* is translated as "occurrence appearing of itself." In Hinton's hands, *ziran* becomes mysterious and unfolding.

In all three translations, it's worth pointing out differences in the poem's numbers. Hightower takes the Chinese measures of space and, in converting them to Western equivalents, the ten Chinese units of land become "a couple of acres," while the eight or nine units of rooms become "four or five rooms." Owen retains the numbers—"ten acres" and "eight or nine rooms"—while Hinton, like Hightower, goes with "nearly two acres" and "four or five rooms," which makes the house modest in size. In line 4, all three translators choose to ignore the literal text, which clearly says "thirty years," and use "thirteen years" instead. Hightower asserts that thirty years makes no sense; that the time of government service was probably close to thirteen years, and so he transposes the "ten" and the "three" (ten plus three, instead of three times ten). Owen and Hinton follow suit.

In contrast to these translations, I chose to retain "thirty years" and want to offer a justification. First, the text clearly says "thirty years"—no one disputes that—and, although thirty years is not literally true, there's a figurative justification for it. "Thirty years" has shock value, and it's also justifiable in that one can conceive of thirty years as half a lifetime. In Chinese astrology, there are twelve zodiac creatures and five elements (wood, earth, air, fire, water), so one cycle with each of the five elements requires sixty years. That cycle can be seen as a completed lifetime. I take Tao Qian's phrase to mean that once one departs from the true path, it may take half a lifetime to discover it.

Returning to Fields and Gardens I

When I was young, I did not fit in
with others, and simply loved the hills and mountains.
By mistake, I fell into the dusty net
and before I knew it, it was thirty years!
The caged bird longs for the old forest.
The fish in the pond misses the old depths.
I cultivate land along the southern wilds,
and, keeping to simplicity, return to fields and gardens.
Ten acres now surround my house;
it is thatched, and has eight, nine rooms.
Elms and willows shade the back eaves.
Peach and plum trees are lined out the front hall.
The distant village is hazy, hazy: and
slender, slender, the smoke hanging over houses.
Dogs bark in the deep lane, and a rooster
crows on top of a mulberry tree.
My house untouched by the dust of the world—
ample leisure in these bare rooms.
I was held so long inside a narrow bird-
cage, but now, at last, can return to nature.

translated by Arthur Sze

In the end, there are things to admire in all of these translations, but there's no substitute for reading and experiencing the poem in Chinese. Tao Qian's rhythmical pulse, clarity of images imbued with Taoist insight, spontaneity, and rigor are untranslatable. It's a poem to return to again and again.

San Juan de la Cruz/ St. John of the Cross

(Spanish, 1542–1591)

TRANSLATIONS BY
Roy Campbell, John Frederick Nims,
Antonio de Nicolás

....

COMMENTARY BY
Willis Barnstone

¡Oh llama de amor viva!

¡Oh llama de amor viva,
  que tiernamente hieres
de mi alma en el más profundo centro!
  Pues ya no eres esquiva,
  acaba ya si quieres,
rompe la tela deste dulce encuentro.

  ¡Oh cauterio suave!
  ¡Oh regalada llaga!
¡Oh mano blanda! ¡Oh toque delicado,
  que a vida eterna sabe,
  y toda deuda paga!
Matando, muerte en vida la has trocado.

  ¡Oh lámparas de fuego,
  en cuyos resplandores
las profundas cavernas del sentido,
  que estaba oscuro y ciego,
  con extraños primores
calor y luz dan junto a su querido!

  ¡Cuán manso y amoroso
  recuerdas en mi seno,
donde secretamente sólo moras:
  y en tu aspirar sabroso
  de bien y gloria lleno
cuán delicadamente me enamoras!

San Juan de la Cruz (1585?)

Song of the soul in intimate communication and union with the love of God

Oh flame of love so living,
How tenderly you force
To my soul's inmost core your fiery probe!
Since now you've no misgiving,
End it, pursue your course
And for our sweet encounter tear the robe!

Oh cautery most tender!
Oh gash that is my guerdon!
Oh gentle hand! Oh touch how softly thrilling!
Eternal life you render,
Raise of all debts the burden
And change my death to life, even while killing!

Oh lamps of fiery blaze
To whose refulgent fuel
The deepest caverns of my soul grow bright,
Late blind with gloom and haze,
But in this strange renewal
Giving to the belov'd both heat and light.

What peace, with love enwreathing,
You conjure to my breast
Which only you your dwelling place may call:
While with delicious breathings
In glory, grace, and rest,
So daintily in love you make me fall!

translated by Roy Campbell (1951)

The Living Flame of Love

Songs
of the soul in its intimate communion
of union with God's love

O living flame of love!
how soothingly you wound
my soul in its profundity—that center
you once made havoc of,
Oh finish! Take me soon!
Tearing the veil away in love's encounter.

O cautery that freshens!
O treasure of a wound!
Caresses light as air! affectionate palm
with settlement past measure!
the taste of heaven around!
Death done, you lift us living from the tomb.

O lamps of fire, whose light
streams in the cavernous soul:
through mighty hollow, dazzled from above
(once dungeons) see tonight
auroras pole to pole!
lavishing warmth and brilliance on their love!

How lovable, how loving
you waken in my breast,
stirring in nooks, no, none are sharers of!
With your delicious breathing
all health and heavenly rest
how delicately I'm caught afire with love!

translated by John Frederick Nims (1979)

Love's Living Flame

*(Songs that the soul sings in her intimate union with God,
her beloved Bridegroom.)*

O Love's living flame,
Tenderly you wound
My soul's deepest center!
Since you no longer evade me,
Will you, please, at last conclude:
Rend the veil of this sweet encounter!

O cautery so tender!
O pampered wound!
O soft hand! O touch so delicately strange,
Tasting of eternal life
And canceling all debts!
Killing, death into life you change!

O lamps of fiery lure,
In whose shining transparence
The deep cavern of the senses,
Blind and obscure,
Warmth and light, with strange flares,
Gives with the lover's caresses!

How tame and loving
Your memory rises in my breast,
Where secretly only you live,
And in your fragrant breathing,
Full of goodness and grace,
How delicately in love you make me feel!

translated by Antonio de Nicolás (1989)

Commentary by Willis Barnstone

San Juan de la Cruz (1542–1591) was a poet of paradox. He wrote few poems, or, if he wrote more than we have, made little effort to preserve them. Yet in the eleven central poems of his work, we have a poet unsurpassed in the Spanish language. He was widely eclectic and openly derivative, yet he was among the most original poets in any tongue. He was not concerned with his place as a poet, yet poetry was so important to him that he considered it as he writes in his commentaries, the only means of expressing the ineffable.

In San Juan we overhear deepest solitude, although his theme is union. He seeks freedom from the senses, although his own poems comprise the most intensely erotic literature written in the Iberian peninsula from the time of the Moors to Federico García Lorca. Although he was a monk who took vows of chastity, his allegory to express oneness with an absolute being was the sexual climax of lovers. He always wears a mask—normally that of the female lover—yet behind the mask, the lyrical speaker of the poems is both universal and, in an almost spatial sense, deeply the poet himself. He withdraws from the world to merge with God, yet nature and human love are the metaphorical keys to his poetry; the word "God" is absent from his poems.

San Juan de la Cruz's father was a Jewish *converso* who married a Moor. After Queen Isabella expelled the Jews, in 1492, the price for remaining in Spain was conversion to Christianity. But San Juan suffered no trauma because of his mixed ethnic and religious background. His ordeal—incarceration in an unlit, windowless closet cell in 1577—came as a result of conflict in the Carmelite order, which pitted the shoed, or *calced*, monks and nuns against the shoeless (*discalced*), who pledged themselves to poverty, prayer, and contemplation.

San Juan states that the experiences behind his poems came as a result of mystical knowledge, and in his commentaries he endeavors to explain the poems as a systematic sequence of steps, from purgation, to illumination, to divine union. San Juan speaks of his journey as a negative way, a passive night of the soul, an unknowing through which comes mystical understanding. His thought is not unrelated to John Keats's idea of negative capability, or to the Socratic idea of knowing more because one knows nothing. These notions have a common basis: one must erase habitual patterns of thinking to achieve a tabula rasa in order to see, understand, and create. *De nada a todo.* From nothing to all.

"O Living Flame of Love," about human and divine love, uses the voice of a woman. By theological convention, the Western soul (anima) is feminine and seeks union with God, who is canonically masculine. With the exception of Jorge Guillén, Spanish literary critics have denied or avoided the immediate mystico-erotic level of the love experience in San Juan's poetry. His poems have been "cleaned up" and misread again and again, both in commentary and in evasive translations.

The poem's first words, *Oh llama de amor viva*, provide the key. The expected title might be "O Flame of Living Love," with "living" (*viva*) an adjective magnifying love, as it appears in many translations. But *viva* is feminine and so must refer to *llama*, not to *amor*, which would require the masculine. By making "living" modify "flame," San Juan changes a cliché into a paradox that works on multiple levels, suggesting not only a fire that destroys and causes pain, but also one that gives life and extreme pleasure. Much of the poem's emotional power resides in paradox: only when the lover is thoroughly detached from the body and earthly desire is she prepared to enter into a physical relationship with her lover, which in turn signifies spiritual consummation.

After the "living flame" is declared, the penis begins to pierce the vagina (here in my translation):

> O living flame of love,
> how tenderly you wound
> my soul in her profoundest core!
> You are no longer shy.
> Do it now, I ask you:
> break the membrane of our sweet union.[1]

San Juan, speaking as the woman, declares herself ready: *ya si quieres, / rompe la tela deste dulce encuentro.* The *tela*, meaning "cloth," "veil," or "membrane," is also the veil separating her from her inner self. In Juan's commentary, the veil separates God outside from the soul inside, yet God is also inside and to be encountered there when the veil is torn away.

While the poem has a beginning, a central movement, and an end, a tone of physical, emotional, and spiritual climax continues through a cycle of fiery, ecstatic orgasm, meditative plunges, and serene continuation of the act of love. The sequence does not proceed from A to Z, but rather moves in a confusion of tenderness, speculation, pain, and rapture—obedient to love, not to rules of doctrine.

The second stanza contains four exclamations, and a last line, no less intense, of explanation:

> O soothing cautery!
> O wound that is a joy!
> O gentle hand! O delicate touch
>   tasting of eternity,
>   repaying every debt.
> Killing, you turn my death to life.

First the fire image is picked up in an incredible metaphor of pleasure and pain: *Oh cauterio suave.* Using no verbs, San Juan cites the pleasure of healing fire (cauterization refers to the medical process of using a hot iron to heal skin), and repeats the image of the broken membrane in the second line, *Oh regalada llaga.* In the third and fourth lines, *Oh toque delicado, / que a vida eterna sabe,* the poet explores the ambiguity of *sabe a,* which is an idiom denoting "taste" that also retains the connotative meaning of "know," *sabe.* San Juan knows through tasting, effectively conveying both physical and intellectual experience. By making "touch" taste of eternity, he also endows the physical with the supernatural.

The last line of the second stanza, *Matando, muerte en vida la has trocado,* has a powerful finality. Now there is not simply a wound, but death

itself. The language is more clearly mystical: by killing my earthly life, you turn me alive into yourself; that is, into God. On the human level one thinks of Renaissance diction, as in John Donne's "The Canonization," in which "death" means the moment of ejaculation.

In the third stanza we find a curious psychological duality, for while San Juan continues to speak as the woman, in the last line the lover becomes *su querido,* meaning, literally, "her lover": in this stanza of extreme eroticism, San Juan steps back from the female persona and seems to participate as both man and woman. The fire image continues, with *lámparas de fuego* ("lamps of fire") to light up and fathom *las profundas cavernas del sentido* ("the lowest caverns of the senses"), clearly the vagina. From former darkness, the female lover wakes to light, warmth, and strange beauty, preparing us for the last stanza, which is distinct in tone from the preceding stanzas.

The human reality of the love scene is emphasized here:

> How lovingly and soft
> you make my breasts recall
> where you alone lie secretly;
>   and with your honeyed breath,
>   replete with grace and glory,
> how tenderly you make me love!

The word *recuerdas,* in "you make my breasts recall," is common to the mystic's diction; here it suggests that the act proceeds not only in the present but through the memory of eternity. Then, after using the word *gloria,* which is both a lover's compliment and a sign of divinity, San Juan ends with the exquisite line *cuán delicadamente me enamoras!* This is the intended closure, or non-closure, of the poem.

The line echoes line 2 of stanza 1, *que tiernamente hieres* ("how tenderly you wound"), in which the adverb *tiernamente* emphasizes the paradox of antithetical pain and pleasure. Here the adverb *delicadamente* has the strength of full understatement, without paradox. It is drawn out slowly, dominating the line, suggesting sensitivity, thoughtfulness, consciousness—the traits of happy lovers.

The discussion above applies directly to the human sexual level, yet clearly the poem functions on the level of the rapturously divine. The first level is real; if this resonant language is to work, it must be read literally, and not, as so often is done, as not meaning what it says. Earlier translations and most interpretations rush into the theological explanation to downplay the immediate meaning of the poem. The divine, insofar as it exists—and it is surely San Juan's intention that it be present—proceeds from the human. Juan goes further than other metaphysical poets in giving us the fullness of love, for while he soars he remains faithfully human. Wherever we go with our figures and transformations, here in the ecstasy of the living flame of love, the real woman and man lie secretly (*secretamente*) alone.

Three Versions

Before the twentieth century, there were many translations into English of the poems of San Juan de la Cruz, all sentimental and piously Catholic. But we know that San Juan's central poems are secular in diction, relating a mystico-erotic love between a woman and man. Among the few twentieth-century translations, three come to mind: those by Roy Campbell, John Frederick Nims, and Antonio de Nicolás.

A South African, Roy Campbell lived most of his life in England, where he wrote verse that was classical and belligerently anti-experimental. In his first decades in England he endeared himself to many of the creative elite, to those whom he attacked in rhyming lampoons written in heroic couplets, and to those who shared his views, if not his aesthetic. But when he became a fervent Catholic who strongly supported Mussolini and Franco, Campbell became the bête noire among the liberal establishment.

One perceived enemy was the poet Stephen Spender. At Spender's public reading of poems about the Spanish Civil War, Campbell rushed onstage and punched Spender, who did not press charges, saying, "He is a great poet . . . and we must understand." Soon after, he awarded Campbell the 1952 Foyle Poetry Prize for his verse translations of San Juan, which won

Campbell worldwide praise from as far away as Buenos Aires, from Jorge Luis Borges.

San Juan's poem is written in the *lira*, a form borrowed from Italian poet Bernardo Tasso, who was imitating Horace. A *lira* consists of four indented heptasyllabic and two longer hendecasyllabic lines—rendered into English by both Campbell and Nims as iambic trimeter and pentameter. Campbell does not indent lines 1, 2, 4, and 5, as one would in the typical *lira*, but his form is regular throughout, the rhyme exact and the meter consistently iambic.

In the poetry of San Juan, the use of the *lira* corresponds to the ordinary speech of the *canción* (song) and *romance* (ballad). Those who translate San Juan usually fail to use an austere but plain diction, and Campbell's version goes up and down the rhetorical ladder. In the eighth line, "Oh gash that is my guerdon!," the word "gash" is strong and alliterates with "guerdon," which correctly translates the Spanish *regalada* ("reward"), but depending how you feel about this translation, the line may seem wonderful, strong, and fresh, or forced, with the remote word "guerdon" not fluent with San Juan's speech.

Exact attention to form is no doubt a reason for many of the small additions Campbell makes. These include the following, in which the words italicized by me have no equivalent in Spanish:

> Oh cautery *most* tender! (line 7)
> Oh gentle hand! Oh touch *how* soft*ly thrilling*! (line 9)
> Oh lamps of *fiery blaze* (line 13, instead of simply "fire")
> The deepest caverns of my soul *grow bright* (line 15)
> In glory, grace, *and rest* (line 23)

The prioritizing of form also creates some interrupted and inverted syntax, as in lines 3 and 4: "How tenderly you force / To my soul's inmost core your fiery probe!" or the last line, "So daintily in love you make me fall!" In the latter, Campbell does catch the dominant meaning ("you make me love"), as others have not.

Other choices may be matters of interpretation. The introduction to Campbell's translations is by Jesuit priest Martin C. D'Arcy, S. J., a Catholic intellectual and philosopher. He advises that "*clichés* of love" must be read only symbolically ("The touch of God is entirely spiritual"), and warns that critics who see "human passion" in San Juan's poem "are victims of some pathological disorder." Campbell's own evasions of physicality suggest agreement with D'Arcy, as in the sixth line, which he translates as "for our sweet encounter tear the robe." *Tela* can mean "cloth" or "membrane," but here, in this most sexually specific of all of San Juan's poems, it clearly refers to the hymen. "Robe" takes us away from this sexual meaning.

John Frederick Nims had a distinguished career as scholar, poet, and, above all, translator. He is perhaps best known today for his versions of the poetry of San Juan de la Cruz, which utilize his poetic expertise, full knowledge of Spanish, and a Spanish text based on the original edition.

Despite abundant straying from the original for purposes of prosody, which Nims intends, his form is splendid: he reproduces San Juan's *lira* effortlessly and adroitly. It is true that the poet he creates in English has very little of the plain, strong voice of San Juan; we hear instead the accomplished poet—and, in the concluding stanzas, an echo of Gerard Manley Hopkins, also a major religious poet. We have to look at Hopkins's magnificent "Wreck of the Deutschland" to find the extravagant particulars of Nims's last two stanzas.

Nims's re-creations are first-class if we do not seek too much of San Juan in them. On the spectrum of closeness to the voice and the prosody of the original, most good translators find themselves in the middle, where we can place Nims, along with W. S. Merwin, Robert Bly, and Stephen Mitchell.

Antonio de Nicolás was born in Spain around 1930, and eventually became a professor of philosophy in the United States. He has published a number of volumes of which he is sole author or coeditor, including *St. John of the Cross (San Juan de la Cruz): Alchemist of the Soul; His Life, His Poetry (Bilingual), His Prose.*

Nicolás's book is very useful. It contains all San Juan's poems in Spanish, his own English translations, a compact biography of San Juan, an abundant selection of his prose in translation, and a foreword by Seyyed Hossein Nasr, which relates San Juan's poems to Near Eastern poetry. Nicolás's translation is in common speech, all for the good, though it also attempts to reproduce some of the original's rhyme and rhythm. While his translation has some vivid lines, it sometimes sacrifices the most obvious meaning to exigencies of prosody, as in "Killing, death into life you change!" (line 12), and the last line, "How delicately in love you make me feel!" Though the line has the same inversion as Campbell's translation, "delicately" is much more accurate (and perhaps more implicitly erotic) than Campbell's "daintily."

Nicolás is a Spaniard who knows the full compass of the Spanish lines, and has done much work to enlighten us in his translation of both poetry and prose commentary, and in his own fascinating introduction. Fortunately, his translations have none of the extremely sentimental piety found in earlier translations by clergymen and others.

Nearly five hundred years ago, Saint John of the Cross was born in Old Castile. His texts will find new light, to be sure, over and over again. *Como Juan de la Cruz, no hay dos*: like John of the Cross, there are not two.

Note

1. In keeping with the agreement for these essays, I do not include my own version but do use it in this discussion of the original poem. For my full translation see Willis Barnstone, *The Poems of Saint John of the Cross* (New York: New Directions, 1976).

Bashō

(Japanese, 1644–1694)

TRANSLATIONS BY
Basil Hall Chamberlain, Harold G. Henderson,
Nobuyuki Yuasa

....

COMMENTARY BY

Hiroaki Sato

枯枝に烏のとまりたるや秋の暮

Kare'eda ni karasu no tomaritaru ya aki no kure

Bashō (1680)

かれ朶に烏のとまりけり秋の暮

Kare'eda ni karasu no tomarikeri aki no kure

Bashō (1689)

The end of autumn, and some rooks
Are perched upon a withered branch.

translated by Basil Hall Chamberlain (1902)

On a leafless bough
A crow is sitting: — autumn,
Darkening now —

translated by Harold G. Henderson (1925)

A black crow
Has settled himself
On a leafless tree
Fall on an autumn day.

translated by Nobuyuki Yuasa (1966)

Commentary by Hiroaki Sato
Singular or Plural?

The translator from Japanese into English often faces a question: is this word singular or plural? That's because most Japanese nouns don't distinguish between countable and uncountable, whereas most English nouns do. It is a feature that Chinese, for one, shares. In fact, it was a British-trained Chinese scholar, James J. Y. Liu, who chose to exalt this linguistic trait as one of the superior aspects of Chinese over English as a medium of poetic expression. His example was the second half of a quatrain by Wang Wei:

月出驚山鳥
[moon rise surprise mountain bird]
時鳴春澗中
[occasionally cry in spring valley]

To the Chinese poet, "it is of no consequence whether 'mountain,' 'bird,' and 'valley' are singular or plural," concerned as he is with "the essence of a mood or a scene rather than with accidental details," Liu observed. This embodies Aristotle's idea of the universal versus the particular. "As Chinese does not require any indication of 'number,' the poet need not bother about such irrelevant details and can concentrate on his main task of presenting the spirit of a tranquil spring night among the mountains."

This argument, in Liu's book *The Art of Chinese Poetry*, was sure to provoke a rebuttal, and it did. In *Chinese Lyricism*, Burton Watson countered Liu's "assertion of the superiority of the generalized over the particular" from the angle of what the modern English reader would want. Baptized by imagism, such a reader would demand "real toads in his imaginary garden," à la Marianne Moore, or declare that there are "no ideas but in things," à la William Carlos Williams, Watson wrote—although he, who studied classical Chinese in Kyoto, did not neglect to add: "To be sure, English, by distinguishing so importantly between 'one' and 'more than one,' and then leaving us in the dark as to how many more, presents almost as fuzzy a picture."

But, as I was saying, the absence of a clear distinction between one and more than one in Japanese nouns often flummoxes the translator. When I collected English translations of the most famous haiku of all, Matsuo Bashō's about the old pond and the batrachian, for *One Hundred Frogs: From Renga to Haiku to English*, I found that most translators think the poem describes just a single creature, while some do not, even though the latter constitute an absolute minority. One of those few is Lafcadio Hearn, the Greek Irish writer who was naturalized in Japan.

Old pond—frogs jumped in—sound of water

Hearn is known to have asked his wife Setsu, a samurai's daughter, to tell him old Japanese stories and poems in her own words, so we may assume this "translation," too, is directly based on her description, free of extraneous speculations on Zen import and such.

So I wasn't surprised to find in Charles Trumbull's Haiku Database a similar numerical split among the translators of another of Bashō's famous haiku, the one about the crow. (Trumbull, who served as the editor of *Modern Haiku* from 2006 to 2013, is meticulously compiling translations of haiku into English, and occasionally other languages as well.) Here, too, there are those who think the poem describes just one animal and those who think otherwise; though, again, the latter are the minority.

There is, however, one interesting difference between the frog and the crow haiku: for the frog haiku, no contemporary painting with Bashō's inscription on it has been found, whereas for the crow haiku, at least two paintings have been found, and they give two diametrically differing pictures, one showing a single crow and the other, many—to be exact, twenty-seven.

There is said to be a third, but I haven't seen it. It is "a sketch of three crows huddling on a leafless branch," according to Basil Hall Chamberlain, the great Victorian Japanologist who also left immortal words on the amphibian haiku: "From a European point of view, the mention of the frog spoils these lines completely; for we tacitly include frogs in the same category as monkeys and donkeys, —absurd creatures scarcely to be named without turning verse into caricature." Chamberlain thought there was only one frog specimen, but more than one bird, evidently because of the sketch he saw. So "some rooks" in his translation, cited here.

If you set aside the picture of three huddling crows for the moment, the question may be: why such a wide discrepancy between one and twenty-seven? The simple answer may be that Bashō changed his view over time, from naturalistic to conceptual.

The painting with many crows came first, perhaps in 1682, though, according to the haikai scholar Kira Sueo, Bashō's inscriptions were not officially authenticated as his until 1973. (*Haikai* is a genre that includes the sequential poetic form of *renga*, or "linked verse," and the *hokku*, or "opening phrase" of the sequence. *Hokku* is what is now called haiku.) The painter's name is not known, but Bashō may well have given him an idea. The painting presents a panoramic landscape in color. To the right, toward the bottom, a bare tree stands with seven crows perched on a couple of branches near the top, with twenty crows in the spacious air above it, altogether a lively bunch of birds. To the left are two pine trees with mountains beyond them, the farther one white, seemingly covered with snow. And to the left of the pine trees is a human figure in traveling garb, apparently looking toward the crows to the far right.

This painting combines autumn and winter landscapes, perhaps to accommodate Bashō's inscriptions, which consist of three parts. Toward the right edge is the crow haiku, in the middle space is a prose piece in praise of travel hats, and on the white mountain toward the left is another haiku suggesting the onset of winter.

In contrast, the painting with a single crow is an ink drawing, and it focuses on the bird. Looking dejected and turning the other way, it is perched on a single, drooping branch. Bashō's inscription is limited to the haiku, placed above the crow with some blank space between. Its painter was one of Bashō's top disciples, Morikawa Kyoriku, a samurai said to have been accomplished in six fields: spearsmanship, swordsmanship, horsemanship, calligraphy, painting, and haikai. That's why, some conjecture, Bashō gave him the haikai name Kyoriku, meaning "six permissions." He became Bashō's

disciple in 1692, just two years before the master's death. That means he made the crow painting during those few years, most likely discussing with Bashō how to present the bird.

Now, considering that crows tend to be gregarious and communal, you might say that the first painting better reflects nature as it is. What about the second painting? Traditionally, it has been suggested that in this piece Bashō is restating in a haikai the Daoist ideal of autumnal desolation expressed in the phrase (枯木寒鴉) ["withered tree cold crow"] and that therefore it can't involve a crowd of crows. Here again, the phrase doesn't indicate whether there is one or more birds shivering on one or more branches.

Having noted this, though, I must also note that in a 2010 paper exploring the Chinese sources of this haiku, Chao Chi-yu translates the phrase as "withered wood and chilly crows" and the haiku as "Crows flew to take a rest on withered branches in an autumn day at dusk," suggesting that at least one Chinese scholar doesn't think either that the original phrase necessarily depicts a single crow or that the haikai's recasting of it should.

In the end, this numerical determination may not be a major problem. Many translators may not even be aware of the multi-crow painting, but knowledge of it does not guarantee the expected result. For example, the scholar Makoto Ueda was thoroughly familiar with the painting when he wrote, in *Bashō and His Interpreters*, that, of the three known paintings with Bashō's inscriptions on them, the "one assumed to be the earliest depicts seven crows settled on a leafless tree, with twenty others flying in the sky." Yet he translates the haiku this way:

> on a bare branch
> a crow has alighted . . .
> autumn nightfall

When it comes to haiku translation in general, how to deal with the form may be a larger question. Most haiku translators employ a tercet or triplet, with rhyme or without, on the apparent grounds that the Japanese haiku is made up of three sections of five, seven, and five syllables. In fact, this form has been so frequently used since it reached the West more than a century ago that outside Japan most people mistakenly assume that haiku are always written in three lines.

There are some translators who employ different forms, as the citations at the outset of this essay attest, but they are a minority. Of the about fifty English translators of the crow haiku that Charles Trumbull assembled, only four (including Nobuyuki Yuasa, included here) use the quatrain, and two (including Basil Hall Chamberlain) the couplet. Whether they make use of couplet, tercet, or quatrain, these translators imply that some familiar English poetic forms are applicable to the Japanese form. Some also use rhyme, as does Harold G. Henderson (also included here).

The monostich is also a legitimate form, but it is less familiar. I made use of this in my own 1981 translation ("On dead branches crows remain perched at autumn's end") because the absolute majority of Japanese haiku poets—that is, those who stick to the set form of five, seven, and five syllables per phrase—treat the poem as a monolinear verse (albeit written vertically), except when written for aesthetic presentation. On these occassions, they break it up as variously as they please, from one to several syllables per line.

At the same time, there are also haiku poets who ignore the set form, and they, too, mostly treat what they write as one-liners. When the writer lineates his haiku, I lineate it in translation, too. In addition, the poets who usually write in the set form sometimes employ hypersyllabic phrases, as Bashō does in the crow haiku. In fact, there are two versions of the poem, but both with a hypersyllabic middle phrase: the first one has ten syllables rather than the standard seven and the second one nine syllables.

As to the aesthetic presentations, in the painting with many crows, Bashō writes his haiku this way:

Kare'eda ni karasu no	(9 syllables)
tomaritaru ya	(6 syllables)
aki no kure	(5 syllables)

In this version, the first and second lines are written so close to each other that at first glance they may not appear separate. In the painting of a single crow, Bashō writes the haiku like this:

Kare'eda ni	(5 syllables)
karasu no tomarikeri	(9 syllables)
aki no kure	(5 syllables)

In Japanese, such "lines" are normally written to be read from right to left, but in another famous haiku, *Michinobe no mokuge wa uma ni kuwaretari* ("The roadside hibiscus has been eaten by my horse"), Bashō breaks it into nine-, three-, and five-syllable lines to be read from left to right. This poem comes with his own lovely painting of a pink hibiscus.

The ten-syllable middle phrase in the many-crow version includes *ya*, a *kireji* ("cutting word"): an exclamation or interjection that is frequently expressed in English translation by a colon, an exclamation mark, or a dash; very few translations retain the *ya*. *Tomaritaru*, "(to) be perched," stresses the settled-down state of the act of perching, and grammatically modifies what follows, *aki no kure* (see below). In the nine-syllable middle phrase of the single-crow version, *tomarikeri* means more or less the same thing except that its stresses marvel at the act.

Has anyone tried to reproduce the hypersyllabic differences in a translation? No one I have found.

And how about the different meanings of the verbs in the middle phrases? American poet Cid Corman, who lived in Kyoto for many years, imagines the precise movement of the crow in his 1991 translation:

on a bare branch a
crow finally gets a grip
fall night coming on

This arresting, precise image compares favorably with that of William N. Porter's translation eighty years earlier, titled "Sunset":

> The autumn day is done,
> The crows upon a withered branch
> Blink at the setting sun.

Finally, in the upper five syllables, *kare'eda*, "withered branch" (as in Chamberlain's translation as well as Porter's) is understood to mean a branch of a dead tree, not of a tree that has shed its leaves, as Henderson's and Yuasa's translations would suggest. And the lower five syllables, *aki no kure*, is traditionally ambiguous, meaning either "an autumn evening" or "late autumn" or both.

Giacomo Leopardi

(Italian, 1798–1837)

TRANSLATIONS BY
Kenneth Rexroth, Eamon Grennan,
Jonathan Galassi

....

COMMENTARY BY
Susan Stewart

L'infinito

Sempre caro mi fu quest'ermo colle,
E questa siepe, che da tanta parte
Dell'ultimo orizzonte il guardo esclude.
Ma sedendo e mirando, interminati
Spazi di là da quella, e sovrumani
Silenzi, e profondissima quiete
Io nel pensier mi fingo; ove per poco
Il cor non si spaura. E come il vento
Odo stormir tra queste piante, io quello
Infinito silenzio a questa voce
Vo comparando: e mi sovvien l'eterno,
E le morte stagioni, e la presente
E viva, e il suon di lei. Così tra questa
Immensità s'annega il pensier mio:
E il naufragar m'è dolce in questo mare.

Giacomo Leopardi (1819)

The Infinite

This lonely hill has always
Been dear to me, and this thicket
Which shuts out most of the final
Horizon from view. I sit here,
And gaze, and imagine
The interminable spaces
That stretch away, beyond my mind,
Their uncanny silences,
Their profound calms; and my heart
Is almost overwhelmed with dread.
And when the wind drones in the
Branches, I compare its sound
With that infinite silence;
And I think of eternity,
And the dead past, and the living
Present, and the sound of it;
And my thought drowns in immensity;
And shipwreck is sweet in such a sea.

translated by Kenneth Rexroth (1950)

Infinitive

I've always loved this lonesome hill
And this hedge that hides
The entire horizon, almost, from sight.
But sitting here in a daydream, I picture
The boundless spaces away out there, silences
Deeper than human silence, an unfathomable hush
In which my heart is hardly a beat
From fear. And hearing the wind
Rush rustling through these bushes,
I pit its speech against infinite silence—
And a notion of eternity floats to mind,
And the dead seasons, and the season
Beating here and now, and the sound of it. So,
In this immensity my thoughts all drown;
And it's easeful to be wrecked in seas like these.

translated by Eamon Grennan (1997)

Infinity

This lonely hill was always dear to me,
and this hedgerow, which cuts off the view
of so much of the last horizon.
But sitting here and gazing, I can see
beyond, in my mind's eye, unending spaces,
and superhuman silences, and depthless calm,
till what I feel
is almost fear. And when I hear
the wind stir in these branches, I begin
comparing that endless stillness with this noise:
and the eternal comes to mind,
and the dead seasons, and the present
living one, and how it sounds.
So my mind sinks in this immensity:
and foundering is sweet in such a sea.

translated by Jonathan Galassi (2010)

Commentary by Susan Stewart
Translating Leopardi's "L'infinito": An Infinite Task

Thoroughly canonized as they are, Leopardi's poems have long been considered untranslatable. The problems they raise may at first seem typical of those facing any translator working from Italian into English: differences in pronoun usage, syntactical order, contractions; the messy task of moving clear Italian rhymes and assonance into the more subtle repertoire of English rhymes; the incommensurability of two very different stress conventions; the difficulty of transposing hendecasyllabic verse into English blank verse; the struggle to maintain the coherence of lines while giving some sense of the play of sounds.

Yet translators of Leopardi must overcome historical obstacles as well, including the unique range of the poet's learning and his borrowings from ancient Greek and Latin, often pastoral, forms. Constantly negotiating between an Enlightenment classicism and a nascent Romanticism, Leopardi shifts rapidly between an active and a passive voice, between rational intention and metrical surrender. His diction is another obstacle as he evokes the speech of his provincial hometown in the Marche and at the same time the sophisticated and precise vocabulary he developed in his magnificent notebooks on aesthetics, the *Zibaldone*. In those pages he praises the beauty of the *indefinito*, the undefined and indeterminate, and the *vago*, the hazy and uncertain. And he celebrates the necessity of invention, indicated by his fondness for the verb *fingere*, to feign, pretend, or imagine. He develops in the *Zibaldone* as well a sharp distinction between two kinds of words: *termini*, terms referring to the concrete, exact domains of science and the empirical, and *parole*, words calling up myriad historical associations.

"L'infinito," composed and published in 1819 when Leopardi was twenty-one, is exemplary not only for its beauty and the power of its thought, but as well for its resistance to English translation. From the start, the three most distinguished recent English renderings of the poem offer different titles: Kenneth Rexroth's "The Infinite," Eamon Grennan's "Infinitive," and Jonathan Galassi's "Infinity."

Rexroth stayed close to Leopardi by twice printing his translation under the Italian title and twice using "The Infinite." Galassi's "Infinity" is puzzling, since *infinità*, the mathematical term, cannot encompass "the infinite" and its matrix of predecessors—Longinus, Edmund Burke, and Immanuel Kant—concerned with the psychological and emotional consequences of sublime experience. Relying on a tertiary meaning in Italian, Grennan's choice of the grammatical term "infinitive" is even more baffling. Rainer Maria Rilke, in his 1938 translation of "L'infinito" into German, also simply used the Italian title. Since the titles of poems as well-known as "L'infinito"—or, say, "The Waste Land"—eventually refer to the works' monumental status as much as to their themes, perhaps the original title remains the best choice for a translator.

As for the form, there are only so many features of Leopardi's variable hendecasyllabics that can be carried over into English. The poem's ingenious metrical effects are striking and particular to the elisions and accents of Italian: consider the calm symmetry of line 6: *Silenzi, e profondissima quiete* [u + u / u u + u u / u + u] or the mimetic effect of the tipping shipwreck, with its core sweet spot, in line 15, the poem's final line: *E il naufragar m'è dolce in questo mare* [u u u + u / + / u u u + u]. Looking for correspondences, all three poets follow Leopardi in employing frequent enjambment. The only end-stopped line is at the dramatic ending to the third line: *esclude*, a stop mimetic of the very blockage it describes. Grennan and Galassi both include it.

Grennan and Galassi also stick with the fifteen-line (sonnet) form and follow Leopardi's own loose *versi sciolti*. Literally "melting or loosened verses," and sometimes inaccurately translated as "blank verse," this term indicates a flexible use of a basic hendecasyllabic line accompanied by frequent enjambment. Rexroth, however, pays little attention to the original lineation and ends up with an eighteen-line poem. Rexroth and Galassi both rhyme "immensity" and "sea" at the end of the poem, yet such a final rhyming closure is not in the original. Leopardi's overall rhyme pattern can be written as AAABBACCCACADCA: each end-word has a rhyme except for the thirteenth line's *questa*. Rexroth's only rhyming end-words are "eternity," "immensity," and "sea." Grennan has some resonant internal sound play: in the opening lines he pairs "loved" and "lonesome," and as his translation goes on, he builds a breathless sense of motion through his use of "hedge," "hides," "horizon," "human," "hush," "heart," and "hearing." Yet his only repetition of end-of-line sound comes with "silences" and "silence." Galassi provides a clever nod to the original by including four analogical rhymed words: the opening "me," line 4's "see," and the closing couplet's "immensity" and "sea." He thereby makes an allusion to Leopardi's final couplet's *mio / mare* ("my . . . sea") as he rhymes his first and last lines.

But of course Italian words rhyme more often than not, and the sound play of the poem exists on a more sophisticated level. For example, as the distinguished Leopardi scholar Margaret Brose points out in a 1983 essay on "L'infinito," Leopardi carefully builds a chiasmus between the poem's first and last lines: *caro / mare // dolce / colle* and also creates a phonetic and semantic rhyme between *spaura, naufragar,* and *mare*. None of these features appear in the English translations, but the transposition Grennan creates between "easeful" and "seas" as he drops the significance of *dolce* ("sweet") has something of Leopardi's wordplay even as he loses one of Leopardi's key terms.

"L'infinito" opens with an instance of inverted syntax, delaying the appearance of the predicate nominative *colle* until the end of the line. From the start, then, an inherent tension crops up between the adverb *sempre* and the verb *mi fu: sempre* indicates a continuous action and *mi fu* is an instance of the reflexive use of the *trapassato remoto*. The *trapassato remoto* is a recognizably literary tense, but it indicates an action *completed* in the remote past and so cannot be truly "always." Jonathan Galassi comes closest to the verb form by using the past tense "was"; nevertheless, risking awkwardness, the translators might have turned to "long ago" or another term of temporal distance so the separation between past and present could be emphasized.

At the poem's opening we also find the adjective *ermo,* a Greek-derived archaism, and a good example of a typical Leopardian *parole*. Its meaning is a shade between "isolated" and "lone" or "sole." Rexroth and Galassi choose "lonely," Grennan the slightly more folksy "lonesome"—and so the word becomes attached to the hill like an emotion. But the meaning of "lone" or "sole" can also indicate something singular, and it is this quality of the hill as a distinctive, isolated point on the landscape that attracts Leopardi's attention. Indeed, the poet's dear "hill" is nearby Monte Tabor. The Adriatic Sea lies beyond Monte Tabor just as the Sea of Galilee lies beyond its Biblical namesake, Mount Tabor. The mountain, as a singular feature of the landscape, beyond which lie other spaces and meanings, will lead the way to the poem's profound and watery close. In the end, an unfolding horizontal view will pull us toward the vertical depths of sky and sea. To move from a succession of sounds into silence, from actual horizontality into imaginative depth, is indeed the central work of the poem.

In the next set of lines Leopardi performs an ekphrastic feat difficult to replicate: after his initial view of the singular hill, he describes how a line of vegetation almost (*da tanta parte*) blocks the view of the farthest horizon. The effect is like looking in turn through each end of a pair of binoculars. Grennan comes closest to the ordinary word *siepe* with "hedge," while Rexroth loses the horizontal form with "thicket" (which in Italian would more likely be *boschetto*), but Galassi understands that a hedge in a landscape in the early nineteenth century was in fact a "hedgerow." Galassi's more exacting turn to the Wordsworthian term (the "hedge-rows hardly hedge-rows" and elevated view of the opening of "Tintern Abbey" come to mind) indicates a horizontal line capable of blocking a vista.

As he sets out these early lines, Leopardi thereby draws the horizontal schema of the landscape and lets the *ultimo orizzonte* represent its most distant point. Rexroth picks this up as "final," Galassi as "last," but Grennan inexplicably uses "entire" horizon, losing Leopardi's trick of depth. Influenced by post-Copernican astronomy, Leopardi implies an unending, unfolding universe. Only Galassi indicates this vision, with his accurate, if somewhat plodding, "superhuman." Unfortunately Galassi's use of "depthless," with its dual valence of the immeasurable and the shallow, halts the reader just at the moment when it is time to dive in. Grennan's "unfathomable" seems closer; Rexroth's "uncanny" adds an awkward Freudianism.

Because the Italian drops the pronoun, the subject or agent of the observations in the poem is often only implied—a feature Leopardi emphasizes when he uses the gerunds *sedendo* and *mirando* in the fourth line and again with *comparando* in line 11. None of the English versions can exactly follow this construction; they must introduce an "I" where there is none. Grennan and Galassi capture the semantic turn effected by *ma* ("but") in line 4, but Grennan unhappily introduces "a daydream" and the verb "picture"—neither of which exist in the original. Both terms are counter to the meaning of *mirando* as a pointed or aimed kind of gazing/looking.

Throughout the poem, the speaker is made the object of feelings, motions, and effects that are expressed not only by means of gerunds, but also via reflexive verbs and passive constructions. We see this strategy at work in the four instances of first-person reflexive forms: *mi fu*; *mi fingo*; *mi sovvien*; *m'è*. Significantly, *il pensier mio* ("my thought") also is acted upon through a reflexive verb: *s'annega* ("drowns itself"). These brief reflexive loops emphasize the role of invention and memory in the progress of the speaker's observations. They move in tension with the poem's deictic *termini*—pointed moments of attention that dissolve increasingly into abstraction: *quest'ermo colle*; *questa siepe*; *quello / Infinito silenzio*; *questa voce*; *questa / Immensità*. Yet of the three translators, only Galassi maintains the relationship between *quello / . . . silenzio* and *questa voce* ("*that* silence" and "*this* voice").

The dense middle lines of the poem—7, 8, and 9—understandably give each translator trouble. Since Leopardi uses the verb *fingere* to mean not only "to pretend," but also "to simulate or imagine," the reflexive form indicates something of the daydreaming Grennan introduces in an earlier line—to invent or imagine or pretend to be. Leopardi indicates that for a little while (*ove per poco*), the heart does not feel fear (*si spaura* is another reflexive verb). A parallel reflexivity between imagined thoughts and a fearful heart is thereby introduced.

The subsequent lines, with their torqued syntax and enjambment, recreate a sequence of sensations. First we discover the sound of the wind rustling in the trees. The plural *piante*, indicating plants or trees, is only one letter away from *pianto* ("crying"), a connection difficult if not impossible to bring over into English. The speaker hears this sound and compares "that infinite silence" to "this voice." Here another set of parallels is introduced, but it is difficult to determine their relation: is the wind rustling in the trees an infinite silence, or is this silence some other silence beyond it? Or is "that infinite silence" elsewhere and "this voice" meant to indicate the voice of the wind? Or, yet another possibility, is the voice the speaker's own, the voice of his thoughts?

This clotted and complex set of lines exemplifies very well Leopardi's use of poetic *parole* and metaleptic constructions. The paired thoughts and heart, the auditory triplet of wind, infinite silence, and voice—words become at once both connected and possible substitutes for one another. At the same time, Leopardi demonstrates brilliantly the impossibility of using deictic terms like "that" or "this" when trying to point to a moving, invisible force such as the wind or a voice, or to something too large to indicate—the sublime silence of the universe. Here the problem is not so much the limits of English as Leopardi's nod to the limits of poetic representation itself.

In all the versions here, *ove per poco* vanishes and the translations lose the halting pace of the original. Rexroth changes the lineation and scrubs things down to: "and my heart / Is almost overwhelmed with dread. / And when the wind drones in the / Branches, I compare its sound / With that endless silence." Galassi similarly strips the lines: "till what I feel / is almost fear. And when I hear / the wind stir in these branches, I begin / comparing that endless stillness with this noise." Leopardi's heart and voice have thereby disappeared. Grennan attaches the phrase "an unfathomable hush" to "In which my heart is hardly a beat / From fear. And hearing the wind / Rush rustling through these bushes, / I pit its speech against infinite silence." Grennan's adaptation significantly changes the meaning: the heart is now more afraid than ever; the agonistic "to pit" has replaced the cooler and slower "to compare"; the wind is now rushing and rustling and the voice no longer ambiguously refers to the speaker as well as to the wind—it is now only the wind's speech. Leopardi's wind rustles (*stormir*—a word linked etymologically to *stormo*, a flight or flock); "rustling" is not, as Rexroth indicates, "droning." Galassi chooses "stirring," a word that nicely helps set up the contrast between stillness and motion, but he ends by introducing the vague and bland "noise." This might have been the place to link the images of rustling leaves and a bird stirring in a tree.

One of Leopardi's simplest and most elegant effects of motion arises from his repetition of *e* ("and"). Throughout, the conjunction both joins and sets into sequence. In the first line the statement *Sempre caro mi fu quest'ermo colle* is followed by a comma, and *E questa siepe* follows as an additional "dear" object and an afterthought. The gerunds *sedendo* and *mirando* similarly are not simultaneous—sitting is the precondition of the focused look. In lines 5 and 6 (*e sovrumani / Silenzi, e profondissima quiete*) and again in line 8 (*E come il vento*) the conjunction also works as both a device of augmentation and continuing thought. These three conjunctions introducing end-of-line phrases are beautifully symmetrical to the anaphoric use of the conjunction *e* in lines 12, 13, and 15. The device continues, in a veritable crescendo of speeding connections, in the internal parallels of lines 12 and 13 as *e la presente* and *e il suon di lei*. The conjunctions of course are easily translated and all three translators carry them over with varying degrees of fidelity to the phrasing.

In lines 11 through 14, leading to the closing line, Leopardi shows the mind at work, revealing the interplay between phenomenal details and abstractions, so readily analogous to his later distinction between *termini* and *parole*. As thought of *l'eterno* ("the eternal") arises, the focus becomes more concrete: the "dead seasons" are followed by the present, living one, and a sense of sound increases. *Il suon di lei* ("the sound of it") plays upon the previous lines, 8 through 10, with their wind in the trees, infinite surrounding silence, and *questa voce*—the undefined term that could indicate either the speaker's own voice or the sounds and silence around him. Rexroth and Galassi stay close to Leopardi, but Grennan introduces "the season / Beating here and now," echoing his earlier mention of the heart as "hardly a beat / From fear." Given that Leopardi's original seems to have a kind of volume control, as sounds are amplified to the point of near chaos and then turned down to an equally overwhelming silence, Grennan's "beat" evokes both the wind and the heart's beat and is not so farfetched as it might first appear.

Here the translator faces new difficulties. Immensity drowns the speaker's thoughts as he cries out that it is sweet to be shipwrecked in *questo mare* ("this—such a—sea"). Galassi chooses "my mind sinks." This is a vivid image, tied to becoming disheartened, yet we can "sink" into a chair or bed as well as into water, and Leopardi's drowning/sea imagery is key to the transit of the poem toward the Adriatic. Grennan chooses a plural—"my thoughts"—and so loses the abstraction of *il pensier mio*; thought itself is drowning, not specific ideas, and Leopardi is moving back from the phenomenal to the indefinite. Both Rexroth and Galassi carry over the predicate adjective "sweet," so important to both the meaning and the metrical emphases of the original poem.

The noun *il naufragar*—"the shipwreck"—frames the last line (literally "and shipwreck is sweet to me in such a sea") and the entire close of the poem as it has unfolded from line 11 onward. Rexroth drops the reflexive aspect of the verb: "And shipwreck is sweet in such a sea." Grennan says "to be wrecked," relying for context on "seas like these" and once again turning a single noun (*mare*) into a plural. Galassi uses "foundering," which relies on the word's Latin etymology, *fond*, or "bottom," but the Latin *naufragar* indicates the more active, and visible, process of shipwreck. This choice has vivid consequences for the ending of the poem—with Galassi's version the waters are closing, or have closed, over; in Grennan and Rexroth's, thought is suspended, drowning before our eyes.

Translation is a practice of hard choices, but as well an art of love. As Rexroth writes in a 1959 essay, "The Poet as Translator," "The ideal translator . . . is not engaged in matching the words of a text with the words of his own language. He is hardly even a proxy, but rather an all-out advocate." Grennan and Galassi have followed Rexroth's lead, for these are three true translations of "L'infinito," not merely versions in the style of Ezra Pound or Robert Lowell. Rexroth has brought Leopardi into contemporary American English. Grennan has made a vivid and memorable English poem. Galassi has exercised unprecedented care. The twenty-one-year-old Leopardi, so famously unfortunate and unhappy, is lucky to have as his advocates these three patient and ingenious poet-translators writing so indefinitely, so invisibly, far in his future.

Charles Baudelaire

(French, 1821–1867)

TRANSLATIONS BY

Rosemary Lloyd, Keith Waldrop,
Louise Varèse

· ·

COMMENTARY BY

Cole Swensen

Un plaisant

C'était l'explosion du nouvel an: chaos de boue et de neige, traversé de mille carrosses, étincelant de joujoux et de bonbons, grouillant de cupidités et de désespoirs, délire officiel d'une grande ville fait pour troubler le cerveau du solitaire le plus fort.

Au milieu de ce tohu-bohu et de ce vacarme, un âne trottait vivement, harcelé par un malotru armé d'un fouet.

Comme l'âne allait tourner l'angle d'un trottoir, un beau monsieur ganté, verni, cruellement cravaté et emprisonné dans des habits tout neufs, s'inclina cérémonieusement devant l'humble bête, et lui dit, en ôtant son chapeau: "Je vous la souhaite bonne et heureuse!" puis se retourna vers je ne sais quels camarades avec un air de fatuité, comme pour les prier d'ajouter leur approbation à son contentement.

L'âne ne vit pas ce beau plaisant, et continua de courir avec zèle où l'appelait son devoir.

Pour moi, je fus pris subitement d'une incommensurable rage contre ce magnifique imbécile, qui me parut concentrer en lui tout l'esprit de la France.

Charles Baudelaire (1869)

A Prankster

The New Year's celebrations were in full swing. A chaos of mud and snow, traversed by a thousand carriages, glittering with toys and sweets, bristling with greed and grief, a city's official delirium, destined to disturb the mind of the strongest recluse.

In the midst of this uproar, a donkey trotted briskly along, harassed by a whip-bearing lout.

As the donkey was about to turn the corner of a footpath, a handsome gentleman, gloved and polished, cruelly cravatted and imprisoned in brand new clothes, bowed ceremoniously to the humble beast, and said to him as he raised his hat: 'A happy and prosperous New Year to you!'. Then he returned to his companions with a fatuous air, as if to ask them to crown his contentment with their approval.

The donkey did not see this fine prankster, and went on zealously trotting to wherever his duty called him.

As for me, I was suddenly seized with a boundless rage at this manifest imbecile, who seemed to me to concentrate within him all the wit of France.

translated by Rosemary Lloyd (1991)

A Joker

Explosive New Year's Day: chaos of mud and snow, criss-crossed by a thousand carriages, sparkling with toys and toffee, crawling with greed and despair, standard delirium of a metropolis, made to disturb the brain of the sturdiest solitary.

In the midst of bohu and din, a donkey trotted briskly, hard pressed by a rascal with a whip.

As the donkey came to turn a corner, a gentleman, gloved, polished, imprisoned in cruel necktie and spanking new duds, bowed ceremoniously to the humble beast and, doffing his hat, addressed it, "All the best for you in the new year," turning then to I know not what companions with a fatuous air, as if praying them to approve his own satisfaction.

The donkey, oblivious to this high-class joker, continued its trek as duty directed.

For my part, I was taken suddenly with an incommensurate rage against this ostentatious imbecile, who seemed to me to concentrate in himself the whole spirit of France.

translated by Keith Waldrop (2009)

A Wag

Pandemonium of New Year's Eve: chaos of snow and mud churned up by a thousand carriages glittering with toys and bonbons, swarming with cupidity and despair; official frenzy of a big city designed to trouble the mind of the most impervious solitary.

In the midst of this deafening hubbub, a donkey was trotting briskly along, belabored by a low fellow armed with a whip.

Just as the donkey was about to turn a corner, a resplendent gentleman, all groomed, gloved, cruelly cravated and imprisoned in brand new clothes, made a ceremonious bow to the humble beast, saying as he took off his hat: "A very happy and prosperous New Year to you!" Then he turned with a fatuous air toward some vague companions, as though to beg them to make his satisfaction complete by their applause.

The donkey paid no attention to this elegant wag, and continued to trot zealously along where duty called.

As for me, I was suddenly seized by an incomprehensible rage against this bedizened imbecile, for it seemed to me that in him was concentrated all the wit of France.

translated by Louise Varèse (1970)

Commentary by Cole Swensen
The case of:

The untranslatable title: ah! always a sign of a particularly promising project! It allows the translator to admit defeat right at the start—to simply get it over with, dispelling at once the illusion that translation might actually be possible, and thus getting immediately to the heart of the promise of impossibility, which is the infinity that every impossibility makes suddenly available. For if we undertake the possible, we admit that there's an end to be achieved; we admit that there's a correct solution, and even if there are many, this is terribly limiting.

Baudelaire's "Un plaisant" is a case in point—in fact, it's a poem full of words that just happen to pose curious problems—not huge ones, but ones that demand that the translator stop and puzzle, choose and doubt. It's not a poem that presents overall content problems—it's easy enough to convey what it says; instead, its content problems occur at tiny, precise, and crucial points, such as the title. The three solutions chosen by these translators—"A Prankster," "A Joker," and "A Wag"—are all excellent solutions, but they all feel a little odd in the mouth. When was the last time you used any of those words in a conversation? Or anywhere, for that matter? But what other word could you use? My grandfather would have said "a wise guy"—but I wouldn't. What *would* I say? And why this gap? Is it that we don't have people who act this way anymore? Hardly that! Or do we prefer to avert our eyes and ignore such behavior? Or do we express it as a verb—he's just clowning around, etc.—thereby allowing the action to pass and not adhere to the person, labeling him forever?

Whatever our reasons, we're left in this case with three options that all sound and feel just slightly off-kilter. Which is fitting, as the French word *plaisant* has the same feel in a French mouth—or so my native French-speaking friends tell me; it's rather outdated and a bit bumbly, for though adjectives are routinely turned into nouns designating a person with that attribute (*le pauvre* for "the poor person," for instance), the more usual term today would be *plaisantin*. Though still a bit odd, the term *un plaisant* was more usual in Baudelaire's day, and so it holds within it the 150 years between then and now, and delicately imparts some of the flavors and scents of that distant time—an attribute that all three of these translations have captured beautifully.

The poem contains several other words that similarly contain distilled time: *joujoux, tohu-bohu, malotru*. The fact that they all rhyme says, I think, something about the way that the poem is held together internally and the way that words communicate privately among themselves, strengthening their affinities, but that may be merely fanciful. As for the words themselves, it's not that they are never heard in today's French, but that they aren't heard often, and when they are, there's a whiff of the antique in the air; one finds oneself suddenly thinking of one's great-aunts. Unfortunately, there's not much English can do with *joujoux* except "toy," which is what all three translators wisely chose, though Keith Waldrop managed to get a little of the sound play of the French *de joujoux et de bonbons* with his alliterative "toys and toffee."

Tohu-bohu presents a more difficult problem, in both its onomatopoeia and its etymology; it comes from the Biblical Hebrew *tohu wa-bohu*, which appears in Genesis 1:2 and describes the condition of the earth before there was light. It is usually translated as "waste and void" or "formless and empty"—so rather the opposite of the scene that Baudelaire is evoking, thus introducing into the poem both the tension of a contradiction and a profoundly originary element that casts the novelty of the new year in literally Biblical terms. Apparently, it's also an English word, as it appears in the *Oxford English Dictionary*. Waldrop took advantage of this in his construction "bohu and din," choosing for his second term a word that, to my ear at least, has a similarly ancient, archetypal ring to it, though I find Rosemary Lloyd's direct, leonine "uproar" equally satisfying. Louise Varèse chose to retain the onomatopoeia with "hubbub," also a very satisfying sound, and one that additionally invites the image of a traffic hub, so appropriate here.

The third term, *malotru*, takes us back to the issue with which we started—an outdated word for which English has no exact equivalent, and one for which all options, even the approximate ones, are equally outdated—but then, that's what we want: the feeling of time and its intolerable pastness present in the poem. Varèse chose "low fellow," Lloyd chose "lout," and Waldrop chose "rascal." Again, when did you last use any of those words seriously? (Though the thought of leaning out the car window and screaming, "You rascal! You lout! You *lowww fellowww!*" the next time someone cuts you off in traffic is pretty appealing.)

Just as the poem begins with a particular difficulty, it ends with one as well: *tout l'esprit de la France. Esprit* becomes a particularly slippery word when it travels from French into English. It can mean "spirit" in all the senses of the English word—from "ghost" to "soul" to "verve" to "personal nature" or "mental attitude"—but another of its principal meanings in French is "mind," while its additional meanings include "finesse" (*resoudre les problèmes avec esprit*), and in compounds it can take on many other nuances, such as *avoir de l'esprit*, "to be witty." Baudelaire's original line maximizes the ambiguity of the term. He seems to be aiming for the most open set of interpretations possible, as if in an attempt to further destabilize this famously unstable word, which has the effect of blowing the poem open right at the end, where we expect closure. Unfortunately, the choice of any English word eliminates at least some possibilities; each of the three solutions chosen by these translators operates differently, but all ingeniously avoid that closing-down as much as possible. Both Lloyd and Varèse chose "wit," which focuses on the social dimension, and sends us back to the middle of the poem, to the description of the dandy, a distinct mid-nineteenth-century Parisian type emblematic of the revolution in social structure and social conditions occasioned by the urban transformation of Paris in the 1850s and 1860s. The choice locks the line into a particular historical moment within a twenty-year span and opens the poem out into a pointed social critique, which is complicated by the fact that Baudelaire would have been placed by onlookers, through his dress and social bearing, in the same class as this *plaisant*. There's an element of self-mockery and frustration around social classification latent in the poem that this choice foregrounds.

Waldrop, on the other hand, chose "spirit," which allows him to retain many more of the French word's meanings and nuances while broadening the field of frustration and extending the social sphere that he's implicating—here, it's *all* of France, and for all time, both past and future. He effectively claims an eternal spirit for France—and damns it—not majestically, not Faustianly, but foppishly. This feels less self-referential, and instead casts the incommensurate rage as a gesture of rupture with and an attempt to escape from the spirit of nationalism that was so virulent in France throughout the nineteenth century.

Though there is an unusual concentration of idiosyncratic, charged vocabulary in this poem, no translation is really about individual words; it's about gathering them into higher syntactical orders, which is where the signatures of poet and translator both come through, in this case revealing three quite different sensibilities—all in the very first phrase. It's an extremely dramatic one: *C'était l'explosion du nouvel an.* The poem begins literally explosively, exploding into the new, challenging the translator to retain the high energy and clipped tone, the compressed equation that the off-rhyme between *"explosion"* and "an" so concisely suggests in the original. These three translators have all found fabulous solutions: Waldrop's "Explosive New Year's Day" keeps it clipped, compact, and much closer to Baudelaire's line, while moving the explosion to an even more immediate position; Varèse's line also positions the explosion in the opening word, but she changes the word—"Pandemonium" (by its very nature spangled and missing from a zoo . . .). What a fabulous way to enter a poem! In contrast, Lloyd's "The New Year's celebrations were in full swing" is more stately, more formal in its normative sentence structure, and thus longer in its approach, putting the emphasis at the very end with an idiom ("in full swing") that captures the reeling motion of the scene.

I love these three translations because they all leap into the poem's many difficulties with verve and zeal, and the ingenious choices that each translator makes resound only more masterfully when compared with the others. It's a particularly good poem to consider in light of the act of translation, too, because its central event is its own kind of translation: at the moment of encounter, an exchange takes place in which an animal takes on the dignity normally expected of a man, while the "ass" slides not only from animal to man, but from a literal term to a figurative one.

However, like all good translations, these three include an element that can't be translated; in this case, it's the connection, visual and somewhat sonic, between the words *an* ("year") and *âne* ("donkey") that in the French allows an animal, here cast as the hero of the tale, to become a figure for the year, which, too, is ultimately impervious to human intervention. All translations need an absolutely untranslatable moment to remind us that any translation is, in fact, impossible—and thus unlimited.

Stéphane Mallarmé

(French, 1842–1898)

TRANSLATIONS BY

Roger Fry, Daisy Aldan,
Peter Manson

....

COMMENTARY BY

Jennifer Moxley

Sonnet

Ses purs ongles très haut dédiant leur onyx,
L'Angoisse ce minuit, soutient, lampadophore,
Maint rêve vespéral brûlé par le Phénix
Que ne recueille pas de cinéraire amphore

Sur les crédences, au salon vide: nul ptyx,
Aboli bibelot d'inanité sonore,
(Car le Maître est allé puiser des pleurs au Styx
Avec ce seul objet dont le Néant s'honore.)

Mais proche la croisée au nord vacante, un or
Agonise selon peut-être le décor
Des licornes ruant du feu contre une nixe,

Elle, défunte nue en le miroir, encor
Que, dans l'oubli fermé par le cadre, se fixe
De scintillations sitôt le septuor.

Stéphane Mallarmé (1887)

Sonnet

Her pure nails very high dedicating their onyx,
Anguish, this midnight, upholds, the lampbearer,
Many vesperal dreams by the Phenix burnt
That are not gathered up in the funeral urn

On the credences, in the empty room: no ptyx,
Abolished bibelot of sounding inanity
(For the Master is gone to draw tears from the Styx
With this sole object which Nothingness honours.)

But near the window void Northwards, a gold
Dies down composing perhaps a decor
Of unicorns kicking sparks at a nixey,

She, nude and defunct in the mirror, while yet,
In the oblivion closed by the frame there appears
Of scintillations at once the septet.

translated by Roger Fry (1936)

Its pure nails offering very high their onyx....

Its pure nails offering very high their onyx,
Anguish, this midnight, bears, like a candelabra,
Many an evening dream consumed by the Phoenix
Not gathered up in any funeral amphora

On the credenzas, in the empty salon: No seashell,
Vanished curio of sonorous emptiness,
(For the Master has gone to draw tears from the Styx
With this sole object in which the Void takes pride).

But near the window open to the north, a gold
Is dying composing a kind of decor
Of unicorns hurling fire at a nixie,

She, a dead nude in the mirror, although,
In the oblivion enclosed by the frame, at once
The scintillations of The Seven Stars are fixed.

translated by Daisy Aldan (1999)

Its pure nails raised to consecrate their onyx,
Anguish, this midnight, holds up, lampadephore,
many a vesperal dream burned by the Phoenix
that is gathered in no cinerary amphora

on the credences, in the empty salon: no ptyx
abolished bauble inanely echoing,
(for the Master has gone to draw tears from the Styx
with this one object on which Nothing prides itself).

But near the cross-pane vacant to the north, a gold
is dying, perhaps in sympathy with the décor
of unicorns kicking fire against a nixe,

she, defunct nude in the mirror, even
though, in oblivion closed by the frame, at once
the septet of fixed scintillations settles.

translated by Peter Manson (2012)

Commentary by Jennifer Moxley
Mallarmé's Unyielding "Sonnet en -yx": Three Encounters

British art critic, painter, and advocate of beautiful rooms Roger Fry; American poet, pedagogue, and visionary editor of *Folder* Daisy Aldan; contemporary young Scottish lyric poet Peter Manson: who among them can see into the mysteries of Stéphane Mallarmé's "Sonnet," often referred to as the "Sonnet en -yx" because of its rhyme scheme? Who can *English* the symbolic vision of that celebrated opening line *Ses pur ongles très haut dédiant leur onyx*?

The "Sonnet en -yx" has been called Mallarmé's "first truly hermetic poem." It is a Petrarchan sonnet with a punishingly restrictive rhyme scheme that alternates between masculine and feminine rhymes on *-yx/-ixe* and *-or/-ore*. All are phonetically identical in French. The poem opens on the image of the personified Anguish bearing a torch with onyx fingernails. Many dreams, burned to cinders by the Phoenix, remain ungathered for burial. A vacant urn sits atop credenzas in a formal room. Therein enters the poem's lexical Greta Garbo—*ptyx*, a word that Mallarmé hoped was meaningless. Though it is the poem's star, the *ptyx* is not actually in the room, nor is the named "Master"—a figure many believe to be the poet. With the *ptyx* he has left for the Styx on a tear-gathering mission. After the sonnet's turn, the complexities only mount. We learn of *un or* ("a gold") dying near a window, which may make up part of a tableau in which unicorns are subjecting a water sprite to a species of torturous fire. For those not adequately baffled, hold on for the *pièce de résistance*: a lifeless nude water sprite mirror-reflected alongside seven stars shining through the window of the empty room.

In their translations, Fry, Aldan, and Manson resist the temptation to unknot this sonic tangle of Mallarméan themes. All, thank goodness, also choose to include prose explanations alongside their English versions. Fry's were written by his friend the French critic Charles Mauron, while Aldan and Manson wrote their own. They share with us the revelations of many hours of labor. All three thought better than to reproduce the rhyme scheme in its strictest guise, opting instead to gesture in the direction of Mallarmé's soundscapes. Thus all partially sacrifice the vortex of *-yx*, which may be the poem's point; as a result they have bequeathed us three experimental English sonnets, acceptable post–*vers libre*, that is to say, post-Mallarmé.

What words do Fry's, Aldan's, and Manson's translations of the "Sonnet en -yx" share? In the first quatrain: "pure nails," "their onyx," "Anguish, this midnight," "many," "by the Phoenix," and "gathered." Translating *purs* as "pure" makes sonic sense, and *ongles* can really only mean one thing: "fingernails." "Nails" approximates the rhythm of the French, but by leaving off "finger" a small ambiguity creeps in, since in English "nails" can also be driven into two-by-fours, whereas if you wanted to build something in French you would need a box of *clous*. Words like "onyx" and "Phoenix," virtually the same in both tongues, leave the translators no choice, though the homophonic pun that emerges between "en -yx" and *onyx* in the French is lost. *Ce minuit* and *maint* are not contextually dubious, and so move unproblematically over, becoming "this midnight" and "many."

A surprise consensus arrives with the word "Anguish" for the French *Angoisse*, though Fry genders his "Anguish" feminine with "her," while Aldan and Manson opt for the neuter "its." "Anguish" has some sonic resemblance to *angoisse*, but there is a nuance of denotative difference between them. *Le Robert* defines *angoisse* as "1. Psychic and physical unease, caused by the sense of some immanent danger, characterized by a diffuse fear, which can move from disquiet to panic and through painful feelings of gastric and laryngeal constrictions (heart in one's throat). 2. Metaphysical disquiet caused by the contemplation of existence" (my translation). The second definition best describes the figure of *angoisse* in the "Sonnet en -yx." So in French *Angoisse* is primarily psychological, though it may have physical effects. The English "anguish," by contrast, divides the psychological and the physical: "1. Excruciating or oppressive bodily pain or suffering, such as the sufferer writhes under," or "2. Severe mental suffering, excruciating or oppressive grief or distress" (*Oxford English Dictionary*). Here the latter, psychological sense seems but a metaphorical mirror of the former.

But what English word might Fry, Aldan, and Manson have chosen in lieu of "anguish"? "Anxiety" or "angst" perhaps? Unambiguously psychological, "anxiety" must have been a tempting choice. Like *angoisse*, "anxiety" is an "uneasiness or trouble of mind about some uncertain event" (*OED*). Though a sonic departure from *angoisse*, "anxiety" would have provided another instance of the sonnet's fetishistic "x." That the word has become watered down with overuse wouldn't have been the case in Fry's time, and I would have thought "anxiety" an obvious choice for Aldan, coming from the psychoanalysis-mad midcentury (W. H. Auden didn't resist). In an early essay, Freud names a complex *Angstneurose*, which the French render as *névrose d'angoisse* and James Stratchey translates as "anxiety neurosis." Thus "angst," *angoisse*, and "anxiety" are strangely bound together—though none lead to "anguish."

The ritual gesture Anguish makes with its fingernails depends on the French word *dédiant*. Present participle of the verb *dédier*, *dédiant* is one of the poem's many words with religious connotations. "Dedicating" (Fry), "offering" (Aldan), and "consecrating" (Manson) are all good equivalents, though "consecrating" brings the religious aspect of the word forth with more force.

Mallarmé delays the revelation that Anguish is the subject of the poem's opening pronoun until line 2, and then creates a further postponement by leaving *lampadophore*—either an adjective describing Anguish or a noun in apposition to it—until that line's end. The word *lampadophore*, which is of Greek origin and means "torchbearer in a ceremony or footrace," is uncommon in French and there is no consensus as to its English equivalent. Manson opts for "lampadephore," hoping to replicate the strangeness of Mallarmé's word choice. Fry and Aldan choose, respectively, "lampbearer" and "candelabra." How one reads the poem's setting clearly influences these choices, for both lamps and candelabra pertain to domestic interiors, whereas torches decidedly do not. Yet torches, with their raging flame, do prepare us for the poem's Phoenix. Does the poem begin in the open air of "this midnight" before moving indoors, as some commentaries claim? Or does it, as Fry and Aldan believe, begin and end in the empty room? All three versions follow Mallarmé's non-normative syntax, but Aldan takes the liberty of creating a simile: "Anguish, this midnight, bears, *like* a candelabra" (my emphasis). This clears things up rather nicely, but changes the French quite a bit.

The next two lines describe a death-rebirth cycle and introduce the first of the poem's figures of emptiness: a funeral amphora empty of ashes. In rendering this image, Manson departs from Fry and Aldan—who both stress the fact that the dreams are *not* gathered—by shifting the negative onto the urn itself: "that *is* gathered in *no* cinerary amphora" (my emphasis). It is a radical departure that yet may lead to the same network of interpretive possibilities. The efficient cycle of birth-death-rebirth that the Phoenix represents precludes the waste of ashes but not necessarily the act of gathering. The ashes *are* gathered—back into more dreams inside the head of the poet, *not* in an urn, which Mallarmé equates with the poem itself: a container for *dead things*.

The poem now shifts its focus to the empty room, which is paradoxically bursting with objects. There one finds at least two "credences" (Fry and Manson) or "credenzas" (Aldan). A "credence" is either a buffet table or a table used for the Eucharistic elements—literally a "table of belief." This meaning is rare and should be rendered in English as "credence table," such that Fry's and Manson's use of "credences" on its own is a tad misleading, since it suggests the abstract noun meaning just "beliefs." The use of "buffet," however, might have jarred even more in this context of consecrations and urns.

On the credence tables, in the empty room, there is "no ptyx." Many attempts have been made to trace the etymology of this word. Both Fry and Manson wisely keep "ptyx" in their English versions. Only Aldan—breezing past it with nary a note in her commentary—embraces one of the dubious etymological possibilities, translating the word as "seashell." Her combination of "credenzas" and "seashell" squarely sets us in a secular bourgeois room. Searching dictionaries for the missing "ptyx" is, in some sense, unnecessary, since line 6, *Aboli bibelot d'inanité sonore*, does serve as a kind of definition, albeit a puzzlingly poetic one. The variety of solutions to this line arrived at by Fry, Aldan, and Manson invites wonder at the wealth of synonyms for *bibelot*. Fry uses the cognate, Aldan "curio," and Manson "bauble." The bibelot/curio/bauble is *aboli*, a favorite word of Mallarmé's. Fry and Manson render it as "abolished," which preserves the meaning and some of the sound. Aldan uses "vanished," which brings in a visual effect such as we might see in a Cocteau film, but takes away the sense that this absence has a measure of violence behind it. The bibelot/curio/bauble is of a "sounding inanity" (Fry), a "sonorous emptiness" (Aldan), or is "inanely echoing" (Manson). Fry's is closest to the French, but if one believes that Mallarmé is describing a poem, Aldan's solution is best. It stresses the theme of empty spaces already so present. Manson takes a risk with "echoing," which is a stretch for *sonore* (one can get there through "resound"), but "echoing" has the bonus of describing what end rhymes—in which this sonnet is so deeply invested—are so good at.

Line 7, "For the Master has gone to draw tears from the Styx," is the most uncontroversial. Fry writes "is gone" rather than "has gone," and Manson leaves "for" lowercase, but otherwise all three versions are identical. We then return to "ptyx," the "sole object" with which *le Néant s'honore*. *Néant* is one of those words that French does well, English not so well. Because of Sartre, one is tempted to hear it as "Nothingness," but only Fry, whose work predates Sartre's, uses the term. Aldan chooses "Void"; Manson, "Nothing." Fry's "Nothingness" packs the most nominal force, the suffix usefully evoking its ineffable quality. "Void" cannot shed its verb form and sounds rather cosmic. "Nothing" can never completely separate from the material world, which may be a good quality, depending on your understanding of Mallarmé's meaning here.

We have now reached the sonnet's turn. It begins with a "but," after which the empty room becomes a flurry of activity. "A gold" is seen in its northern corner near or through *la croisée . . . vacante*. *Croisée* means both "crossroad" and "window." The setting argues for "window," but with it we lose the connotation of a "cross," foregrounded in the French, and crucial in that the cross-like letter "x" dominates the poem's sound and images. Manson solves this by coining the kenning-like "cross-pane," which evokes both the cruciform shape of a mullion and the pane it contains. It is a brilliant solution.

The gold at the window is dying, which makes no sense until we realize that Mallarmé is describing fire. The French is difficult. Mallarmé uses *agonise* to describe the fire, followed by *selon*, which means "according to" (as in "The Gospel according to . . ."). *Agonise* is a false cognate with "agony," except possibly in the context of Christian history. We are meant to understand it as death throes. *Selon* is rendered by Fry and Aldan as "composing," a decision that clarifies the image, but which I cannot etymologically reconstruct. Manson renders *selon* as "in sympathy with," arriving there, I imagine, via the word "accord." Though an interesting decision, it is difficult to fathom the idea of a fire dying in sympathy with a decor it is arguably a part of. I sincerely believe all three translators did their best with this recalcitrant line, yet none of the English versions altogether satisfies.

The fire takes part in the oddest, and arguably silliest, scene in the poem: a "decor" of unicorns aggressing a nixie. Fry's commentator Charles Mauron sees this mythological battle as an imaginative flight of the window-gazing poet, "as we fancy monsters in a fire"; Aldan agrees: "he beholds in the sky a golden reflection which . . . assumes the likeness of a unicorn hurling fire at a dying water-nymph." Manson provides a gloss on *nixe* that leads us to Wagner's Rhine Maidens, but curiously changes the gender of Mallarmé's sprite by using the masculine "nixe." No doubt he was driven to this sex change in his search for a true rhyme for "ptyx," perhaps trusting that few readers would care about the gender of water sprites. Yet gender is never neutral in Mallarmé, so the change is a risk, especially given that this male "nixe" is later referred to as "she."

By the final tercet the unicorn-bullies have done in the nixie. She is now a *défunte nue* reflected in a mirror. The French *défunte* has the same root as the English "defunct," meaning "deceased," but *nue* can mean both "nude" and "cloud." If the nixie/unicorn scene was indeed a fancy imagined while gazing at a sunset intermixed with clouds, the double entendre in the French redeems a species of realism for the poem. It is utterly lost in English. Fry and Manson keep "defunct," but Aldan chooses the more shocking "a dead nude," which I rather like. "Defunct" feels fussy and formal, while "dead" is straightforward and leaves no ambiguity (not very Mallarméan, I admit).

The image of the dead nixie leads Manson to make the speculation that Marcel Duchamp's *Étant donnés* "might be, in part, an attempt at a literal visualisation of the Mallarmé sonnet." This enticing suggestion, while almost too good to be true, has the advantage of illuminating *both* works as studies in perspective and framing, with violence against a female subject at their core. It highlights the way Mallarmé's poem is using image not as a simple mental representation of the visual world but rather as Pound defined it, as "an intellectual and emotional complex in an instant of time."

Now to the complex image in the poem's finale, an image that, according to Mauron, uses riddle logic: what is "of scintillations at once the septet"? he asks of Fry's translation. Answer: "the Great Bear." Had Mallarmé not mentioned in a letter that he meant to evoke "a stellar and incomprehensible reflection, of Ursa Major," the "septet" in the poem might have remained "incomprehensible." The image has many facets: the mirror in which we see the nixie simultaneously encloses *l'oubli* ("oblivion" in all three versions) and reflects the *scintillations* ("scintillations" in all three versions) of a seven-starred constellation. Aldan changes the constellation Mallarmé intended by translating *septuor* as "the Seven Stars." Her note reminds us that the Pleiades is "a significant constellation in esoterica" (not to mention in French poetry), which perhaps motivated her decision, for she believes the sonnet is essentially about a transmission "of the Spirit to cognition." Fry and Manson keep the riddle by sticking with "septet," a direct translation of *septuor*. Mallarmé wants to evoke the night sky, the visual drama of white stars against black, but by using a musical metaphor he makes the scintillations sing, infusing the "sonorous emptiness" with suspended stellar music.

The words *encor*, *que*, and *sitôt* control the spatial and temporal dance between the deceased nixie, oblivion, and the constellation. The nixie is "in the mirror, while yet" (Fry), "although" (Aldan), "even / though" (Manson) the scintillations of the constellation are fixed there as well. The syntactical position of *sitôt* is perverse: *se fixe / De scintillations sitôt le septuor*. Fry preserves the word order as well as the confusion: "there appears / Of scintillations at once the septet." Aldan, the translator most willing to stray from the original, moves the position of *sitôt*, and uses a hyperbaton, gaining another terminal "x": "at once / The scintillations of The Seven Stars are fixed." Manson changes the syntax to make sense of *sitôt*, but then splits *se fixe* into adjective and verb: "at once / the septet of fixed scintillations settles." *Se fixe* has become both "fixed" and "settles." All three are compelling solutions to a very difficult image.

Though the mysteries of the "Sonnet en -yx" may never be completely revealed, even to French readers, I feel grateful that as English readers we have access to these three compelling versions. Each distinctly reflects the tightly framed "scintillations" of this mysterious and beautiful poem.

C. P. Cavafy

(Greek, 1863–1933)

TRANSLATIONS BY

John Mavrogordato,
Daniel Mendelsohn, Avi Sharon

· ·

COMMENTARY BY

George Kalogeris

τὰ ἄλογα τοῦ Ἀχιλλέως

Τὸν Πάτροκλο σὰν εἶδαν σκοτωμένο,
ποὺ ἦταν τόσο ἀνδρεῖος, καὶ δυνατός, καὶ νέος,
ἄρχισαν τ' ἄλογα νὰ κλαῖνε τοῦ Ἀχιλλέως·
ἡ φύσις των ἡ ἀθάνατη ἀγανακτοῦσε
γιὰ τοῦ θανάτου αὐτὸ τὸ ἔργον ποὺ θωροῦσε.
Τίναζαν τὰ κεφάλια των καὶ τὲς μακρυὲς χαῖτες κουνοῦσαν,
τὴν γῆ χτυποῦσαν μὲ τὰ πόδια, καὶ θρηνοῦσαν
τὸν Πάτροκλο ποὺ ἐνοιώθανε ἄψυχο – ἀφανισμένο –
μιὰ σάρκα τώρα ποταπὴ – τὸ πνεῦμα του χαμένο –
ἀνυπεράσπιστο – χωρὶς πνοὴ –
εἰς τὸ μεγάλο Τίποτε ἐπιστραμένο ἀπ' τὴν ζωή.

Τὰ δάκρυα εἶδε ὁ Ζεὺς τῶν ἀθανάτων
ἀλόγων καὶ λυπήθη. "Στοῦ Πηλέως τὸν γάμο"
εἶπε "δὲν ἔπρεπ' ἔτσι ἄσκεπτα νὰ κάμω·
καλύτερα νὰ μὴν σᾶς δίναμε ἄλογά μου
δυστυχισμένα! Τί γυρεύατ' ἐκεῖ χάμου
στὴν ἄθλια ἀνθρωπότητα ποὔναι τὸ παίγνιον τῆς μοίρας.
Σεῖς ποὺ οὐδὲ ὁ θάνατος φυλάγει, οὐδὲ τὸ γῆρας
πρόσκαιρες συμφορὲς σᾶς τυραννοῦν. Στὰ βάσανά των
σᾶς ἔμπλεξαν οἱ ἄνθρωποι." – Ὅμως τὰ δάκρυά των
γιὰ τοῦ θανάτου τὴν παντοτεινὴ
τὴν συμφορὰν ἐχύνανε τὰ δυὸ τὰ ζῶα τὰ εὐγενῆ.

C. P. Cavafy (1897)

The Horses of Achilles

But when they saw that Patroklos was dead,
Who was so young, and strong, and brave of heart,
The horses of Achilles so did start
To weep; and their immortal part rebelled
Against the work of death they there beheld;
Shaking their heads, waving their manes unshorn,
And tramping on the ground, as if to mourn
For Patroklos, knowing his soul was fled
Away from empty flesh,—his spirit shed,—
Without breath,—weaponless,—
Returned from life to the great Nothingness.

The tears of the immortal horses there
Zeus saw and grieved. "At Peleus' wedding-day"
He said "unwise and thoughtless was my way;
Better my horses never to bestow
Unfortunate! What would you down below
With wretched man who is the toy of fate,
Horses whom death and age no wise await?
The woes of time torment you, and men snare
In their own miseries." Yet for the care
Of death perpetual
The noble horses let the tears downfall.

translated by John Mavrogordato (1951)

The Horses of Achilles

When they saw Patroclus had been killed,
he who'd been so brave, and strong, and young,
the horses of Achilles began to weep:
their immortal nature was indignant
at this work of death, which it now beheld.
They'd shake their heads and toss their flowing manes,
and with their feet they'd stamp the ground and grieve
for Patroclus who they knew was lifeless—undone—
shabby flesh by now—his spirit vanished—
left without defenses—without breath—
returned from life unto the great Nothing.

Zeus beheld the tears of the immortal
horses and grieved. "At Peleus's marriage,"
he said, "I should never have committed such great folly.
Better never to have given you away, my
unhappy horses! What business have you down here
with wretched humanity, the plaything of fate.
You, for whom neither death nor old age lie in wait,
are oppressed by passing misfortunes. Men have snared you
in their afflictions." —And yet their tears,
for the everlasting calamity
of death, the noble creatures kept on shedding.

translated by Daniel Mendelsohn (2009)

The Horses of Achilles

When they saw Patroclus lying dead
who was once so brave, so strong and young,
the horses of Achilles began to weep;
their immortal natures stood aghast
at that masterwork of death.
They reared their heads and shook their manes,
they stomped the ground with their hooves
and mourned for Patroclus,
lifeless, destroyed, mere flesh and bone,
defenseless now, his spirit gone,
a castaway from life, now naught.

Zeus saw the tears of the immortal steeds
and grieved, saying, 'It was my mistake,
it was my thoughtlessness at Peleus' wedding.
We should never have given you as a gift, poor horses!
What business did you have among wretched
humankind, plaything of destiny, you whom neither death
nor the sorrows of old age torment. Men have tangled you
in their own miseries.' Yet the two noble horses
continued to pour out their tears
for the eternal misfortune of death.

translated by Avi Sharon (2000)

Commentary by George Kalogeris

There is, perhaps, in all the Iliad *nothing more deep in significance—there is nothing in all literature more perfect in human tenderness, and honour for the mystery of inferior life, than the verses that describe the sorrow of the divine horses at the death of Patroclus, and the comfort given them by the greatest of the gods. You shall read Pope's translation; it does not give you the manner of the original, but it entirely gives you the passion.*

John Ruskin, *Fors Clavigera*

Cavafy's poem has been called a "fairly close adaptation" of a famous passage from Book 17 of the *Iliad*. In places it reads like a direct translation, although as David Ricks has pointed out, in his book *The Shade of Homer*, Cavafy's phrasing is actually closer to that of Alexander Pope's *Iliad*. What gives this poem its originality and force is the way in which Cavafy remains so attentively subject to, yet not subjected by, the basic circumstantial pressures of Homer's passage. Adaptation, translation, original work—call it what you will, the corresponding verbal energies generated by this kind of reading back, and rendering into, are just another way of saying that poetry is doing what it has always done; or, in Virgil's beautiful formulation: "song replying to song replying to song."

For the poem's title Cavafy uses the demotic term for horses, *aloga*, rather than the purist or classical term, *ippoi*. The vernacular term humanizes (up to a point) the Olympian horses, and, as the phrase is repeated, helps to keep the sense of their suffering on our level, and to make them less like the equestrian steeds on a marble frieze. Of course there is no way to render the fullness of this effect into English, since English lacks any kind of clearly divided "higher" and "lower" classification system when it comes to levels of diction. (Daniel Mendelsohn has tried to make a case for using Latinate words in those instances where Cavafy uses *katharevousa*, or "purist diction," but this method of translation rests on a false analogy: English words based on Anglo-Saxon roots are used in combination with Latinate

terms all the time in our everyday speech, and there doesn't seem to be any immediately recognizable raising or lowering of the verbal register based on the lineage of the words alone.) But the more crucially insoluble problem is that the Greek word for "horse" is constructed with an alpha privative before its root: *a-logos*. At its most literal, the meaning of the term is "speechlessness." The drama of the poem is in the title: the horses of Achilles have been rendered speechless before the unspeakable, struck dumb by their grief for Patroclus, over whose body the Greeks and Trojans will carry on a fierce struggle. Cavafy's title reminds us that these are magic horses, divine creatures that (with Hera's assistance) are able to speak—and in their refusal to speak they are denying their immortality. (In Book 19, though, when Achilles whips the horses into battle, the steed Xanthus will turn its glorious head back to Achilles, and speak with the power of divine Logos, reminding the hero of his prophesied doom.)

In the first line of Cavafy's poem, the use of the word "dead" at the end of the line, in both the Avi Sharon and John Mavrogordato versions, is more effective than Daniel Mendelsohn's "had been killed"—more effective in its end-of-the-line, end-of-a-life abruptness, which is the cold realization of the horror as it is happening. (Part of Cavafy's genius here is in not using the word "corpse," as if that term had yet to enter the immortal horses' vocabulary, at least not while the body is still warm.) Mendelsohn is more literally accurate with respect to the Greek σκοτωμένο, but the past-tense particles soften the suddenness of the brute reality, bearing reference to the fallen body rather than to the unbearable actuality of experiencing the mangled flesh itself, for which the dull, indelible, monosyllabic thud in the sound of "dead" is so viscerally poignant.

Mavrogordato's use of "but" at the beginning of the first line is not only effective in establishing his iambic meter; it also plunges us into the action in medias res—like the opening line of the *Iliad*. As if preempting all the Olympian knowledge the horses possessed when they entered the human world, that "but" enhances the swiftness of the divine creatures' collision with mortality, their transformation from *ippoi* to *aloga*. It is the start of a sentence that will leave them forever stupefied by human suffering.

I'd like to cite my own version of the first stanza here, in relation to a particular point of translation in the fourth and fifth lines of Cavafy's poem, where the horses bear witness to "the work of death"—a phrase that is not in Homer but is used several times by Pope, whose magisterial rendering Cavafy seems to have been very familiar with. Mendelsohn's "indignant" lacks the taut force of Mavrogordato's "rebelled," which, in its rhyme with "beheld," at the end of the next line, has the back-turning strain of the held-back reins in it. Sharon's sonorously proximate terms "aghast" and "master-work" create a darkly sardonic effect, and bring to life the consummately macabre *techne* of Death. (Similarly, Stratis Haviaris, in his very fine translation, depicts Hades's craft and sullen art as "handiwork.") Here's my version of the first stanza:

> When the horses of Achilles turned and saw
> Pátroclus dead, that beautiful young man,
> So brave and strong, they both began to weep.
> Suddenly that Olympian breed felt bewildered
> By death's outrageous display of what it is.
> No matter how they arched their necks, and tossed
> Their wild, luxuriant manes, or stamped their hooves
> As if to wake him up, they couldn't shake off
> What they were seeing, seeing it there in the dirt:
> That heap of flesh and bones with the pitiful look
> Of Pátroclus. Their rider's breath was gone.
> Now he was nothing—nothing now and nowhere.

Although I wasn't able to produce anything like the lucidly simple, effusion-resistant concentration in Cavafy's outraged lines about the outrageous work of death, I felt that "display" might suggest, within the guts of its grammar, the splayed limbs of dead Patroclus. "Of what it is" attempts to get at the horses' bewilderment as the shock of death is sinking in; the unknowable, anonymous neuter and neutering "it" is meant to emphasize the unspeakable horror of what the horses are experiencing, as it is happening. I wanted the pronoun "it" to serve as a way of confronting the horses with the work (ἔργον) of death "it-self"—in that hideous instant when what it is becomes known only by what it does.

Another difficulty—or opportunity, depending upon how one chooses to interpret the lines—occurs at the end of the first stanza and involves Cavafy's weighty phrase τὸ μεγάλο Τίποτε, which Mavrogordato translates as "the great Nothingness." To my ear, the simplicity of Mendelsohn's slightly variant "the great Nothing" has a starkly hollow ring, conveying the right kind of emphatic nullity, a black hole to which no suffix can affix itself: "the great No-thing." The overwhelming power of Hades for the ancient Greeks, a place without water or light or speech, is captured in Ajax's prayer in Book 17 of the *Iliad*. Massive Ajax, surrounded by Trojans and swarms of dust clouds, invokes great Zeus to kill him "in the light of day"—a raw plea for one more moment of earthly clarity, under the Homeric light of the sun.

The phrase χωρὶς πνοή ("without breath") is missing from Sharon's translation, but is vital to the sense of utter fragility that Cavafy's passage conveys, the sorrow for the irrevocable loss of the life breath made palpable by the staccato rhythms and dashes that break up the breathing of the Greek lines. Here, too, I can't help but hear an allusion to the *Iliad*, specifically to Achilles's great speech about the sheer vulnerability of human mortality (Trojans included) in Book 9. Refusing the embassy's offer of gifts contingent upon his return to the battle, he says: "But a man's breath cannot come back to him again, cannot be raised up or recaptured once it has passed beyond the little fence [*orkos*] of the teeth" (literal prose mine).

Mavrogordato's version, so eloquent in the pacing of its mourning, duplicates Cavafy's intricate rhyme scheme, and attains an especially elegant effect in the couplet cinch of "weaponless" and "Nothingness." The polysyllabic rhyme seems to melt away the body's defenses before our eyes, and with its anguished pathos, and maybe even a deeply ironic insistence, it endeavors to remind us that the hero is weaponless against Hades. (As in Pausanias's memorable description of the famous painting of the underworld by Polygnotos, in which Theseus and Perithous are helplessly holding out their swords, as if the blades were still thirsting for blood. The weapons that were once the means of their κλέος, the glory that insures the hero's remembrance, are now useless down there—down there in the dark and the dust, where the heroes are vanquished shades like everyone else.) In places the easy availability of the rhymes, along with occasionally old-fashioned diction (e.g., "no wise await" in the second stanza), makes Mavrogordato's version seem less hard-pressed by the fact of atrocity that so tongue-ties the horses, and more vulnerable to undiscerning sentiment; but here the flaying, sibilant sounds of "flesh" and "shed," "weaponless" and "Nothingness," in the sheerness of their sensuous tissue, are implicitly convincing.

Sharon, too, very finely gets something of the bitter, abysmal bleakness of Hades's vacuousness, in the punning, compressed astringency of "now naught." And in his translation of ἐπιστραμένο ἀπ' τὴν ζωή (literally "turning back from life") as "a castaway from life," the Greek strophe is brilliantly attuned to its English turn, and what could have been a throwaway phrase in English now carries the destitute weight of a victim's life, cast away in the merciless catastrophe of war.

In my own translation, like in Sharon's, I avoid using the big abstraction ("the great Nothingness") but opt for a less-concise approach, using a full line for the one phrase "Now he was nothing—nothing now and nowhere." I have chosen to make use of the word "no" as a term of ultimate negation in order to convey the high premium, for the Greeks, on the here and now, and within that the concomitant terror of death. I want the reader to feel the inexorable force of this realization, in the way that the terms of negation (and their particular metrical stresses) reify that negation as they are moving across the iambic pentameter line. The "no" in "now" becomes the "no" in "nothing"—or "no thing." And then the "no" in "now" and the "no" in "nothing" become the "no" in "nowhere"—or "now where?"—as if the words were enacting the horses' discovery of the awful truth, the nonnegotiable, absolute negation of life. As the sensitive horses ponder the insensate body of the beautiful hero lying in the dirt, I want those implacably dismayed, spasmodic repetitions of "no" to suggest the pounding hooves Cavafy so wrenchingly mentions earlier (a detail not in Homer): the horses stomping on the ground like children trying to wake a sleeping father. And in the steady beat of the line, one "no" for each iambic (or trochaic) stress, the horses keep coming up against the impediment that gives their grief its impetus, until their everlasting, flowing tears punctuate the end of the poem.

The second stanza begins with Zeus looking down, presumably from the clouds of Olympus, oblivious to the death of Patroclus. And yet just one book of the *Iliad* earlier, Zeus looks down at the battlefield with great anguish, unable to alter the fate of his human son Sarpedon. In a phrase redolent with wounded, archaic grandeur (perhaps not unlike "long-suffering" Yahweh in the Hebrew Bible), Homer says that Zeus weeps "tears of blood." Cavafy's Zeus is pensive but dry-eyed, the sky god pondering the inconsolable tears of the horses, but dismissive of human suffering. By way of implicit allusion, Cavafy's scene is set in juxtaposition to the Sarpedon scene—which is a reading back into the epic I feel Cavafy must have wanted, imperative as it is to one of the central concerns of the poem: that the sympathy of the gods is transitory, but human suffering is everlasting. Wilfred Owen's "reciprocity of tears," suggesting a balance struck between the mutually maimed, is a transaction not possible with the gods of Olympus. (It should be noted that in Homer's horses of Achilles passage there's a much fuller and grander portrayal of Zeus, and though his haughty pity for the human race is abstract, he's still a more sympathetic figure, however vastly superior.)

Later on in this stanza there is a phrase that, translated directly into English, becomes riskily acquiescent to the encrustations of classical trope: "toys of fate." Mendelsohn's "plaything of fate" is not only closer to the Greek, cognate as it is with παίγνιον, but also more faithful to the arbitrary brutality manifest in the word "thing." Simone Weil, in her great essay on the *Iliad*, writes that the hero of the epic is force, force that turns a human being into a thing, whether victor or vanquished: the hero becomes a thing dragged behind a chariot in the dust, a chariot driven around and around the city walls by a thing that is also a hero. Mendelsohn's ominous rhyme of "lie in wait" with "plaything of fate" has its own vicious suggestion of inescapable circularity.

Here's my version of the poem's ending lines, beginning midway through Zeus's address to the horses:

"... What on earth were the two of you doing down there,
Yoked to the cars of such pathetic creatures?
Mortals are nothing but the dust at your heels.
Old age and death can never catch up with a horse
That flies like the wind. And yet you carry on
As if men had bridled you to their misery."

But those two gallant creatures kept right on weeping,
Weeping for Pátroclus, still shedding their tears
As if there was no end to what they felt.

"Τί γυρεύατ' ἐκεῖ χάμου," Zeus says, which means something along the lines of "What are you doing down there?" It is also worth noting that the commonplace Greek expression has the verb for turning (γυρίζω) in it, as if Zeus were telling the horses that they were only going around in circles. Rather than translating "human wretchedness" directly, the vernacular energy of the Greek, so alive to Zeus's disparaging tones with their implications of vertiginous futility, provides impetus for my interpretive line "Mortals are nothing but the dust at your heels." Human wretchedness is no plainer than when the horses spell it out for us in the Iliadic dust, as when Hector is tied by the heels to Achilles's chariot and dragged around the walls of Troy. And Death never catches up with the immortal horses, but is always breathing down our mortal necks.

Cavafy's poem ends with his sublime lines about the tears of the horses falling onto the ground. It is the tears themselves that are immortal, and the horses' grief is now as immortal as the disaster of death. In my version I wanted the ending line to be entirely monosyllabic, to give the salience of the tears a simple, irreducible finality. But I couldn't get anything like the huge-hearted heartbreak of Cavafy's sweeping τοῦ θανάτου τὴν παντοτεινὴ τὴν συμφορὰν ("the everlasting calamity / of death"—Mendelsohn), which means that my concluding lines don't allow for the dense pitch of the horses' rich perplexity, the poem's intractable pathos that, like the *Iliad*, becomes the undying replenisher of generous tears, eternal eyes elaborating a world of woe. Or as Pope so beautifully puts it:

The big round drops coursed down with silent pace,
Conglobing on the dust.

Rainer Maria Rilke

(German, 1875–1926)

TRANSLATIONS BY
M. D. Herter Norton,
J. B. Leishman, Robert Bly

· ·

COMMENTARY BY

David Young

Archaïscher Torso Apollos

Wir kannten nicht sein unerhörtes Haupt,
darin die Augenäpfel reiften. Aber
sein Torso glüht noch wie ein Kandelaber,
in dem sein Schauen, nur zurückgeschraubt,

sich hält und glänzt. Sonst könnte nicht der Bug
der Brust dich blenden, und im leisen Drehen
der Lenden könnte nicht ein Lächeln gehen
zu jener Mitte, die die Zeugung trug.

Sonst stünde dieser Stein entstellt und kurz
unter der Schultern durchsichtigem Sturz
und flimmerte nicht so wie Raubtierfelle

und bräche nicht aus allen seinen Rändern
aus wie ein Stern: denn da ist keine Stelle,
die dich nicht sieht. Du musst dein Leben ändern.

Rainer Maria Rilke (1908)

Archaic Torso of Apollo

We did not know his legendary head,
in which the eyeballs ripened. But
his torso still glows like a candelabrum
in which his gaze, only turned low,

holds and gleams. Else could not the curve
of the breast blind you, nor in the slight turn
of the loins could a smile be running
to that middle, which carried procreation.

Else would this stone be standing maimed and short
under the shoulders' translucent plunge
nor flimmering like the fell of beasts of prey

nor breaking out of all its contours
like a star: for there is no place
that does not see you. You must change your life.

translated by M. D. Herter Norton (1938)

Archaic Torso of Apollo

Though we've not known his unimagined head
and what divinity his eyes were showing,
his torso like a branching street-lamp's glowing,
wherein his gaze, only turned down, can shed

light still. Or else the breast's insurgency
could not be dazzling you, or you discerning
in that slight twist of loins a smile returning
to where was centred his virility.

Or else this stone would not stand so intact
beneath the shoulders' through-seen cataract
and would not glisten like a wild beast's skin;

and would not keep from all its contours giving
light like a star: for there's no place therein
that does not see you. You must change your living.

translated by J. B. Leishman (1960)

Archaic Torso of Apollo

We have no idea what his fantastic head
was like, where the eyeballs were slowly swelling. But
his body now is glowing like a gas lamp,
whose inner eyes, only turned down a little,

hold their flame, shine. If there weren't light, the curve
of the breast wouldn't blind you, and in the swerve
of the thighs a smile wouldn't keep on going
toward the place where the seeds are.

If there weren't light, this stone would look cut off
where it drops clearly from the shoulders,
its skin wouldn't gleam like the fur of a wild animal,

and the body wouldn't send out light from every edge
as a star does . . . for there is no place at all
that isn't looking at you. You must change your life.

translated by Robert Bly (1981)

Commentary by David Young

I have put M. D. Herter Norton's version of this poem first, not only because it is the earliest, but because it is so straightforward and sensible, giving the reader good access to the poem and not trying for any particular grandeur or originality. Her Rilke versions, kept in print for many years (the original copyright is 1938), have always served Rilke's readers in English well: faithfully, modestly, and with integrity. That said, the temptation to be a bit more ambitious, in the direction of literary achievement with English, will always persist.

The first issue that confronts the would-be translator of this poem is the fact that it's a modified Petrarchan sonnet, rhymed ABBA, CDDC, EEF, GFG. The urge to duplicate can be very strong, which is why I've included the J. B. Leishman version, for many years the available (British) alternative to Herter Norton's. Readers can explore the sacrifices that have been made to achieve the rhyme scheme. They are sometimes considerable, the "giving/living" rhyme being perhaps the most egregious. A comparably dubious, fully rhymed version by C. F. MacIntyre is still in print from the University of California; in MacIntyre's case the syntax also suffers substantially from the effort to replicate the formal rhyme scheme. I do not think it gets us close to the spirit and sheer wonder of Rilke, but one must appreciate the courage and commitment that sent both Leishman and MacIntyre in this difficult direction.

Robert Bly's version, in reaction to all this formalism, is much more literal and emphatically colloquial. Here and there it may overexplain a little ("If there weren't light"), turn clumsy (lines 11 and 12), or skate toward absurdity (those swelling eyeballs!), but Bly's overall sense of the poem's muscular vigor is both persuasive and exciting. I just wish he had a better ear for the poem's rhythm; his first line, for example, is pure prose.

I came to the project of translating the *Sonnets to Orpheus* in 1978, around the same time that Bly was doing his selections (he never undertook the sequence as a whole). I was fresh from a translation of the *Duino Elegies* (which were written at the same time, in the culminating creative burst of Rilke's career as a poet). In that project I had solved the problem of the long German elegiac line by borrowing William Carlos Williams's triadic line with variable feet, a more comfortable and expressive mode for American speaking and listening. The success of that made me think, at first, that I could do something comparably innovative with the Orpheus sonnets: even, perhaps, treat them as prose poems!

I soon learned that a sonnet wants to remain a sonnet and will accept no substitutes. It's a two-part structure with two subdivisions, and there's a kind of fierce integrity to the form. But since fully rhymed translations in English almost always turn out to be disastrous, the tail wagging the dog, I settled finally on a kind of middle way (later also the choice of Edward Snow, Stephen Mitchell, and Galway Kinnell) that tries to preserve the movement and feel of the sonnet without committing to a full and exact rhyme scheme. That worked well enough with the Orpheus sequence that I found I wanted to use it when I came, later, to translating poems, many of them sonnets, from the *Neue Gedichte*.

I found that I could use off-rhyme and internal rhyme while always being careful not to distort the sense. The sureness of movement and the verbal music may not match the original exactly, but they belong, always, in the foreground.

> We've never known the legendary head
> where the eye-apples ripened. But
> his torso glows still, like a candelabrum
> in which his gaze, turned down,
>
> contains itself and shines. Otherwise
> the breast-curve wouldn't blind you so, nor would
> the hips and groin form toward that smile
> whose center held the seeds of procreation.
>
> And then this stone would stand here, short and broken,
> under the shoulders' clear cascading plunge
> and wouldn't ripple like a wild beast's fur

and break with light from every surface
like a star: because there is no place
that doesn't see you. You must change your life.

translated by David Young (1994)

Three further points:

1. Rilke definitely says that eye-apples ripened in the now-missing head of the statue. I think translators should not ignore this strange and wonderful metaphor.
2. As Leishman points out, *Kandelaber* could mean, in Rilke's time, a branching streetlamp, gas-burning, that could be brightened or dimmed. That's how the notion of a candelabrum ("candelabra" is the plural) being turned down can be present in the poem, a puzzling notion unless you think of, say, a gas-burning chandelier.
3. The verb *flimmern* suggests light, e.g., "glisten," "glimmer," "flicker," "gleam," but I decided that movement (my "ripple") was even more crucial, given the context in which the illumination is about to take place. The stone surface of the sculpture turns first to the hide of a wild beast, alive with movement. Then it becomes a dazzling star.

Rilke realized that gazing hard at an object could lead to the revelation that it also may be gazing hard at you. That happens with his famous panther; it happens here, too, unforgettably. This is how I describe it in *Six Modernist Moments in Poetry*:

Here the gazer, a casual museum visitor imagining the missing head and glancing at the break just above the genitals, is abruptly exposed to the glare of the sun god's regard. The looker is looked at and seen so irrevocably that that person's life must change. There is no going back from this moment when apparently dead stone returns to its godhead and godhood, locking us into its gaze. Light breaks from every surface of the statue, but light is also everywhere around us, like sunlight, and in it we are illuminated and visible to everything. Our being seen is universal.

Yahya Kemal Beyatlı

(Turkish, 1884–1958)

TRANSLATIONS BY

Roger Finch,
Sidney Wade and Yurdanur Salman,
Bernard Lewis

....

COMMENTARY BY

Sidney Wade

Gece

Kandilli yüzerken uykularda
Mehtâbı sürükledik sularda.

Bir yoldu parıldayan, gümüşten,
Gittik . . . Bahs açmadık dönüşten.

Hulyâ tepeler, hayâl ağaçlar . . .
Durgun suda dinlenen yamaçlar . . .

Mevsim sonu öyle bir zaman ki
Gaaip bir mûsikiydi sanki.

Gitmiş kaybolmuşuz uzakta,
Rü'yâ sona ermeden şafakta . . .

Yahya Kemal Beyatlı (1940)

Night

As Kandilli flowed through sleep's first quarter,
We dragged moonlight along in the water.

We walked on silver the moon made glisten;
We did not speak and we did not listen.

The hills were spectral, dreamlike were the trees . . .
Slopes stood still in pools that listed no breeze . . .

Time seemed to be locked with a year-round key
Closed in music invisibility.

Our disappearance fades where we have gone;
Before it concludes, our dream is at dawn.

translated by Roger Finch (2006)

Night

While Kandilli floated in clouds of sleep,
We pulled the full moon through the unruffled deep.

The path through the water was a shimmering burn.
We went . . . and never spoke of the return.

Dreaming slopes and phantom trees . . .
Hillsides in water taking their ease.

The season's nearing end was strewn
With the notes of an old and distant tune.

We lost ourselves in that long, far drift
Until it put us ashore in the dawn, and left.

translated by Sidney Wade and Yurdanur Salman (2004)

Night

Kandilli floated upon sleep—
We trailed the moonlight on the deep

We took a shining silver track
And spoke no word of turning back

Phantom trees on the dreaming crest
Pensive slopes where the waters rest

The season's end was such a time
The distant note of a hidden chime

We passed and vanished far away
Ere the dream was lost at break of day

translated by Bernard Lewis (1978)

Commentary by Sidney Wade

Turkish is an agglutinative language. That is to say, a word's meaning can be elaborated on and added to by the attachment of suffixes. In fact, there is a single word in Turkish that can express the following English sentence: "You are not one of those who can be turned into a New Yorker." Here it is: *Nevyorklulastiramadiklarimizdansiniz.* Because of this structural frame, it is an intensely compact and economical language, which creates difficulties, sometimes, for the translator who wants to honor original forms and syllable counts.

Examining these three translations, some of the priorities held by the translators become apparent. Bernard Lewis's choice of a compact line (in fact, regarding the number of syllables, he uses fewer than the original, which is rather remarkable—the original contains approximately ten per line, whereas Lewis allows himself only eight) surely reflects his desire to bring across the structural economy of the language, as well as harkening back to the ancient balladic rhythm of so much traditional English verse. My own choice in this respect was to allow myself liberties with the line length in order to express the deep lyricism of the original music—my lines range from seven to twelve syllables. Roger Finch works within a perfect ten-syllable line, from which he never varies, even though Beyatlı allows himself an occasional nine-syllable line within the more predominant count of ten.

As for the issue of cleaving to the literal meaning of the text, each of us took some liberties, some of us, ahem, more than others. There is no key or lock in the fourth stanza of the original, as Finch's translation suggests, there are no "clouds," as I inserted into the first line; nor is there a "hidden chime," as Lewis has it in the fourth stanza. I suppose I took the longest steps away from the literal, as I turned the dream of the original's final stanza into a metaphorical "long, far drift" that has agency and purpose and physical strength. Both Lewis and I turned to the old English metaphor "the deep" to express what in the original is, simply, "water."

The most interesting issue in comparing these three translations, to me, is that both Finch and I tried to provide links that do not exist in the original, in order to make narrative (and perhaps cultural) sense out of the many mysterious gaps between Turkish and English, whereas Lewis leaves logical connections up to the reader. In his introduction to *Eda: An Anthology of Contemporary Turkish Poetry*, editor Murat Nemet-Nejat asserts that the essence of the Turkish language resides in its fundamental structure, which insists on the mysterious, hidden relations of things. According to Nemet-Nejat,

> the underlying syntactical principle is not logic, but emphasis: a movement of the speaker's or writer's affections. Thinking, speaking in Turkish is a peculiarly visceral activity, a record of thought emerging. The nearer the word is to the verb in a sentence, which itself has no fixed place in the sentence, the more emphasis it has. This ability to stress or unstress—not sounds or syllables; Turkish is syllabically unaccented—but words (thought as value-infested proximity) gives Turkish a unique capability for nuance, for a peculiar kind of intuitive thought.

The language, because of its structure, requires a fair dose of patience and intuition, as often one cannot understand the true intention of the speaker, or even the sense of the communication, until one gets to the end of a very long sentence, where the operative verb, with its person, time, and number signifiers, often resides.

I attempted to create a holistic narrative out of the original materials by turning the mystery of the final two stanzas into something more concretely metaphorical and, oddly, less mysterious, and it seems to me Finch is attempting the same sort of thing. Lewis leaves us to our own devices and wishes us well in connecting the literal sense of the five stanzas. At the very literal level, what the words of the final two stanzas say in Turkish is this: "The season's end was such a time / It was as if an invisible (or absent) music // We left we got lost in distance / Dream's end before at dawn." Lewis, in his minimalist way, most faithfully represents, in English word order, the literal meaning. In the final line, he uses the (to my ear) antique-sounding adverb "ere" in his solution to the problem of connecting the literal dots; Finch uses "before"; my choice is "until." I considered shortening that to "till," but ultimately rejected it because I felt the line moves more musically with the two syllables of "until."

I very much admire Lewis's choice to minimally punctuate the poem. Both Finch and I chose standard English punctuation, but there is something magical about the tone of this poem that is nicely reflected in the subtle uncertainties of the unpunctuated translation. This choice also brings to the foreground the essential intuitive mystery that characterizes the Turkish language itself.

Anna Akhmatova

(Russian, 1889–1966)

TRANSLATIONS BY

Gerard Shelley, Andrey Kneller,
Stephen Berg

. . . .

COMMENTARY BY

Joanna Trzeciak Huss

Песня последней встречи

Так беспомощно грудь холодела,
Но шаги мои были легки.
Я на правую руку надела
Перчатку с левой руки.

Показалось, что много ступеней,
А я знала – их только три!
Между кленов шепот осенний
Попросил: «Со мною умри!

Я обманут моей унылой,
Переменчивой, злой судьбой».
Я ответила: «Милый, милый!
И я тоже. Умру с тобой...»

Это песня последней встречи.
Я взглянула на темный дом.
Только в спальне горели свечи
Равнодушно-желтым огнем.

29 сентября 1911
Царское Село

Anna Akhmatova (1911)

Song of the Last Meeting

My heart grew chill so helplessly,
Although my footsteps seemed so light.
In all my anguish I was drawing
My left-hand glove upon my right.

There seemed to be so many steps,
Although I knew there were but three.
The breath of autumn in the maples
Seemed to whisper: "Die with me!

I have been deceived by fate
That hath neither faith nor rue."
And I answered in a whisper:
"So have I. I'll die with you."

This is the song of our last meeting.
I glanced toward the house in the night:
Only the bedroom lights were burning
With an uncaring yellow light.

translated by Gerard Shelley (1942)

Song of the final meeting

How helplessly chilled was my chest, yet
My footsteps were nimble and light.
I unconsciously put on my left hand
The glove that belonged on my right.

It seemed that the stairs were endless,
But I knew—there were only three!
Autumn, whispering through the maples,
Pleaded: "Die here with me!

I was blindly deceived by my dreary,
Dismal, changeable Fate." "And I too,"
I responded, "My darling, my dear one,
And I'll also die here with you."

This is the song of the final meeting.
I looked up at your house, all dark inside.
Just the bedroom candles burned with a fleeting,
Indifferent and yellowish light.

translated by Andrey Kneller (2011)

Last Meeting

I was helpless, my breasts were freezing.
I walked one foot on tiptoe,
I put my left glove on
my right hand, like an idiot.

There seemed to be so many steps then
but I knew there were only three.
Autumn whispered through the maples
"Die, like me:

that sick, truculent liar, Fate,
has stripped me, for the hell of it."
"I've been flayed like you," I remember answering
as I left, "and I'll die when you do."

This is our last meeting—this place, this voice.
I looked back at the shape of the dark house.
Candles guttered in the bedroom window;
behind them, eyes and a torso.

translated by Stephen Berg (1981)

Commentary by Joanna Trzeciak Huss

There are few poets of whom it can be said that they ushered in a new century. One such poet is Anna Akhmatova (1889–1966), born Anna Gorenko. It has been argued that poetry was still in the nineteenth century until she burst onto the scene, but as with all things Akhmatova, there is a great deal of mythology framing the available facts.

Her first collection, *Evening* (1912), in which "Song of the Last Meeting" appears, brought poetry back to earth from the metaphysical musings of the symbolists and found a ready public. Her poems are marked by great emotional intensity expressed with concreteness and compactness. Akhmatova's is a poetry of physiology—botanical, corporeal, emotional, spiritual. Trees in Akhmatova are not just trees, but maples, lindens, elms, oaks, spruces, and poplars, and have been chosen for their distinctive physical properties or cultural resonance. The heart is not a symbol—it is an organ. Its beating intensifies and attenuates in strength and rate in concert with changes in emotional pitch. The physiology of motion is continuous with that of emotion. As Boris Eikhenbaum observed in 1923, it was through the description of movements and gestures, a technique borrowed from the nineteenth-century novel, that Akhmatova was able to attain, with such brevity, such a depth of feeling. Her lines are short, yet within a single sixteen-line poem one can find distilled a narrative situation worthy of a lengthy prose work.

Akhmatova's "Песня последней встречи"

What stands out in this poem is the objectivity with which it treats subjective experience. One device for achieving this is to have the subjects of sentences not coincide with the poetic persona—"I" and "my" are scarce—but rather with body parts, as in the first line, where it is the "chest"/"breast" that grows chill, not the person. This yields a sense of estrangement: one is rendered an observer to one's own bodily states. The grip of emotions on the body is not complete, as we witness in the second line: the gait remains light, unaffected by the helplessness with which the chest is growing cold. Upper and lower bodily states are independent not only of their subject, but of one another, as if subject to different laws. The poetic persona seems to experience simultaneously alienation and a strange kind of self-discovery.

In the absence of a conversation with the lover, there is a dialogue with nature, who responds sympathetically to the poetic persona. The mode of address here utilizes *ты*, the informal form of "you," as opposed to *вы*, the formal "you," a distinction present in Russian but archaic in English ("thou" versus "you"). While the poem is written in the past tense, consistent with a reflection on past events, the tense shifts into the present when the dialogue with autumn begins. The informal pronoun, which lends the conversation a note of intimacy, combined with the shift to the present tense, which grants the exchange an immediacy that vaults the reader into the scene, demonstrates the role that grammatical choices play in eliciting aesthetic engagement.

Formal elements are important in Russian poetry, which is one reason it is difficult to translate. This poem follows the rhyme scheme aBaB, with feminine (two-syllable) rhymes in the first and third lines, and masculine (one-syllable) rhymes in the second and fourth lines of each stanza. For example, in the first quatrain, there is the feminine rhymed pair *холодела / надела* and the masculine rhymed pair *легки* and *руки*.

The poem consists of four quatrains, starting in anapestic trimeter, which shifts into a Russian verse form called *dol'nik*, marked by a fixed number of stressed syllables per line (here three). A key shift occurs in the final line of the first quatrain, whose disrupted meter conveys the emotional state of the poetic persona. The poem has many rhythmic breaks, which emerge naturally from the flow of its colloquial language. Consider the second line of the second stanza: *А я знала, – их только три!* ("But I knew—there were only three!"—Kneller). Rhythmic breaks provide minor anticipatory syncopations throughout the poem. It has been said of Akhmatova that her soul turned grief into song, and her pen turned song into poetry. This poem is truly a song.

Gerard Shelley's Translation (1942/1949)

Translation is never a voice from nowhere. Each translation is influenced by contingencies embodied in the person of a given translator. An early translation of Akhmatova's "Song of the Last Meeting" is by Gerard Shelley (1891–1980). An Englishman, Shelley spent considerable time in Russia, and was a translator not only of Russian poetry but of memoirs, works of history, and folktales. As Constance Garnett did for the nineteenth-century Russian novel, so Shelley did for the Russian poetry of his day, proudly delivering it to a receptive English readership.

One is struck by the melodiousness of Shelley's translation. Its song-like quality is apparent from its rhyme and regular meter (iambic tetrameter), a modified ballad stanza with the exception of lines 8 through 12, where there is more metrical variation, setting off the dialogue with the wind. Shelley departs from the original verse form, but makes metrical choices that carry the conversational character of the poem. The poem shifts to a standard ballad stanza—alternating tetrameter and trimeter—in the final quatrain.

It is worth paying attention to Shelley's diction. In reading rhymed, metered verse we can distinguish between those poems that appear to have *discovered* the music lurking in language and those that appear to have *imposed* it. In the first couplet, there are several signs of imposition: "*so* helplessly," "*so* light," "*was* drawing" (italics mine). The adverbial modifier "so" contributes the front end of an iamb, but is a semantically superfluous filler word (although arguably erecting a useful parallelism between "helplessly" and "light"). Similarly, "was drawing" would be more naturally expressed as "drew," were it not for material considerations. Moreover, "In all my anguish" has been added to the first stanza, presumably to achieve the right line length, and detracts from the translation by stating what is left unsaid in the Russian, losing some of the economy of Akhmatova's verse. Generally, though, Shelley's translation offers the reader more of a journey of musical discovery than a labored imposition of meter and rhyme. His translation also avails itself of metrical contrast in the line "I glanced toward the house in the night." This metrical turn mirrors the bodily turn of the poetic persona toward the venue of the final encounter.

The rhyme scheme is ABCB. Shelley opts for masculine rhymes, which are simple without being hackneyed (with the exception of "night" and "light"). There is no evidence of shoehorning here, perhaps because Shelley has chosen not to replicate with perfect fidelity the rhyme and meter of the Russian. Ironically, this choice may be what carries the song.

Andrey Kneller's Translation (2011)

Andrey Kneller's 2011 collection *Final Meeting* gives us the Russian originals and English translations on facing pages. Kneller emigrated from Russia to New York at the age of ten, and is both a poet and a translator of Russian poetry.

Kneller's title, "Song of the final meeting," stresses—more than "last" does—the end of an affair. The translation varies metrically, but for the most part maintains three stresses per line throughout. Like Shelley, Kneller gives us a song, also using an ABCB rhyme scheme, but with a decidedly different lilt. Economy of expression is paramount.

The pervasive presence of possessives in the first quatrain ("my chest," "my footsteps," "my left hand," and "my right") reduces the distance between the voice of the poetic persona and the physical description of bodily state. A subjectivity creeps in that gives an effect of introspection rather than the dispassionate observation for which Akhmatova is lauded. Yet Kneller, like Akhmatova, consistently uses the past tense, which allows for a dual consciousness. The poetic persona is (now) consciously aware that she had been acting unconsciously. This duality mirrors the contrast between being "helplessly chilled" from the waist up, yet "nimble" below.

Despite the constraints of rhyme and meter, Kneller's translation exhibits a surprisingly natural word order, especially in the first two stanzas. There, meter seems to have emerged rather than to have been imposed. That said, in the first stanza the word "unconsciously" is introduced to keep the meter, but at the expense of economy, making explicit what Akhmatova leaves unsaid. In the third stanza, in the response of the poetic persona to the pleas of autumn, "here" is added: "I'll also die here with you." Nothing in the Russian suggests or requires anything regarding *where* the poetic persona will die, only *that* she will die.

There is a bit of a loss of poetic control after the first two stanzas. In the third stanza, the register turns formal: "dreary, / Dismal, changeable." Furthermore the syntax is a bit strained, and there is some awkward redundancy: "and I too" / ". . . / And I'll also die here with you." In the final stanza, there is a decisive break in the rhyme scheme, an addition of feminine rhymes in the first and third lines.

Stephen Berg's Translation (1981)

Stephen Berg (1934–2014) was an American poet as well as the founder and editor of the *American Poetry Review*. He did not know Russian, but rather worked from Richard McKane's translation of Akhmatova, initially to create a version of the poem for his volume *Grief* (1975). Later he revisited his version and, for his 1981 collection, *With Akhmatova at the Black Gates*, he rewrote it. Whether the resulting poem should be considered a translation, an adaptation, a version, or even a palimpsest is a subject worthy of debate.

Berg makes no pretense of giving us a song—witness his title, "Last Meeting." His poem is written in free verse, and drops the "song" of Akhmatova's original title. The opening quatrain, its first three lines each beginning with "I," unflinchingly foregrounds the intense self-awareness, self-obsession, and, ultimately, self-deprecation of the poetic persona. The emphasis here is less on the objective description of physical detail and more on the poetic persona's subjective experience. Where Shelley has the heart growing helplessly chill, a concession to autonomous physiology, Berg's poetic persona is the one who is helpless, evoking a sense of inadequacy and deficiency. Berg's version depicts the poetic persona as victim, an object of pity and self-deprecation ("like an idiot"). This is not to say he eschews descriptive detail: his depiction of physical movement is vivid and highly specific ("I walked one foot on tiptoe").

Berg's handling of temporal cues in his choice of verbs and adverbs brings into sharp relief the cognitive and epistemic dimensions of the poem. The mise-en-scène is pushed backward in time by some of the translation choices. To the end of the first line of the second quatrain Berg appends "then," yielding the impression that the scene being recounted belongs to a past that stands at a temporal remove. Here we have a voice of metacognition. Thought process and mental state are rendered dual and explicit: "I remember answering."

Despite his colloquialisms, Berg makes some jarring word choices. Fate is a "sick, truculent liar" who has "stripped" Autumn (of foliage, we might presume). Fair enough. Yet a parallel is erected between the stripped Autumn and the speaker, who has been "flayed"—skinned—yielding a violent image.

"This is our last meeting—this place, this voice." The first line of the final quatrain gives pause: with whom is this the last meeting? Perhaps not the former lover. It is not even clear whose voice "this voice" is: That of Autumn? That of the poetic persona? Then or now? Is the meeting between place and voice? Regardless, a curious effect is engendered by the use of the present tense in this version. It is as if to provide a meta-commentary on the scene that has been depicted: what I am describing to you right now is our last meeting—"this place, this voice." Coupled with the indeterminate antecedent of "our," Berg's version takes on the status not of a song, but of a confession. Illuminating the darkness of the bedroom, the "guttered" candles reveal that the speaker's gaze is being returned by an embodied presence: "eyes and a torso." The poem ends on this metonymic representation of the lover, and a bit of a gothic note.

In his foreword to *With Akhmatova at the Black Gates*, Hayden Carruth calls Berg's versions a "fusion of two lives, two minds, and two sensibilities." Those of us who are fans of fusion fare often pride ourselves on our palates, with their sensitivity to the melded morsel, coupled with their uncanny ability to analyze and discern its alchemical components. What do our taste buds bid us to make of Berg's Akhmatova in this poem?

The Three Translations

Different translators have different aims, which must be kept in mind when passing judgment on a translation (one might separately assess the appropriateness of the aims). The resulting translation comes about as a product of the gravitational force of the original and the aims of the translator, which, while not always known, are sometimes explicitly stated, and can sometimes be partly inferred from the translations themselves.

Gerard Shelley, more than many other translators, appears to be focused on the target audience, using the resources of English to produce a song. He does not mimic every feature of Akhmatova's original, but rather re-creates Akhmatova's poem in English. If his aim is to give us an Akhmatova that can be sung, then he has succeeded.

Kneller explicitly states that Russian poetry is a linguistic and artistic lifeline to his first language. In his manifesto on translation, he argues that the translator must attain as close a semblance to the original as possible— a difficult task. It is hard to preserve the rhyme, meter, sense, and reference of the Russian and have it sound natural in English, but Kneller's translation succeeds in achieving its aims to a surprising degree (though his diction ages Akhmatova beyond her years, especially in the latter half).

Stephen Berg appropriates Akhmatova's poem and uses it as a resource for what seems to be an expression of his own emotions, not those of Akhmatova's poetic persona. Thus he says things Akhmatova never would have said in ways she never would have said them.

In his seminal work "The Task of the Translator," philosopher Walter Benjamin (1892–1940) claims that the translator's task is to restore to wholeness a vessel that, after Babel, has been shattered into fragments. He speaks in a metaphysical and somewhat mystical sense about the totality of language, but in a more limited way what we see in these three translations of a single poem is that each fills a crack in the vessel of the whole, although each contains its own cracks. Shelley gives us a song. Kneller attempts to re-create the form of Akhmatova's poem. Berg attempts to inhabit the emotional space of Akhmatova's poem, but on his own terms. This plurality of philosophies of translation helps explain why translation is an ongoing process that is never completed.

Boris Pasternak

(Russian, 1890–1960)

TRANSLATIONS BY

Lydia Pasternak Slater,

Jon Stallworthy and Peter France,

James E. Falen

· ·

COMMENTARY BY

J. Kates

ГАМЛЕТ

Гул затих. Я вышел на подмостки.
Прислонясь к дверному косяку,
Я ловлю в далеком отголоске,
Что случится на моем веку.

На меня наставлен сумрак ночи
Тысячью биноклей на оси.
Если только можно, Авва Отче,
Чашу эту мимо пронеси.

Я люблю Твой замысел упрямый
И играть согласен эту роль.
Но сейчас идет другая драма,
И на этот раз меня уволь.

Но продуман распорядок действий,
И неотвратим конец пути.
Я один, все тонет в фарисействе.
Жизнь прожить — не поле перейти.

Boris Pasternak (1946)

Hamlet

The murmurs ebb; onto the stage I enter.
I am trying, standing in the door,
To discover in the distant echoes
What the coming years may hold in store.

The nocturnal darkness with a thousand
Binoculars is focused onto me.
Take away this cup, O Abba, Father,
Everything is possible to thee.

I am fond of this thy stubborn project,
And to play my part I am content.
But another drama is in progress,
And, this once, O let me be exempt.

But the plan of action is determined,
And the end irrevocably sealed.
I am alone; all round me drowns in falsehood:
Life is not a walk across a field.

translated by Lydia Pasternak Slater (1963)

Hamlet

The buzz subsides. I have come on stage.
Leaning in an open door
I try to detect from the echo
What the future has in store.

A thousand opera-glasses level
The dark, point-blank, at me.
Abba, Father, if it be possible
Let this cup pass from me.

I love your preordained design
And am ready to play this role.
But the play being acted is not mine.
For this once let me go.

But the order of the acts is planned,
The end of the road already revealed.
Alone among the Pharisees I stand.
Life is not a stroll across a field.

translated by Jon Stallworthy and Peter France (1984)

Hamlet

The tumult dies. I enter from the wings.
And leaning in the doorway to the stage,
I seek to catch, within the distant echo,
The shape of what may happen in my age.

Upon my figure from the dark of night
A thousand focused glasses have been trained.
But Abba, Father, if there be a way,
Allow this bitter cup to pass me by.

I cherish your unwavering design
And willingly consent to play this role,
But ask that you release me for a time,
For now another drama's plot unfolds.

But all the acts are written and ordained.
I know the journey's end and hear its toll.
Alone I stand. Pharisaism reigns.
The way through life is not a simple stroll.

translated by James E. Falen (2012)

Commentary by J. Kates
A Little More than Kin

More than a dozen translations of Boris Pasternak's "Гамлет" have appeared in print. Choosing for this essay, I have steered a course between the many-headed Scylla of those that are more imitations than translations and the stony Charybdis of those that try slavishly to reproduce only the superficial form of the poem. My purpose in examining these three is not to tear any of them down, but inevitably I will have to note their omissions as one way of getting to their inclusions—every translation is an existential choice. These are versions I respect and admire.

The first words Shakespeare's Hamlet utters, an aside after King Claudius's smarmy verbal embrace, are "A little more than kin, and less than kind." They come smack in the middle of a busy scene—the Danish prince has been swept onstage with the court in a swirl of political and personal dispensations. He immediately gets caught up in verbal fencing with his uncle-father and his mother. There is no contemplation here, no expectant silence. When the Russian poet Boris Pasternak famously translated Shakespeare, capturing that scene with these lines and successfully reproducing their intricacies of sound, he turned the irony into straight commentary and sacrificed the bitter pun: *И даже слишком близкий, к сожаленью* ("And even too close, unfortunately").[1]

How different is the Hamlet that Pasternak himself imagined, entering to an audience hushed in anticipation. No lines in Shakespeare's play correspond precisely to this coup de théâtre:[2] ("The hum has quieted down. I came out onto the stage")—a brand-new scene. The Russian sentences are in the first person. They are in the past tense. They are those of an actor having directed and blocked his own performance—"I leaned against the door-post." Pasternak's Hamlet, like Shakespeare's, distances and dramatizes himself, but it's not "himself"; he's a fiction of a fiction. That's the first thing to notice: the Russian poet chooses to write in the voice of an imaginary character portrayed by an actor.[3] More than that, the writing of another fiction has been laid between the poet and the reader, thus: one poet (Boris Pasternak) invents another poet (Yuri Zhivago), who has written as an actor assuming the role of Shakespeare's fictional Hamlet, who, we are accustomed to recognizing, is much given to dissembling with "an antic disposition," and who (which *who* is this?) will later in the poem quote as his own the words of still another, even more exalted person, the second of the Trinity. Nevertheless, this "Hamlet" has often been read as a highly individual expression of Pasternak's own situation in the culture and politics of his own time and place. It is clearly no simple walk across an empty stage.

In the third and fourth lines, "Hamlet" locates himself in time as well as space: "I catch in the distant echo / What is happening in my age." We take this *век* ("century/age") to be Pasternak's own, roughly contemporary with his character Zhivago's, although framing a different life story.

Boris Leonidovich Pasternak, born in 1890, lived through all the grim years of the first half of the twentieth century, until 1960, one of the few artists to survive the politics of his time, occasionally by his own equivocating, and under the unsolicited protection of Stalin himself. By 1946, when he wrote the first draft of "Hamlet,"[4] he had seen the fate of his contemporaries and tried to walk his own uneasy line between authority and independence. There is no question that Pasternak suffered a measure of guilt. For instance, he unreasonably held himself at least partially responsible for the fate of Osip Mandelstam. And the age he lived in certainly put everyone onstage. Not just a thousand opera glasses, but a whole judgmental population and an intrusive bureaucracy.[5]

Yet Pasternak embedded "Hamlet" in the fictional biography of a passionate doctor who got caught up more directly in the events of revolution and civil war and who was quite clearly not simply Boris Leonidovich himself. It is through the character of Yuri Zhivago that most English speakers first read the poem, either in a translation by Bernard Guilbert Guerney from the first, hastily contrived English publication in 1960, or in the more recent (2012) translation by Richard Pevear and Larissa Volokhonsky. These versions of "the Zhivago poems" are mechanical and subsidiary to the prose. We want to attend to more-ambitious translations, but first return to the original text.

In the second stanza, the emphasis shifts explicitly from the actor as director to the actor as one who is being observed and directed by others: "On me is trained the twilight of night / A thousand opera-glasses on their axes." And a big jump occurs in the third line of the stanza—"If it is only allowed, Abba Father"—which introduces imagery absent from Pasternak's original two-stanza version, the explicit identification of Hamlet with Christ (Отче isn't just "father"; it's the High Church, the "Father" of the Lord's Prayer, for instance), consummated in the following line by a direct quote from Matthew 26:39, to "let this cup pass." In the original Passion narrative, God as Father and Son is both director and directed, both active and passive, with, in fact, exactly the ambiguity Pasternak has set up for Hamlet in the poem itself.

The next seven lines play out internal desires against external constraints: "I love your stubborn idea / and am agreeable to playing this role. / But right now another drama is going on. / Dismiss me this one time. // But the order of the acts is thought out / and the end of the journey inevitable. / I am alone. Everything drowns in Pharisaism." A word meaning "but" in a strong, oppositional sense, Но repeats awkwardly at the beginning of two nearly adjacent lines. It can't be ignored either time; while it seems to trip up the momentum, it expresses contradictory tensions turning in on themselves and on the speaker. Finally, there is the conclusion, Жизнь прожить—не поле перейти ("To live through life is not to walk across a field"). This sounds to a foreign ear like a profound, melancholy apothegm. In fact, it's a tired proverb, a cliché. After those awkward repetitions of Но, the poem "Hamlet" ends not with a bang but a whimper, a deliberate letdown. Life is not a bowl of cherries.

And that last line is a minefield for a translator. It has to be both idiomatic and specific in its reference, a cultural impossibility in English. With the contrary forces of a commonplace association and a concrete image, Pasternak has reminded the reader that the speaker is not in fact crossing an open field but posing in a theater, observed by a glittering audience. I want to look first at how three different translators have handled this key line.

Lydia Pasternak Slater, the poet's sister, reads her brother's work with the authority of direct communication: "I have tried to translate in the same way as my brother wrote," she says in the introduction to her translations. Yet now her version has become just one among many. "Life is not a walk across a field" is how Slater renders the critical last line. For Jon Stallworthy and Peter France: "Life is not a stroll across a field." Most recently, for James E. Falen: "The way through life is not a simple stroll." All of these capitalize on Pasternak's simplicity of diction in general, and two out of three maintain the polarity of stage and field. But all suppress the action by turning verbs into nouns, and two out of three collapse "getting through" life into the single word "life." They all let go of the banality of the observation, although avoiding any kind of sententiousness. What can a translator do beyond this? Find an equivalent English-language cliché (the "bowl of cherries" above, or "a walk in a park") and substitute that? But that would be to lose, as Falen does, the movement from the beginning to the end of the poem between the theater and the open field. Getting through life *is* walking across a stage. Not just the event but the process matters here.

That process, for Falen and for Stallworthy/France among these three, begins with Pasternak's use of the past tense. Russians often use the past tense to indicate present action. (The common way of saying "Let's get going" in Russian is "We're gone.") Yet there is something crucial in the moment of Pasternak's speaker, who has already committed himself onstage before he confronts his situation. Translations that put the first line into the present tense miss this nuance. Only Stallworthy/France suggest the finiteness of the action: "I have come on stage." This first line introduces the straightforward quality of language that Pasternak sets against a complexity of meaning. Once into the stanza, Slater loses some of this with inversions not comfortable in contemporary poetry: "onto the stage I enter" and "to play my part I am content." Falen and Stallworthy/France are far more idiomatic here, and truer to the original. By the penultimate line of the poem, though, it is these two versions that indulge in inversion, and it is Slater's diction that stands naturally alone.

More problematic for me in Slater's version is her downplaying of the

Christian themes that Pasternak introduces into the Zhivago poem. Except for "Abba, Father" and the single word "cup," she makes no direct allusion to Biblical language, even translating the specific Pharisaism into a vague "falsehood." (In my own translation of "Hamlet," I choose a middle way, replacing the Pharisees with "hypocrites," which at least has scriptural warrant.) Stallworthy/France stay closest to the Bible, and therefore, in this instance, closest to Pasternak—and, perhaps equally important, closest to Zhivago. Falen's editorializing "bitter," I suspect, helps him fill out the rhythm of the line.

Why do all three translations turn the simple "catch" of the third line into seeking and trying to catch? This, too, probably derives from a metric, not a semantic, need. Unfortunately, it falsifies the awareness of the speaker, making Hamlet more tentative than he needs to be. Pasternak's speaker knows clearly what he hears.[6] Falen and Slater are both troubled by the stark last line of the first stanza, and plug it out in pedestrian feet. For me, too, translating that line has proved troublesome; there's too much space for monosyllabic content in plain English. Stallworthy/France negotiate this problem most successfully, by making explicit in the completed poem the future tense of Pasternak's first draft. And yet, if Pasternak changes tenses deliberately from future to present, they contribute to a further misunderstanding.

When Slater writes about "what I regard as essential when translating Pasternak's poetry," she is attending exclusively to the formality of his verse, stressing the rhythm over all other qualities of sound, "because instinctive feeling for rhythm and harmony were inborn qualities of his genius, and he simply could not write differently." Attention to the sound of "Hamlet" is equally critical to Falen. "I wanted," Falen writes, "in addition to conveying the general sense of the poem, to use some form of structured verse, even if it varies from the form of the original. Pasternak's poem seems essentially to be in trochaic tetrameter with alternating feminine and masculine rhymes (some near or inexact rhymes). My version is in iambic pentameter, with fewer rhymes (whether exact or near rhymes), and I have not observed the Russian pattern of alternating masculine and feminine rhymes."[7]

Stallworthy/France feel least constrained by the regularity of the poem's rhythms, choosing for several lines the force of spare diction over the demands of the ear. Their dereliction from strict metrics gives us the intricate, anapestic alliteration and assonance of "I try to detect from the echo." Like theirs, Pasternak's own subtlety of sound effects extends well beyond meter and end rhymes. None of the three translations here has caught, for instance, the echo of Я ловлю / Я люблю ("ia lovliu/ia liubliu"), although Slater could have done it with "discover" and "love," nor the framing chiasmus at the beginning of the second stanza that suggests the brackets of a proscenium stage. Only Stallworthy/France take on directly the anaphora of the two *Hos*.

All of the translators here carefully balance the exigencies of sound against those of sense. The sacrifices they make vary in their intensity, but they all come to bear in the images of the last stanza. Less concerned with the Christian reverberations than the other translators, Slater chooses not to translate *конец пути*, which refers to a journey—not a drama—coming to an end, a movement checked by boundaries, mediated by the single Biblical evocation of drowning in Pharisaism. Falen and Stallworthy/France keep the Pharisees in this stanza, if not the drowning,[8] and even introduce, perhaps, a new point of reference. In both their versions, the speaker is not only not moving, he is not leaning against a door. He "stands," and his standing sounds like Luther at the Diet of Worms, who "can do no other." This is not at all in the original, but it is inconsistent neither with Pasternak's own cultural history nor with the tone of the poem. Does that "stand" distract or enrich our reading? Does it contradict the willingness of the speaker to accede to the demands of the script? Hard to say. And if this introduced allusion sounds far-fetched, either in its inclusion or in my reading of it, what are we to make of another translator,[9] who finds a Mandelstam-inspired pun on *oca* ("wasp") in Pasternak's *ocu* ("axes") and translates the second stanza: "Night blankness pins me to its axis / through a thousand opera-glasses / with a wasp-sting." Difficult as the choices of what to leave out might be for a translator, we all need to be even more cautious of what, accidentally or on purpose, we add. Falen contributes his own "bitter" and "toll," Slater an image of the "sealed" end. Stallworthy/France apparently make it part of their discipline to try not to step at all beyond the boundaries of the original text, but their "stand," like their "try" in the first stanza, shows how difficult this is.

It has been said that Russians believe everything can be translated into their language and nothing can be translated out of it; and while they cite Pasternak's Shakespeare as a paragon of translation, his own poems are deemed untouchable. "A little more than kin, and less than kind" might just as easily express the way readers of original texts tend to dismiss what gets put into English, and might suggest that some even come to cry murder. Yet the translations examined here are far kinder than that, and their kinship, both with the original and with one another, is indisputable. There is, as all of *Hamlet* dramatizes, a glory in words, a falsity in words, and a limit to what words can accomplish. Slater, Stallworthy/France, and Falen each have a piece of the truth of "Hamlet," and none of them has it all, but then none of them claims to have it all. That's not what translations do. Translators and readers of translations need to keep this always in mind, or none should "scape whipping."

Notes

1. I use my own approximate literal translations of the original Russian in the first part of this essay.

2. The play comes closest to that in act 3, scene 1, when Claudius and Polonius ostensibly leave the scene and Hamlet enters with his "To be or not to be" soliloquy. But the business and stage direction there—"*Exeunt* Claudius *and* Polonius. *Enter* Hamlet"—leave no time for an expectant hush.

3. The relationship between Shakespeare the actor-playwright and Hamlet the character-playwright-actor adds another dimension that might take us too far afield here, but which is not completely irrelevant to the complexity of the roles.

4. The poem exists in an earlier version, dated February 1946, eight lines long.

5. "When we met we spoke in whispers, glancing at the walls for fear of eavesdropping neighbors or hidden microphones. When I returned to Moscow after the war, I found that everybody covered their telephones with cushions, because it was rumored that they were equipped with recording devices, and the most ordinary householders trembled with terror in the presence of the black metal object listening in on their innermost thoughts."—Nadezhda Mandelstam.

6. It may or may not be relevant to this moment of the poem, but, in his own notes, writing of Shakespeare's character, Pasternak writes, "*Hamlet* is not a drama of lack of character, but a drama of duty and self-denial."

7. E-mail note from Falen to me, March 20, 2013 (my translation).

8. Slater even anticipates and reinforces the strong verb "drown" with the verb she chooses at the very beginning of the poem, where the murmurs "ebb" instead of merely quieting down.

9. Tony Brinkley. His justification is thus, in the essay "Translating Pasternak's Hamlet": "In the second stanza, *oc*, the Russian for 'axis' is very close to *oca*, the Russian for 'wasp'. Mandelshtam had played on this near-homonym in a Voronezh poem where he is 'armed with the vision of narrowing wasps' as he 'listen[s]' while they 'suck the earth's axis'. Throughout the Voronezh poems mark the serendipity that the syllable *oc* is common to both Mandelshtam's and Stalin's given names (Osip, Josif). At the same time as a reference to the 'axis' powers, *oca* names Stalin's fascism. Perhaps Mandelshtam hoped that for the leader this 'wasp-sting' could work a little like Hamlet's 'mousetrap.'"

César Vallejo

(Spanish, 1892–1938)

TRANSLATIONS BY

Clayton Eshleman, Rebecca Seiferle,

Barry Fogden

••••••••••••••••••••••••••••••

COMMENTARY BY

Cindy Schuster

Los heraldos negros

Hay golpes en la vida, tan fuertes . . . Yo no sé!
Golpes como del odio de Dios; como si ante ellos,
la resaca de todo lo sufrido
se empozara en el alma . . . Yo no sé!

Son pocos; pero son . . . Abren zanjas oscuras
en el rostro más fiero y en el lomo más fuerte.
Serán talvez los potros de bárbaros atilas;
o los heraldos negros que nos manda la Muerte.

Son las caídas hondas de los Cristos del alma,
de alguna fe adorable que el Destino blasfema.
Esos golpes sangrientos son las crepitaciones
de algún pan que en la puerta del horno se nos quema.

Y el hombre . . . Pobre . . . pobre! Vuelve los ojos, como
cuando por sobre el hombro nos llama una palmada;
vuelve los ojos locos, y todo lo vivido
se empoza, como charco de culpa, en la mirada.

Hay golpes en la vida, tan fuertes . . . Yo no sé!

César Vallejo (1918)

The Black Heralds

There are blows in life, so powerful . . . I don't know!
Blows as from the hatred of God; as if, facing them,
the undertow of everything suffered
welled up in the soul . . . I don't know!

They are few; but they are . . . They open dark trenches
in the fiercest face and in the strongest back.
Perhaps they are the colts of barbaric Attilas;
or the black heralds sent to us by Death.

They are the deep falls of the Christs of the soul,
of some adored faith blasphemed by Destiny.
Those bloodstained blows are the crackling of
bread burning up at the oven door.

And man . . . Poor . . . poor! He turns his eyes, as
when a slap on the shoulder summons us;
turns his crazed eyes, and everything lived
wells up, like a pool of guilt, in his look.

There are blows in life, so powerful . . . I don't know!

translated by Clayton Eshleman (2007)

The Black Heralds

There are blows in life, so powerful . . . I don't know!
Blows like God's hatred; as if before them,
the undertow of everything suffered
were to well up in the soul . . . I don't know!

They're few; but they exist . . . They open dark furrows
in the most ferocious face and the most powerful loins.
Perhaps they're wooden horses of barbaric Attilas,
or black messengers that Death sends to us.

They're profound lapses of the soul's Christs,
of some adorable faith that Destiny blasphemes.
Those bloodthirsty blows are cracklings of some
bread that in the oven's door burns up on us.

And man . . . Poor . . . poor man! He turns his eyes, as
when a slap on the shoulder calls us by name;
he turns his crazed eyes, and everything he's lived
wells up, like a pool of guilt, in his gaze.

There are blows in life, so powerful . . . I don't know!

translated by Rebecca Seiferle (2003)

The Black Heralds

You get knocks in life, so vicious . . . It beats me!
Blows as if from God's hate; as if under their rain,
the backwash of everything you've suffered
stagnates in your soul . . . It beats me!

Not many; but you get them . . . They open up dark sluices
in the fiercest face and in the strongest back.
Perhaps they're the mounts of barbarian Attilas;
or the black heralds sent to us by Death.

They're the falls to earth of the Christs of your soul,
of some worshipful faith that Destiny blasphemes.
Those bleeding blows are the crackings
of a loaf burning away on us in the oven door.

And man . . . Wretched . . . wretched! He looks round,
as you do when a clap on the shoulder gets your attention;
he turns his mad eyes, and all the life he has lived
puddles, like a pool of guilt, in his gaze.

You get knocks in life, so vicious . . . It beats me!

translated by Barry Fogden (1995)

Commentary by Cindy Schuster

A preeminent figure in Hispanic letters, César Vallejo (Santiago de Chuco, Peru, 1882–Paris, 1938) is renowned as one of the most original poetic voices of twentieth-century Latin America. "The Black Heralds" is the title poem of his first book of poetry, published in 1918. Though influenced by the *modernista*[1] movement, the poems in this collection nevertheless challenge the movement's conventions with the introduction of the unorthodox imagery, transgressive metaphors, and disarticulated language that would come to characterize his later work.

There have been many translations of "The Black Heralds."[2] The three presented here were chosen because of the intriguing contrasts that become apparent when we juxtapose them, and because they tangibly illustrate each translator's distinct approach. Ultimately, my concern is with how these translators function as intermediaries between the poem and the reader.

Clayton Eshleman began translating Vallejo in the early 1960s, yet it was not until 2003 that he turned to *The Black Heralds*, which appears in his comprehensive *The Complete Poetry* (2007). Eshleman affirms a strong position against interpretive translation; his goal is "to respect the original at every point . . . , to aim for a translation that was absolutely accurate *and* up to the performance level of the original." For Eshleman, who maintains that he was "psychically opened up" by the Peruvian poet, the project of translating Vallejo was a transformational experience that became profoundly enmeshed with his own process of self-realization as a poet.

In the introduction to her translation of *The Black Heralds* (2003), Rebecca Seiferle, who also translated *Trilce* (1992), Vallejo's most original and experimental work, argues that he is still being read and translated according to Western paradigms that view him as "a shadow to our prevailing modes, representing whatever we ourselves have left out." Vallejo was *mestizo*—his grandfathers were Spanish Catholic priests and his grandmothers were indigenous women—and Seiferle is critical of approaches to his work that obscure his autochthony and his marginality. She discusses her "sense that Vallejo's work was still being colonized," and asserts that he

is "much more intelligible . . . on his own terms." Vallejo, she insists, is "always replying to the language of empire."

Barry Fogden is an English poet whose translation of *The Black Heralds* was published in 1995. Fogden's brief translator's note does not discuss his approach to Vallejo's poetry, but his translation demonstrates a bent for interpretation and colloquiality that I suspect underlies an intention to make Vallejo more accessible to the average reader.

"The Black Heralds" expresses the existential anguish of a subject who endures crushing blows from which there is no salvation. The poem's movement is circular; the last line is identical to the first, and leaves us hanging with its failure to comprehend, much less transcend, suffering and loss. Ellipses inscribe gaps into the poem where language is aborted and thought trails off into silence. As Efraín Kristal observes in the introduction to the Eshleman translations, "one feels the breath knocked out of the poetic voice." Faith offers no solace; the iconographic language of the sacred is ruptured and Christian doctrines are turned upside down. The poet throws in his lot with the rest of humanity, but his compassion and solidarity are insufficient: there will be no alleviation of suffering, no expiation of guilt.

Without delving into the technicalities of Spanish metrification and rhyme, we should note that Vallejo's lines follow, for the most part, a regular rhyme scheme, and that he makes ample use of internal rhyme as well. The assonance of the long, stressed "o" that echoes mournfully through the poem underscores the sense of anguish and despair. For example, in Gol*pes* c*o*mo *del o*dio *de* Dios (line 2), the insistent repetition of the sound intensifies the relentless buffeting of the blows, and in *Y el* hom*bre* . . . P*o*bre . . . p*o*bre! (line 13), it heightens the pathos of a line already punctuated by loss (emphasis mine).

We can discern a regular rhyme scheme in Eshleman's first three stanzas ("know"/"know," "trenches"/"death," "soul"/"door"), and Seiferle offers some end rhymes as well, though not in predictable patterns ("some"/"us," "name"/"gaze"). Both use assonance and slant rhyme to reproduce the long stressed "o" throughout their translations, with words such as "blows," "so," "powerful," "know," "soul," "open," "door," etc.

Seiferle and Eshleman begin with identical translations of line 1, and register only minor differences in the rest of the stanza. Fogden, on the other hand, employs a more colloquial, informal register: *golpes* is rendered as "knocks," and *Yo no sé!* becomes "It beats me!," which creates a rather unfortunate pun. In line 2 he translates those same *golpes* as "blows," and *ante ellos* as "under their rain," which repositions the subject, who in Spanish faces the blows; the expression "rain" of blows, moreover, contradicts line 5, which states that the blows are infrequent. His translation of *fuertes* (line 1) as "vicious" adds a sense of malicious intent to "God's hate," not present in the other translators' more accurate "powerful." In lines 3 and 4 *la resaca . . . / se empozara* is translated by Eshleman as "the undertow . . . / welled up" and by Seiferle as "were to well up," implying that suffering flows like an undercurrent below the surface, filling the soul to the brim. Fogden opts for "the backwash . . . / stagnates," which emphasizes the persistence of the suffering, whose aftermath lingers unmoving in the soul. He also introduces the pronoun "you," which is not present in the Spanish: "You get knocks," rather than the more literal "there are" for *hay*. He continues this strategy throughout: "everything you've suffered," "your soul," etc. We might read these forms of "you" as the nonspecific "one," and/ or as attempts to bring the reader directly into the poem.

The elliptical phrasing that precedes the caesura in line 5 of Eshleman's translation foregrounds the sense of the insufficiency of language and the truncation of expression we find in the original text. The second "they are" in "They are few; but they are" is quite literal and leaves the line suspended with the same ambiguity we find in the Spanish: it can be read as emphasizing the existence of the blows (they *are*) as well as indicating the failure of language to express or represent them adequately (they are . . . *what?*). Both Seiferle ("They're few; but they exist") and Fogden ("Not many; but you get them") opt for the former meaning, and Fogden again diverges somewhat from the original by inserting "you" and employing a more colloquial register.

In the same line, Seiferle's "furrows" and Eshleman's "trenches" are the most literal translations of *zanjas*; "furrows" is less strange and gives us the image of a "real" face, inasmuch as we might say "a furrowed brow" in English. *Lomo* in Spanish usually refers to the back or the loins of a quadruped; in the poem it carries the connotation of a beast of burden, of the subject bent under a great weight despite having "the strongest back" (Eshleman and Fogden). Seiferle's "powerful loins" conveys this metaphorical sense as well, and allows for a consistent translation of *fuertes*. Notwithstanding, it also introduces the quite different sense of male virility.

We can begin to discern hints of the indigenous experience in Seiferle's translations of the next two lines. For example, she translates *potros* as "wooden horses," in contrast to Eshleman's literal "colts" and Fogden's generic "mounts." The wooden horse is another name for the rack, a torture device used by the Spanish Inquisition, which established a tribunal in Peru that functioned for 250 years. The use of this acceptation of *potros* calls attention to the violent oppression of Peru's indigenous population by colonial powers, and "barbaric Attilas" could easily refer to the Spanish conquistadors. I wonder about Seiferle's translation of *heraldos* as "messengers" in this line, inasmuch as she opts for "heralds" in the title. While it might be a stretch, it would be consistent with her reading of the poem to speculate that she is making an allusion to the Incan messengers who brought news of the arrival of the Spaniards. It is also worth noting that she ends the stanza with "us," thus subtly bringing the reader into the poem as we linger, albeit for just a beat, on that word.

In the third stanza Vallejo undermines Catholic doctrine by pluralizing Christ, and then by locating these Christs in the human soul. As Kristal observes, "It is not the soul of man that falls within a Christian framework, but Christianity itself within a humanistic one. . . . In Vallejo's religious rhetoric, humanity is not awaiting Christ's salvation. On the contrary, and with intended blasphemy, a Christ 'falls' each time the soul is battered by the blows of life." Eshleman's translation of *las caídas hondas* as "the deep falls" is quite literal and preserves the difficulty of the line, while Seiferle's "profound lapses" suggests a moral slippage or fall from grace. Fogden opts for "the falls to earth," which provides an apt image for the mind to wrap itself around. In line 10, the Spanish *fe adorable* can be understood as a "faith worthy of adoration." While "adorable" (Seiferle) is technically a cognate in English, given its common meaning as "charming" or "cute," Eshleman's choice of "adored" might be a more felicitous approximation. Fogden's choice of "worshipful" better describes one who worships than it does the faith itself.

In line 11, the adjective *sangrientos* is translated variously as "bloodthirsty" (Seiferle), which points to a violent and savage agency (perhaps another reference to colonialism); "bloodstained" (Eshleman), which describes the marks of the blows on the body, and carries a connotation of guilt as well; and "bleeding" (Fogden), a participial adjective that indicates continuity (the blood is still flowing from the wounded body), and that may also be used as an intensifier in British English. The stanza continues to sabotage the Catholic belief system as the bread—the body of Christ—is burned before it can be consumed. In line 12, *se nos quema* is rendered as "burning up" by Eshleman, which removes the "us" introduced in this line, in contrast to Fogden's "burning away on us" and Seiferle's "burns up on us." Seiferle's "us" is again the last word before the stanza break.

Eshleman's translation underscores the inadequacy of language in his rendering of *pobre* in line 13: "And man . . . Poor . . . poor!" This translation highlights the sense of paralysis and unfinishedness; the repetition of "poor" compounds the pity as it heightens the sense that the poet is at a loss for words. The line reads more oddly in English than in Spanish, where *pobre* is both an adjective and a noun meaning "poor [unfortunate] man" or "poor thing," as in Seiferle's "Poor . . . poor man!," which not only maintains the effect produced by the repetition of "poor," but further intensifies it, by allowing "Poor . . . poor" to directly modify "man." By ending the phrase with "man," she allows our attention to be drawn back to the subject, which is, in turn, a synecdoche for humanity. Fogden opts to avoid any ambiguity the reader might find in "poor," translating *pobre* as "wretched."

In Quechua culture, explains Seiferle, "seeing" is considered to be a principal component of "knowing," and she notes that "*The Black Heralds* is full of eyes, unexpected gazes. . . . In these poems, the agency of sight is inseparable from the condition of being wounded. . . . Throughout, eyes are associated with the autochthonic." In her translation of the phrase *vuelve los ojos*, she preserves the presence of the eyes, as does Eshleman, by opting for the literal "he turns his eyes," in contrast to Fogden's again more naturalized "he looks round" (though Fogden later translates the same phrase as "he turns his . . . eyes" in line 15).

Seiferle's translation of *como / cuando por sobre el hombro nos llama una palmada*—"as / when a slap on the shoulder calls us by name"—conveys a sense of intimacy, whereas Eshleman's slap, in contrast, "summons us," which is more formal and suggestive of a compelling authority. Fogden's "as you do when a clap on the shoulder gets your attention" changes the pronoun from "us" to "you," and is unnecessarily wordy and proselike. In line 16, Seiferle and Fogden both translate *la mirada* as "his gaze," which carries more intensity, and potentially more agency, than Eshleman's "his look." Seiferle further accentuates the "gaze"—the last word of the stanza—by rhyming it with "name" and "crazed."

The last line brings the poem full circle with translations identical to their first lines, as in the original.

We have seen distinct patterns emerge in the work of these three translators. Of the three, Barry Fogden appears to be most concerned with producing a "user-friendly" version of "The Black Heralds." He introduces "you" into the poem from the outset, and his register tends toward the conversational. His is the most expository and assimilationist; he prefers to avoid ambiguity and tends to opt for explication. His use of multiple translations for the same word further highlights this preference. While these strategies may make for an ostensibly easier read, I concur with Antoine Berman's assertion, in "Translation and the Trials of the Foreign," that such "explicitations may render a text more 'clear,' but they actually obscure *its own mode of clarity*."

Clayton Eshleman's translation closely adheres to the original and is the most attentive to Vallejo's linguistic experimentation. One can sense Eshleman's restraint and resistance to interpretation. He does not eschew the strangeness of the original, nor does he attempt to resolve ambiguities or smooth out odd turns of phrase. This preservation of "the foreign" allows the reader to engage with the difficulties of Vallejo's poetics by refusing to obscure them.

Rebecca Seiferle's translation allows Vallejo's indigenous sensibility to become manifest in the poem. She challenges the erasure of his ethnicity that she perceives in other approaches to his work, and gives us a close approximation of the original from this perspective. Seiferle manages, moreover, through the cumulative effect of certain lexical and syntactic nuances, to convey the sense of intimacy with the reader that carries much of the emotional resonance in Vallejo's poem.

Notes

1. Latin American *modernismo* is distinct from modernism in Europe and the United States. The movement developed in the late nineteenth and early twentieth centuries, and is considered to be the first uniquely Latin American form of literary expression. Reacting against a romanticism that had become commonplace, the *modernistas* sought to renew the Spanish and Portuguese languages and create a universal, cosmopolitan aesthetic.
2. Other translators of this poem include Rachel Benson, Richard Schaaf and Kathleen Ross, Robert Bly, and Michael Smith and Valentino Gianuzzi.

Federico García Lorca

(Spanish, 1898–1936)

TRANSLATIONS BY

W. S. Merwin, Catherine Brown,
Michael Smith

....

COMMENTARY BY

Rebecca Seiferle

Gacela de la terrible presencia

Yo quiero que el agua se quede sin cauce.
Yo quiero que el viento se quede sin valles.

Quiero que la noche se quede sin ojos
y mi corazón sin la flor del oro;

que los bueyes hablen con las grandes hojas
y que la lombriz se muera de sombra;

que brillen los dientes de la calavera
y los amarillos inunden la seda.

Puedo ver el duelo de la noche herida
luchando enroscada con el mediodía.

Resisto un ocaso de verde veneno
y los arcos rotos donde sufre el tiempo.

Pero no me ilumines tu limpio desnudo
como un negro cactus abierto en los juncos.

Déjame en un ansia de oscuros planetas,
¡pero no me enseñes tu cintura fresca!

Federico García Lorca (1931–1934)

Gacela of the Terrible Presence

I want the water reft from its bed,
I want the wind left without valleys.

I want the night left without eyes
and my heart without the flower of gold.

And the oxen to speak with great leaves
and the earthworm to perish of shadow.

And the teeth of the skull to glisten
and yellows to overflow the silk.

I can see the duel of the wounded night
writhing in battle with noon.

I resist a setting of green venom
and the broken arches where time suffers.

But do not illumine your clear nude
like a black cactus open in the reeds.

Leave me in an anguish of dark planets,
but do not show me your cool waist.

translated by W. S. Merwin (1955)

Ghazal of the Terrible Presence

I want there to be no channel for the water.
I want there to be no valleys for the wind.

I want there to be no eyes for the night,
no flower of gold for my heart;

and I want the oxen to talk to big leaves,
and the earthworm to die of shadow,

and I want teeth in the skull to gleam,
and the yellows to wash over the silk.

I can see the struggle of wounded night
wrestling in coils with midday.

I can endure a sunset green with poison
and the broken arches where time suffers.

But do not show me your immaculate nude
like a black cactus open in the reeds.

Leave me in longing for shadowy planets,
but do not show me the cool of your waist.

translated by Catherine Brown (2001)

Gacela of the Terrible Presence

I want the stream to lose its banks.
I want no slopes to cradle the wind.

I would have the night eyeless
and my heart yield up its fine gold;

oxen converse with broad leaves
and the worm die of shadow;

the skull's teeth glitter
and the yellows flood the silk.

I can bear to see the grief of wounded night
struggling in the coils of noon.

I withstand a sunset of green venom
and shattered arches where Time mourns.

But do not show me your lucent nakedness
as a black cactus opens out in reeds.

Leave me to yearn for dark planets
but do not show me your young waist.

translated by Michael Smith (2007)

Commentary by Rebecca Seiferle
Black Cactus Open in Reeds

"Gacela de la terrible presencia" is from Federico García Lorca's *Diván del Tamarit*, written between 1931 and 1934 and published posthumously in 1940. The collection contains a sequence of twelve *gacelas* and a sequence of nine *casidas* (from the Arabic forms the *qasida* and the *qhazal*). *Diván*, too, is an Arabic form in which a collection is arranged according to the alphabetical order of the end rhymes. Both in the collection itself and in the individual poems, Lorca does not follow the forms exactly; his approach to the form is "arbitrary," as Emilio García Gómez characterizes it, and yet it is "a moving act of homage." The preoccupation of the collection has been described by Michael Smith as "the passion of tormented love," and by Christopher Mauer as "elegiac" and "the grave utterance of unsatisfied desire in the shadow of death."

We read Lorca as we *have* read him, which is to say that all the various translations (and few Spanish poets have been as variously translated as Lorca) and texts about Lorca himself and his work collaborate to create an understanding of his work for the English reader. For instance, that "shadow of death" is much more poignant to us with our knowledge of Lorca's fate, but its presence in these poems is due more to Lorca's long preoccupation with the juxtaposition of death and desire than to a foreshadowing of his death. If the poems in *Diván del Tamarit* are poems of a tormented love, they are also Lorca's play upon absence and presence, just as his forms play upon the Arabic forms. If desire can be heard in the first words of "Gacela of the Terrible Presence," *Yo quiero* ("I want"), it could also be said that the speaker's desire is equally to *not* desire. The poem's "duel" grows in intensity, through the use of alliteration, parallelism, repetition—but also by means of denial, by saying what isn't wanted in order to increase the intensity of what is.

The three translations discussed here at length, by W. S. Merwin, Catherine Brown, and Michael Smith, span five decades. Reading them, we can hear the changing poetics of our own language. Merwin's translation is notable for its music, Brown's for its clarity, and Smith is most captivated by Lorca's tone. Each of these translations conveys the struggle of desire for a presence that, because it confines and directs the speaker's desire, becomes terrible. The speaker of "Gacela of the Terrible Presence" wants feeling to be left—like the water, like the wind—without that form or presence that contains and directs it. Desire becomes terrible because of its insistence on presence. In the fifth stanza, the speaker sees (in Merwin's translation) "the duel of the wounded night . . . / with noon," a struggle integral to the poem, where, in the beginning, "I want" is followed by "without," and, at the conclusion, "do not" cries out to presence.

At the beginning of the translations, the differences in the translators' strategies already start to exert themselves. What is interesting is how these notable translations all stray from what Lorca says, which is literally, "I want the water left without a channel. / I want the wind left without valleys." *Se quede* means "is left," "remains," "stays." Merwin is closest with "I want the water reft from its bed, / I want the wind left without valleys." But he uses "reft" and "bed," which emotionally poeticize the line. "Reft" adds an element of being violently torn from, and while *cauce* is "riverbed," the shortened form, "bed," almost personifies the landscape, as if the water were a person "reft from [his] bed." Due to the internal rhyme, Merwin does gain in the music of the line.

Brown completely inverts the emphasis here with "I want there to be no channel for the water. / I want there to be no valleys for the wind." She shifts to what isn't wanted (channel, valleys), even though doing so ignores Lorca's desire that the water and the wind remain. This inversion also results in a prosaic, almost explanatory poetic line.

Smith's translation reads, "I want the stream to lose its banks. / I want no slopes to cradle the wind." He, too, adds to the original: his "stream" is much smaller and more specific than Lorca's "water" (furthermore, a stream is channeled, has a direction of flow). Having the stream "lose its banks" makes the water almost active; there's almost a mini-narrative in the line, similar to the mini-narrative of Merwin's "reft from its bed." In his second line, Smith adopts a similar strategy to Brown's, emphasizing what isn't wanted, but he uses "cradle," adding an element both childlike and maternal.

Each of these translators adds to the poem at the beginning, striking certain notes that bring in associations, emotional nuances, shifts away from Lorca's original. Because those notes are struck in the opening lines, they are like a tuning key for the choices that follow. Lorca does not say "reft" or "cradle" or "lose." As the poem develops, each of the translators seeks something more than the original; the "teeth in the skull" (Brown) that literally "shine" in Lorca's poem "gleam," "glisten," and "glitter" in these translations. Brown, having begun with what isn't wanted ("I want there to be no"), must add "I want" to the third and fourth stanzas, to bring some clarity about what *is* wanted back into the poem. Smith's second stanza adds another element altogether with "I would have" and "my heart yield up its fine gold." In Lorca's line, he wants his heart without that gold flower; in Smith's line, that gold flower is now some "fine" treasure that the speaker would have his heart yield up. As in the first lines, Merwin stays closest to the original throughout.

Yet in the following stanzas, the original's complexity eludes all three translators. All three versions have "yellows" that "overflow" (Merwin), "wash over" (Bowman), or "flood" (Smith) the silk. But they all miss the fact that, as Eliot Weinberger has pointed out, "amarillo" refers not only to the color but also to a silkworm disease. We are given the surrealistic Lorca we might expect, but at the expense of both the vivid actuality—a disease that, killing the silkworm, turns its cocoon yellow—and the deeper meaning of the original that conveys the risk of delimited desire, the overwhelming of the creature and its creation.

The image at the center, the "duel of wounded night" that the speaker *can* see, is in some respects central to translating the poem. Admittedly, it is a challenge to the translator! *Luchando* means "struggling, wrestling, fighting," and each of the translations conveys the struggle of wounded night with noon, though Smith sees night's "grief" and has it caught in the "coils of noon," as if it were the prey of noon. Brown's "wrestling in coils with midday" is a decorative and puzzling image that risks redundancy, for how

to envision "wrestling in coils"? By adding "duel" and "battle," Merwin emphasizes the struggle, and does bring in "writhing." However, the challenge in Lorca's lines is *enroscada*, which can mean "coiled, twisted," but also "screwed on or in." None of the translations convey the startling interpenetration of night and noon in this image.

Because the visions that the speaker *can* see and resist are not entirely evoked in the translations, the speaker's anguish and yearning must fall upon Merwin's "clear nude," Smith's "lucent nakedness," and Brown's "immaculate nude." *Limpio* most often means "clean," but here again the language is poeticized—to "immaculate," "lucent," "clear"—even though none of these result in strong elemental images, for what is a "clear nude"? Or a "lucent nakedness"? Or an "immaculate nude"? "Your clean nakedness" would be closest to Lorca, but it's as if, having chosen a kind of poetic diction, each translator must retain his or her loyalty to that language. In the last line, Merwin has "cool waist," Smith has "young waist," and Brown has "the cool of your waist." *Fresca* means "cool," but it also conveys the same meanings that "fresh" conveys in English ("cheeky," "bold," "sassy," etc).

In the three translations' last two stanzas, we might almost be looking at a nude statue, a cool, clear, immaculate presence. What the translations do convey is the distance of the object of desire, but not how it draws too close, interpenetrates night and noon, and directs the speaker, who wants his feeling to flow as freely as water and wind. Oddly enough, it is the terrible presence driving this poem that finally eludes us. Lorca's original is simpler, more elemental than an English reader might guess from these translations, as if his poem, too, were naked, stripped of poetic ornamentation, as direct as that image of a "black cactus open in the reeds."

Xu Zhimo

(Chinese, 1897–1931)

TRANSLATIONS BY

Kai-yu Hsu, Michelle Yeh,
Hugh Grigg

....

COMMENTARY BY

Bonnie S. McDougall

再別康橋

輕輕的我走了，
　　正如我輕輕的來；
我輕輕的招手，
　　作別西天的雲彩。

那河畔的金柳，
　　是夕陽中的新娘；
波光裡的艷影，
　　在我的心頭蕩漾。

軟泥上的青荇，
　　油油地在水底招搖；
在康河的柔波裡，
　　我甘心做一條水草！

那榆蔭下的一潭，
　　不是清泉，是天上虹；
揉碎在浮藻間，
　　沉澱著彩虹似的夢。

尋夢？撐一支長篙，
　　向青草更青處漫溯；
滿載一船星輝，
　　在星輝斑斕裡放歌。

但我不能放歌，
　　悄悄是別離的笙簫；
夏蟲也為我沉默，
　　沉默是今晚的康橋！

悄悄的我走了，
　　正如我悄悄的來；
我揮一揮衣袖，
　　不帶走一片雲彩。

Xu Zhimo (1928)

[A transliteration appears at the end of the commentary, on p. 120.]

Second Farewell to Cambridge

Quietly I am leaving
Just as quietly I came;
Quietly I wave a farewell
To the western sky aflame.

The golden willow on the riverbank,
A bride in the setting sun;
Her colorful reflection
Ripples through my heart.

The green plants on the river bed,
So lush and so gracefully swaying
In the gentle current of the Cam
I'd be happy to remain a waterweed.

The pool under an elm's shade
Is not a creek, but a rainbow in the sky
Crushed among the floating green,
Settling into a colorful dream.

In search of a dream? You pole a tiny boat
Toward where the green is even more green
To collect a load of stars, as songs
Rise in the gleaming stellar light.

But tonight my voice fails me;
Silence is the best tune of farewell;
Even crickets are still for me,
And still is Cambridge tonight.

Silently I am going
As silently I came;
I shake my sleeves,
Not to bring away a patch of cloud.

translated by Kai-yu Hsu (1963)

Second Farewell to Cambridge

Softly I am leaving,
    As I softly came;
I wave my hand in gentle farewell
    To the clouds in the western sky.

The golden willow on the riverbank
    Is a bride in the sunset;
Her luminous reflection in the ripples
    Is swaying in my heart.

Plants in the soft mud
    Wave in the current;
I'd rather be a water reed
    In the gentle river of Cam.

The pool in the elm shade
    Is not clear but iridescent;
Wrinkled by the swaying algae,
    It settles into a rainbowlike dream.

In search of a dream? With a long pole,
    Sail toward where the grass grows greener;
In a skiff loaded with starlight,
    Sing among the shining stars.

But I cannot sing tonight;
    Silence is the tune of farewell.
Summer insects are quiet for me, too;
    Silent is Cambridge tonight.

Quietly I am leaving,
    As I quietly came;
I raise my sleeve and wave,
    Without taking away a whiff of cloud.

November 6, 1928

translated by Michelle Yeh (1992)

Saying Goodbye to Cambridge Again

Lightly I leave,
as lightly I came;
I lightly wave goodbye,
to the sunlit clouds in the western sky.

The golden willows of that riverside,
are brides in the setting sun;
their glimmering reflections in the water,
ripple in the depth of my heart.

The waterlilies in the soft mud,
sway splendidly under the water.
In the gentle waves of the Cam,
I would be a water plant!

That pool in the shade of elm trees,
is not springwater, but a heavenly rainbow;
crumbling amongst the floating grasses,
the settling rainbow seems like a dream.

Looking for dreams? Push a punt,
to where the grass is greener still upstream;
a boat laden with starlight,
singing freely in the glorious light of stars.

But I cannot sing freely,
silence is the music of my departure,
even the summer insects are quiet for me,
tonight's Cambridge is silent!

Quietly I leave,
as quietly I came;
I cast my sleeves a little,
not taking even a strand of cloud away.

translated by Hugh Grigg (2012)

Commentary by Bonnie S. McDougall

"Second Farewell to Cambridge" is perhaps the best-known poem in contemporary China, both on the Mainland and in Taiwan. Its remarkable fame is in part due to its inclusion in school textbooks, so that most native Chinese speakers are familiar with it even in childhood. Its author, Xu Zhimo, was for a long time held in disregard by Mainland authorities because of his opposition to the left-wing literary movements of the 1920s, while for the same reason he was highly regarded in Taiwan. The relaxation of the 1980s that followed the end of the Cultural Revolution allowed the inclusion of Xu Zhimo in the Mainland canon, where the author's romantic life and his inspired poems on love and beauty captured the imagination of a vast new readership.

The Poem and the Poet

One reason for the poem's popularity over almost a hundred years lies in its poignancy: writing on board a ship in the China Sea as he was nearing his homeland, Xu Zhimo laments the foreign land he has left behind while at the same time acknowledging the impossibility of bringing any relic of it home.

Xu Zhimo is famous for his love of English romantic poetry and English culture associated with places like Cambridge University, which he attended briefly in 1922 and twice revisited before his untimely death. Many educated Chinese in the 1920s and 1930s would have had profound sympathy for the poet's reluctant choice, and the same sentiment would also have affected the thousands of Chinese students and other visitors to Cambridge in the present century. In 2008 the university set up a stone inscribed with Xu Zhimo's poem alongside the Cam; it has since become a kind of shrine for Chinese tourists.

The Translators and Their Readers

The lasting appeal of this poem to Chinese readers is matched by the many translations that have appeared in print and on the Internet. For this exercise, I have chosen translations by two native speakers of Chinese resident in the United States, along with one by a native speaker of English. These translators have an excellent knowledge and understanding of both Chinese and English, and, with a few exceptions, their translations either contain no inaccuracies or work imaginatively within the larger meaning of the poem. Michelle Yeh is the most academic of these three; Kai-yu Hsu, himself a poet, addresses a wider audience; and both include the poem in their general anthologies of twentieth-century Chinese poetry, each of which contains a long general introduction plus introductory notes for each author. Hugh Grigg, a student at Cambridge in 2012 when he wrote his translation and published it in a student online magazine, addresses readers who understand Chinese and readily appreciate the poet's dilemma in leaving Cambridge.

The Translations

One of the poem's attractions to translators lies in its resemblance to an English poem: its division into four-line stanzas, the indentation of the second and fourth lines of each stanza, and the rhyme scheme (ABCB) are all common features of the kind of English poetry that the poet admired, and its translators typically copy at least one of these formal qualities. Others among the poem's many translators attempt rhyme; some are less concerned with adhering to the verse form; some provide illustrations. Still, given the huge differences between Chinese and English, the poem presents many translation issues.

A typographical device in English that is not available in Chinese is the use of an initial capital letter at the beginning of each line. From the early years of the twentieth century, poets writing in English have created a sense of radical modernity by omitting this initial capital. Only Grigg among these three translators takes advantage of this type of non-capitalization to signal Xu Zhimo's self-conscious modernity, a modernity that is conveyed to his original Chinese readers in his use of an English verse form.

Another major difference between written Chinese and English is that parallelism and repetition are more common in Chinese. In prose, it is normally desirable to reduce repetition in English by devices such as the use of pronouns and descriptive clauses; in poetry, the choice is not always obvious. In "Second Farewell to Cambridge," the poet sets up a nicely balanced mix of repetitions, links, and echoes that enhance the nostalgic mood of the poem without ever pressing too heavily. The translations here also present the reader with a balance of these repetitions, links, and echoes, although not necessarily in the same places or in the same mix.

A major example of repetitions and echoes in this poem is the adjective/adverb *qingqing de*, which occurs in the first, second, and third lines of the first stanza; Hsu has "quietly," Yeh has "softly/gentle," and Grigg has "lightly." Slightly more complicated is the use of *qiaoqiao de* in the first and second lines of the final stanza, translated by Hsu as "silently" and by Yeh and Grigg as "quietly," while *qiaoqiao* (followed by the copula *shi*) in the penultimate stanza appears in all three translations as "silence."

Two grammatical issues where translators of Chinese into English face tricky problems are the use of definite and indefinite articles, and the distinction between singular and plural forms of nouns; both are often ignored in Chinese, and the translator sometimes has few guidelines in syntax or context. In the case of the word *yuncai* ("cloud/clouds"), the choice is clear: in the first stanza it should be plural and definite (there is rarely a single cloud in the sky at sunset), while in the last stanza it is specifically singular and indefinite. Yeh and Grigg make the same choice, while Hsu avoids the issue (see below).

Another feature of written Chinese is its flexibility in using (and sometimes inventing) binomial words in which each syllable is a word in its own right; these compounds are not necessarily translatable into a single word in English. The word *yuncai* again is a good example. As one word, it simply means "clouds"; as two words it is more like "cloud color/splendor/brilliance." Hsu has "aflame" ("clouds" being understood) in the first stanza and "cloud" in the last, losing the repetition that links the beginning and the end of the poem. Grigg's "the sunlit clouds" and "cloud" ignore the time of day (sunset) mentioned in the second stanza, while Yeh's "the clouds" and "cloud" are appropriately restrained (clouds at sunset are normally highly colored, especially when the poem's theme includes a farewell).

An example that shows the value of research occurs in the first line of the second stanza. Hsu and Yeh both have "The golden willow," but Grigg has "The golden willows," as do some other translators familiar with the stretch of willows along the Cam. However, it has been claimed that this line refers to a single willow near King's College (where the memorial stone now stands); also, a single willow implies a single bride in the next line, where "brides" (Grigg) might seem less romantic.

Only one of the three versions of the final couplet in the second stanza is fully satisfactory:

> *Hsu:*
> Her colorful reflection
> Ripples through my heart.

> *Yeh:*
> Her luminous reflection in the ripples
>   Is swaying in my heart.

> *Grigg:*
> their glimmering reflections in the water,
> ripple in the depth of my heart.

In these couplets, Hsu's restraint is unnecessary and his "colorful" is bland, while Grigg's "in the water" and "in the depths of my heart" are wordy and unimaginative. In contrast, Yeh deftly introduces the light playing on the waves implied in the compound *boguang* ("wave light") by choosing "swaying" (*dangyang*: "undulate, ripple") for the reflection.

In the third stanza the divergence is even more striking:

> *Hsu:*
> The green plants on the river bed,
> So lush and so gracefully swaying

Yeh:
Plants in the soft mud
    Wave in the current;

Grigg:
The waterlilies in the soft mud,
sway splendidly under the water.

In this example, each translator chooses a plural subject, but they differ in regard to case: Yeh's omission of a definite article before "plants" is hardly noticeable, and there is even some advantage in the line's simplicity; on the other hand, a preverbal noun in Chinese is normally definite, so that Hsu's and Grigg's translations give a better sense of the original.

The meaning of the word *xing* is not entirely clear (it does not appear in standard Chinese–English dictionaries). It is given as an equivalent for *xingcai* in Chinese–Chinese dictionaries, which is in turn translated as "banana plant" or *Nymphoides peltata*. The suggestion that any kind of banana grows in southern England seems absurd, and the Latin is hardly more appropriate. In this context, Hsu's and Yeh's choice of "plants" is understandably reductive, while Grigg's "waterlilies" is over-decorative. Yeh and Grigg reasonably consider "green" (*qing*) as a gratuitous modifier for plants; Hsu's "river bed" for "soft mud" is unnecessarily genteel. An example of a binomial compound in this couplet is *zhaoyao*. As two separate words, it can mean "to wave" (as in waving one's hand) and "to shake, rock, wag"; as a compound, it has a special usage, meaning "to act ostentatiously." Yeh follows the poet in repeating "wave" from the first stanza, while Hsu and Grigg both choose "sway" (which here seems very appropriate), focusing on the second word in the compound: here, each solution is accurate and attractive. The translations of the adjective/adverb *youyou de* ("glossy, shiny"; "smoothly, luxuriantly") in the second line, however, are all disappointing: it is over-translated by Hsu ("so lush and so gracefully"), omitted entirely by Yeh, and replaced by the meaningless and inaccurate "splendidly" by Grigg.

The fifth stanza signals a change in theme, introduced by the word "dream" (repeated from the end of the fourth stanza): the poet plays with the idea that dreams can come true and that his voice can rise in song, only to realize that in reality he is no longer able to sing.

Hsu:
In search of a dream? You pole a tiny boat
Toward where the green is even more green.
To collect a load of stars, as songs
Rise in the gleaming stellar light.

Yeh:
In search of a dream? With a long pole,
    Sail toward where the grass grows greener;
In a skiff loaded with starlight,
    Sing among the shining stars.

Grigg:
Looking for dreams? Push a punt,
to where the grass is greener still upstream;
a boat laden with starlight,
singing freely in the glorious light of stars.

There are several infelicities here. Hsu's "even more green" is awkward. The omission of a subject for the person who is poling the boat in Yeh's and Grigg's versions makes the sentence sound like a command, whereas in Chinese it is normal to omit a pronoun subject in a straightforward statement. The boat is just a boat in Chinese, not Hsu's "tiny" boat (the added word may be inserted for rhythm), and in English (and especially in Cambridge) it is more accurately a "punt" (Grigg), not a "skiff" (Yeh).

In the following couplet from the sixth stanza, Grigg's "tonight's Cambridge" stays close to the Chinese grammar, but Hsu's and Yeh's "Cambridge tonight" reads more like English. "Summer insects," the literal translation, preferred by Yeh and Grigg, is better than Hsu's "crickets," which gather around a fire in winter.

Hsu:
Even crickets are still for me,
And still is Cambridge tonight.

Yeh:
Summer insects are quiet for me, too;
   Silent is Cambridge tonight.

Grigg:
even the summer insects are quiet for me,
tonight's Cambridge is silent!

The final couplet in the last stanza contains the poem's unstated message:

Hsu:
I shake my sleeves,
Not to bring away a patch of cloud.

Yeh:
I raise my sleeve and wave,
   Without taking away a whiff of cloud.

Grigg:
I cast my sleeves a little,
not taking even a strand of cloud away.

The main challenges here for the translator are partly grammatical, partly cultural. In Chinese a measure word is normally inserted between a number and the noun it modifies, but measure words are much less common in English, and there is no reason not to translate the expression as "a cloud" or "a single cloud." (It's also possible that Yeh has mistaken "whiff" for "wisp.") The translators have presented three very different interpretations of the motion of the poet's sleeve, *hui yi hui* ("to give a little shake"). It is not clear what Grigg means by "cast," which seems to suggest a throwing action, and Yeh seems to take "sleeve" as metonymy for "arm," and repeats "wave," as in a farewell. Hsu's "shake," on the other hand, echoes the earlier reference to singing by borrowing a gesture from Peking Opera, where with a graceful shake of his long sleeve the performer brings the cuff back across his wrist, allowing him to pause while he recovers his poise, comes to a decision, or conveys strong emotion.

Neither Yeh nor Grigg catches the significance of the final line, ignoring the purposeful construction *bu daizou* ("not to take away"), which indicates the poet's resolution to leave the place he loves so deeply without taking any of its beauty with him. This seems to me the only reading of the poem that makes sense in the context of Xu Zhimo's life and poetry.

According to this reading, the main theme of the poem is that Xu Zhimo is heartbroken at the idea of leaving Cambridge, a city whose natural and architectural beauty, modern and ancient culture, and intellectual richness have captivated him, and where he has found friendship as well as romantic love. Nevertheless, throughout his stay he has remained a foreigner in a country where he has no voice. At the same time, he is conscious of his pressing duty as a Chinese intellectual to return to his homeland, which is suffering under the depredations of native warlords and colonial oppression, and to his family. Apart from the physical impossibility of bringing even the merest trace of Cambridge's beauty with him, he is also aware that its immaterial attractions (signified by the clouds above the Cam) are irrelevant in light of the crises that imperil modern China. Patriotism and personal inclinations pull in opposite directions, but loyalty in the end has a stronger claim. It is a dilemma that many twentieth-century Chinese writers experienced, and Kai-yu Hsu must be numbered among them. While the Chinese tourists who flock to Cambridge are not faced with the same agonizing choice, they are also conscious of the clashes between tradition and modernity—between China and the West—that brought about the conflicted identities of writers like Xu Zhimo in the 1920s and Kai-yu Hsu four decades later. Many readers of the poem's translations will appreciate its charm, and many will also find it relates to their own divided loyalties.

Transliteration:

Zai Bie Kangqiao

Qingqing de wo zou le,
Zhengru wo qingqing de lai;
Wo qingqing de zhaoshou,
Zuobie xitian de yuncai.

Na he pan de jin liu,
Shi xiyang zhong de xinniang;
Boguang li de yanying,
Zai wo de xintou dangyang.

Ruan ni shang de qing xing,
Youyou de zai shuidi zhaoyao;
Zai Kang He de rou bo li,
Wo ganxin zuo yi tiao shuicao!

Na yu yin xia de yi tan,
Bu shi qingquan, shi tianshang hong;
Rousui zai fu zao jian,
Chendianzhe cai hong shide meng.

Xun meng? Cheng yi zhi chang gao,
Xiang qingcao geng qing chu man su;
Manzai yi chuan xinghui,
Zai xinghui banlan li fangge.

Dan wo bu neng fangge,
Qiaoqiao shi bieli de shengxiao;
Xia chong ye wei wo chenmo,
Chenmo shi jinwan de Kangqiao!

Qiaoqiao de wo zou le,
Zhengru wo qiaoqiao de lai;
Wo hui yi hui yixiu,
Bu daizou yi pian yuncai.

Carlos Drummond de Andrade

(Portuguese, 1902–1987)

TRANSLATIONS BY
Virginia de Araújo, John Nist,
Kay Cosgrove

··································

COMMENTARY BY
Ellen Doré Watson

Segredo

A poesia é incomunicável.
Fique torto no seu canto.
Não ame.

Ouço dizer que há tiroteio
ao alcance do nosso corpo.
É a revolução? o amor?
Não diga nada.

Tudo é possível, só eu impossível.
O mar transborda de peixes.
Há homens que andam no mar
como se andassem na rua.
Não conte.

Suponha que um anjo de fogo
varresse a face da terra
e os homens sacrificados
pedissem perdão,
Não peça.

Carlos Drummond de Andrade (1934)

Secret

Poetry is incommunicable.
Stay crammed in your corner.
Don't love.

I hear say there's shooting
and we're in range.
Is it the revolution? Love?
Don't speak.

All is possible, only I impossible.
The seas overflow fish.
There are men who walk on the sea
just like on streets.
Don't tell.

Suppose a burning angel
swept the earth's face
and martyred men
begged pardon.
Don't beg.

translated by Virginia de Araújo (1980)

Secret

You cannot communicate poetry.
Keep still in your corner.
Do not love.

I hear that there is shooting
within reach of our body.
Is it a revolution? is it love?
Say nothing.

Everything is possible, only I am impossible.
The sea overflows with fish.
There are men who walk on the sea
as though they walked in the street.
Do not tell.

Suppose that an angel of fire
swept the face of the earth
and the sacrificed men
asked for mercy.
Beg nothing.

translated by John Nist (1965)

Secret

Poetry is unreachable.
Remain twisted in your corner.
Don't love.

I hear that there is gunfire
within reach of our body.
Is it the revolution? Love?
Don't say a thing.

Everything is possible, only I'm impossible.
The sea spills over with fish.
There are men that walk on the sea
as if they walked on the street.
Don't tell.

Suppose that an angel of fire
swept the face of the earth
and the men sacrificed
begged forgiveness.
Don't beg.

translated by Kay Cosgrove (2014)

Commentary by Ellen Doré Watson
Drummond Incommunicado

What if it's not that "poetry is what gets lost in translation," as our cranky friend Robert Frost famously pronounced, but that poetry itself is innately insular, unable to travel—not simply from one language to another but from one person to another? Should Carlos Drummond de Andrade's mysterious and bossy little poem "Segredo," which makes such a pronouncement in its first line, be heard as serious jest or a cry of desperation? If, as I believe, good poems, even difficult ones, teach us how to read them, then we must count on their translators to recognize and to bring over their embedded signals.

The structural consistencies of this poem include successive imperatives, sonic echoes, word repetition, including the prominent quadruplet of *nao*'s ("no," leading to "don't" in translation) that shape the short, final line of each stanza, the preponderance of end-stopped lines (twelve of seventeen), and the diminishing shape of each stanza. These notes of stability are continually undermined by disruptions of pattern, changes in diction, and the movement from implicit speaker, to inclusion in a "we," to an explicit "I," and back to a veiled speaker. Some of the deviations undermine themselves by establishing new patterns: the irregular number of lines per stanza settling by the end (three, four, five, five); the steady increase in non-end-stopped lines, giving a sense of growing fluidity; and the alternation between an authoritative and a questioning stance that occurs from stanza to stanza. What this adds up to is a poem brilliantly at war with itself, an utterance trying to unsay itself, and then to say itself again.

The poem begins with the blanket statement, as Virginia de Araújo puts it: "Poetry is incommunicable." This claim immediately presents a conundrum, of course: if true, it will get through to no one, since it is delivered in a poem. Kay Cosgrove's version seems a bit off the mark here, since "unreachable" characterizes poetry as equally ungraspable by reader *and* writer, whereas the original allows that the poet might have something to transmit; it simply cannot be transmitted via poetry. John Nist goes even further off the track. Introducing an addressee strikes a more personal tone and sig-

nificantly narrows the meaning, whereas with *incomunicável*, Drummond places the emphasis on poetry's innate incommunicability. (I'd be tempted toward "incommunicado," except that it implies a potentially temporary state, making for a less definitive pronouncement.)

In the absence of an explicit addressee, the reader might well wonder whether the speaker is being ironic or talking to himself, or perhaps both. In any event, *torto*, in the first stanza, presents a translator's nightmare: a word with myriad meanings and connotations that no single English word can bring along. *Torto* means "crooked" ("twisted," "bent," "lame," "awry," "impaired," "dishonest," "torturous") and also: "wrong," "sad," "impotent," "lopsided," "kinky," "warped," "sidelong" (and, as a noun, "clubfoot").

Instead of wrestling with all these layers, Araújo's "crammed" takes a limiting, literal tack, emphasizing the smallness of the corner, while Nist errs in the opposite direction, with "Keep still in your corner." They both sacrifice complexity for clarity, but Nist violates tone as well: rather than a perplexing and insulting command, we get the tepid instruction of a schoolmarm. Cosgrove's version comes closest to the original. While I might have gone with the stronger and more idiomatic "stay" instead of "remain" for the verb, her adjective "twisted" contains both physical and psychological connotations.

Torto is not a commonly used word, but it makes a notable appearance in the opening of Drummond's "Poema de sete faces," the first poem in his first collection, *Alguma Poesia* (Some Poems):

Quando nasci, um anjo torto	When I was born, a twisted angel,
dêsses que vivem na sombra	one of those who live in the shadow,
disse: Vai, Carlos! Ser gauche *na vida.*	said: Go, Carlos, be *gauche* in life.
	translated by John Nist

These lines are among Drummond's most well-known, and would certainly reverberate for many reading "Segredo," which came four years later, in *Brejo das almas* (Swamp of Souls). Given the proximity and positioning of the words *torto* and *gauche*, and the overlap in their meanings, it's almost as if the angel were saying: "Go ahead, be like me, be an oddball, be awkward, sad, wrong, lame." In "Segredo," instead of an angel instructing (or giving permission to) the poet to be who he is, who he was born to be, we have a human speaker commanding we're not sure whom (but someone similarly *gauche*) to hunker down into a kind of desperate nonbeing. This one moment crystallizes the shift from the ironic and active isolation of Drummond's first book to the nihilistic and turbulent stasis of the second. I'm at a loss to understand how Nist and Araújo, both of whom know the oeuvre well, could forgo an echo that captures such a profound change in attitude.

The closing line of stanza 1—like those of the subsequent stanzas—is a curt, negative command. There's neither leeway nor mystery in translating it, only the matter of whether or not to use a contraction (the definitive but colloquial "Don't" versus the more formal and authoritative "Do not"). The dependable symmetry of the word *não* ("no") appearing at the left margin to close each stanza stands in stark in contrast to the poem's irregular line lengths and varying numbers of lines, and the tension between these throws into relief the poem's architecture: a classic if ragged example of pattern and variation. All three translators respect and replicate the poem's overall structure, and Araújo and Cosgrove repeat "Don't" at the beginning of the last line of each stanza, but all three miss opportunities to mirror the original's more subtle use of repetition, and thus a chance to underline the tension between continuity and discontinuity.

Stanza 2 begins by leaving abstractions behind and turning to "shooting." Its most pronounced features include the subtle glue of sonic echoes, a disruption of pattern, and an odd and ungrammatical usage. Beginning with *Ouço*, the first two lines contain six final "o" vowel sounds (in Portuguese pronounced like our long "u"), which echo *torto* and *canto* from stanza 1, and appear again later in *tudo, como, anjo, fogo*. This kind of music is much harder to accomplish in English without creating a singsong quality, so I understand the need to be subtle, but I think the translators could have done more with sound. Nist and Cosgrove give us only "hear" and "reach"; Araújo does

better with "say" and "range," echoing "stay" from above. Even more problematic is the fact that none of the translators makes use of the repetition in the first and last lines of the verb *dizer* (albeit in different forms), the primary definition of which is "to say." "I hear say" ("hearsay"!) in Araújo's first line is fine, but in the last line of this stanza she shifts to the synonym "speak." Interestingly, in the original the last line of stanza 2 contains three words instead of two, like the other final lines. Repeating "say," a transitive verb, would have demanded an object, and thus reproduced Drummond's three-word variation: "Don't say anything." Another variation in stanza 2 is the move from the colloquial voice of the first line to the oddness of the second. I applaud Nist and Cosgrove for honoring this shift by maintaining the unidiomatic "within reach of our body." Araújo ignores it, giving us the idiomatic and less intimately threatening rephrasing "we're in range" (with no "body" at all!).

Translation is surely not only "the art of choice" (Gregory Rabassa) but that of supremely fine distinctions. What's the difference between "all" and "everything"? To my mind, at least in the first line of stanza 3, Araújo's "All is possible" is weaker and more formal than Nist's and Cosgrove's breathy, coming-from-the-chest "everything," spelling out syllable by syllable its all-inclusiveness. To make matters worse, Araújo follows this with the stiff, verbless "only I impossible." Nist and Cosgrove do better, using "everything" and inserting the implied verb, "am" (no doubt to smooth out the English)—and they do so as subtly as possible. The drawback of Cosgrove is that her use of the contraction places the line's heaviest stress on "I'm." In my view, a better choice is Nist's "I am," in which the verb, implicit in the original, still remains almost invisible by virtue of being unstressed, and what stands out is the "I"—the single appearance of the first-person singular pronoun in the original. The lines that follow present little controversy, though I do wonder why Araújo pluralizes "street" and gives us an intransitive verb with a direct, instead of an indirect, object ("overflow fish"). And everybody's third and fourth lines could be less wordy and/or more colloquial: "There are men who walk on the sea / as if walking down the street," for instance. It's worth noting that in the last line of stanza 3 all three translators use "tell," the verb most often paired with the noun of the poem's title.

Drummond begins his last stanza with *suponha* ("suppose"), appearing to step back from the definitive mode with which he began the poem, instead imagining, at least for a moment, a kind of divine intervention. My first impulse in translating a phrase like *um anjo de fogo* would generally be to ditch the prepositional phrase, using instead a one-word adjective, in which case I'd opt for the stronger, literal "fiery," rather than Araújo's "burning angel." Here, though, I think it best to retain the preposition "of," as Cosgrove and Nist do, to take advantage of the Biblical connotation the context demands—in terms of diction and also because fire is not the condition of the angel but his power, the cleansing tool with which he sweeps the earth. Similarly, I think "swept the face of the earth" begs to be maintained (as Nist and Cosgrove do) to convey a grand gesture, rather than Araújo's more matter-of-fact (and up-close-and-personal) "swept the earth's face."

Leaving aside the oddness of Drummond's supposition, with the already-sacrificed men having the temerity to belatedly request forgiveness, it's important to note that the verb for the hypothetical request is *pedir*, most commonly defined as "to ask," and that this verb is repeated in the last line. Nist ignores this, using first "asked" and then "beg," though clearly he's attuned to the symmetry of the poem's structure. In fact, Nist seems to be trying to go Drummond one better, creating a more complicated pattern and variation: his last lines chime, but in pairs ("Do not," "Say nothing," "Do not," "Beg nothing"). If the original structure could not easily and effectively come into English, or if his translation were presented as adaptation or "version," I might have found this alternating pattern clever, but neither is the case. So why sacrifice the four resounding negatives at the left margin? Nist's last line emphasizes the "nothing" rather than the *not doing* that is commanded at the end of each stanza and of the poem entire.

While Cosgrove and Araújo reproduce the verb repetition at the poem's close, they, like Nist, use "beg." I understand the initial appeal of a more concrete, even visual verb, and one that seems to nod both to the quotidian phrase "I beg your pardon" and to the poem's religious content,

but Drummond could have chosen more-specific verbs, such as *suplicar* or *implorar* ("to beg" or "to entreat"); instead he uses the more general, less fraught *pedir*, perhaps so the verb can more easily travel from the Biblical territory of the penultimate line to the cooler, Drummondian world of the last line. "Ask" also echoes the simplicity of the earlier "Do Not"s: "love," "say," and "tell."

Comparing these translations to Drummond's "Segredo" is a humbling reminder to me of how difficult our task as translators is and how easy it is to lose sight of the fact that a poem's every word and element must be taken into account, not only individually but as part of a set of echoes and divergences, gestures and signals that combine to create the full complexity before us on the page.

If "Segredo" seems unyielding and self-contradictory on first look, those adjectives seem no less accurate to me after deep reading; but I find myself fully engaged by the complex thoroughness and power with which Drummond brings us inside the conflict at its heart—which is succinctly contained in the frame or mini-poem of the title and last line alone. What is the "secret"? "Don't ask."

Despite all the *nao*'s, or "don't"s, I don't see this poem as a call for general paralysis, much less, as some critics have it, as a thoroughly theoretical, metalinguistic piece. Shapely and jagged, abstract and concrete, bossy and questioning, it sounds to me like a cry of desperation. Whether the prohibitions are directed at us or at himself, the speaker can neither express himself with impunity nor remain silent. Maybe the poem is tantamount to a message in a bottle, written—with little hope but great panache by someone *incommunicado*—and cast onto the waves. No matter how pessimistic he is that the message will truly reach anyone, there it is, bobbing, witness to a predicament that might just turn out to be temporary.

Sophia de Mello Breyner Andresen

(Portuguese, 1919–2004)

TRANSLATIONS BY

Ruth Fainlight, Richard Zenith,
Lisa Sapinkopf

....

COMMENTARY BY

Alexis Levitin

A pequena praça

A minha vida tinha tomado a forma da pequena praça
Naquele outono em que a tua morte se organizava meticulosamente
Eu agarrava-me à praça porque tu amavas
A humanidade humilde e nostálgica das pequenas lojas
Onde os caixeiros dobram e desdobram fitas e fazendas
Eu procurava tornar-me tu porque tu ias morrer
E a vida toda deixava ali de ser a minha
Eu procurava sorrir como tu sorrias
Ao vendedor de jornais ao vendedor de tabaco
E à mulher sem pernas que vendia violetas
Eu pedia à mulher sem pernas que rezasse por ti
Eu acendia velas em todos os altares
Das igrejas que ficam no canto desta praça
Pois mal abri os olhos e vi foi para ler
A vocação do eterno escrita no teu rosto
Eu convocava as ruas os lugares as gentes
Que foram as testemunhas de teu rosto
Para que eles te chamassem para que eles desfizessem
O tecido que a morte entrelaçava em ti

Sophia de Mello Breyner Andresen (1972)

The Small Square

My life had taken the form of a small square
The autumn when your death was being meticulously organized
I clung to the square because you loved
The humble and nostalgic humanity of small shops
Where shopkeepers fold and unfold ribbons and cloth
I tried to become you because you were going to die
And all my life there would cease to be mine
I tried to smile as you smiled
At the newspaper seller at the tobacco seller
At the woman without legs who sold violets
I asked the woman without legs to pray for you
I lit candles at all the altars
Of the churches standing in the corner of that square
Hardly had I opened my eyes when I saw and read
The vocation for eternity written on your face
I summoned up the streets places people
Who were the witnesses of your face
So they would call you so they would unweave
The tissue that death was binding around you

translated by Ruth Fainlight (1988)

The Small Square

My life had taken the shape of the small square
That autumn when your death was meticulously getting ready
I clung to the square because you loved
The humble and nostalgic humanity of its small shops
Where clerks fold and unfold ribbons and cloth
I tried to become you for you were going to die
And all life there would cease being mine
I tried to smile the way you smiled
At the newsagent at the tobacconist
And at the woman without legs who sold violets
I asked the woman without legs to pray for you
I lit candles before all the altars
Of the churches located on one side of this square
For as soon as I opened my eyes I saw I read
The vocation of eternity written on your face
I summoned the streets the places the people
That had been witnesses of your face
In hopes they would call you in hopes they would unravel
The fabric that death was weaving in you

translated by Richard Zenith (1997)

The Little Square

My life took on the shape of the little square
That autumn when your death meticulously organized itself
I clung to the square because you loved
The humble, nostalgic humanity of the shops
Where clerks would wind and unfurl ribbon and fabric
I tried to make myself you because you would die soon
And all my life ceased being mine there
I tried to smile your smile
At the newspaper vendor the tobacco vendor
And the legless woman who sold violets
I asked the legless woman to pray for you
I lit candles at the altars
Of the churches on the corners of this square
Then with eyes hardly open I discovered I could read
The calling of the eternal written on your face
I summoned the streets places people
That had been the witnesses of your face
So they might call you back might unweave
The cloth death wove in you

translated by Lisa Sapinkopf (1993)

Commentary by Alexis Levitin

Sophia de Mello Breyner Andresen's "The Small Square" is a touching, perhaps even painful, poem about a woman facing the inevitable death of her mother, wishing it could be forestalled, knowing it cannot. It is also a poem about how the daughter understands that the biological imperative will force her to take her mother's place in the world, despite her reluctance to do so.

I translated and published this poem myself in Macmillan's 1983 *Women Poets of the World*. I have included my version at the end of this essay, and will at times refer to my own choices as I examine the practice of the three translators whose work came later.

First of all, there is the title. Both Ruth Fainlight and Richard Zenith choose "small" for their adjective, as do I, while Lisa Sapinkopf opts for "little," though in a recent conversation she agreed that "small" would have been better. My guess is that we all feel "little" rather too self-consciously endearing with its tripping combination of the plosive "t" dwindling toward its unstressed liquid conclusion. This square, after all, represents our "small" world under the aegis of death. A serious matter.

The first two lines of the poem present an interesting problem with the verb *se organizava*. Is the mother's death organizing itself or being organized? Fainlight chooses "when your death was being meticulously organized," implying a larger force behind death, while Zenith sees death as the actor: "when your death was meticulously getting ready." Sapinkopf has elements of each: "when your death meticulously organized itself." I like her vision; in fact, I use the same language myself, but I now suspect that we would have done better using the progressive tense, as do Zenith and Fainlight, since the death of the poet's mother was not sudden, but was building slowly and surely.

The next sentence hinges on the important verb *agarrar*. The poet is hanging on to the square, which her mother loved, because what she really wants is to hold on to her mother. All three translators agree on "I clung to the square" (while I opt for the more desperate "I grasped hold of"). The poignancy of the vain attempt is clear in either version.

The next challenge is in line 5, "Where shopkeepers fold and unfold ribbons and cloth," as Fainlight has it. Zenith and Sapinkopf choose the more modern "clerks," leading them to a rather bolder rhythm. I see "shopkeepers" as more nostalgic, more redolent of the comfort of the past, both in nuance and in sound, but I think either solution will serve. As for the repetitive activity described, I think it essential that the translator repeat the verbal form, as does the original *dobram e desdobram*. Fainlight and Zenith both settle on "fold and unfold," while Sapinkopf chooses two separate verbs: "wind and unfurl." "Unfurl" has a nice and somewhat mournfully ironic touch in a poem about death, but the loss of repetition so essential to the sense of ongoing life is unfortunate.

For me, the next line is all about rhythm:

> I tried to become you because you were going to die (Fainlight)
> I tried to become you for you were going to die (Zenith)
> I tried to make myself you because you would die soon (Sapinkopf)

To my ear, the Zenith solution, with its final three iambs, is the most melodious and the most poetically natural, even as it risks the somewhat inflated diction of "for," instead of the colloquial "because." I notice ruefully that I also chose the less rhythmically satisfying "because." The next line again raises the question of rhythm, and again the best solution to my ear seems to be Zenith's: "And all life there would cease being mine." Fainlight's choice, "all my life there," is not only rhythmically less satisfying but misleading, for the original suggests that all life there in the square, along with the mother, was in the process of abandoning the poet.

Now supporting actors enter the scene. The common folk for whom the poet's mother had a ready smile are, in Fainlight's version, a "newspaper seller," a "tobacco seller," and a "woman without legs." For Zenith, they are a "newsagent," a "tobacconist," and a "woman without legs"; for Sapinkopf, a "newspaper vendor," a "tobacco vendor," and a "legless woman." Lexically, all three are correct. But which is idiomatically satisfying? Which description sounds like real English? I am not fully satisfied by any of the three. To my ear, both "newspaper seller" and "newspaper vendor" sound labored, and "newsagent" seems British, leaving my American instincts a bit uneasy. I myself used "newspaperman," but that term now sounds quite vague to me. I wonder if "newsdealer" might not have been the best solution. Or perhaps the more slangy "paper guy." As for the woman selling violets, the brutality of her suffering is nicely accentuated by the cold directness of "woman without legs."

Now a geographic problem arises. In the Praça dos Leões in central Porto, two churches happen to share a single corner of the rather rambling square. If one has not been there, it is hard to imagine what the poet intended. Fainlight seems to get it right: "I lit candles at all the altars / Of the churches standing in the corner of that square." Zenith also understands the geography, but his language slips toward prose as it strives for touristic clarity: "I lit candles before all the altars / Of the churches located on one side of this square." Sapinkopf's version sounds fine, but she had not visited Porto at the time and so she logically but incorrectly assumed that the churches were on different corners. Hence some encouraging advice to translators: don't visit just the language you love; visit the country from which it comes.

At last we come to the philosophically most challenging lines in the poem, *Pois mal abri os olhos e vi foi para ler / A vocação do eterno escrita no teu rosto*:

> Hardly had I opened my eyes when I saw and read
> The vocation for eternity written on your face (Fainlight)

> For as soon as I opened my eyes I saw I read
> the vocation of eternity written on your face (Zenith)

> Then with eyes hardly open I discovered I could read
> the calling of the eternal written on your face (Sapinkopf)

The original first line is beautifully compact and none of the English versions are able to convey that succinctness. The logic of English grammar requires some explanatory elaboration. As for the second line, I find Fainlight's "the vocation for eternity" interesting in a disturbing way, as it resonates with the presence of our own great Emily Dickinson. However, I feel that "the vocation of eternity" (my own choice as well as Zenith's) is a legitimate and equally disturbing interpretation. Through the two prepositions, we are reminded that despite the illusion that our only calling is life, in fact, as is the case with the poet's mother, in the end our true vocation beyond this life is painfully revealed. (And let me mention, parenthetically, that one of the greatest challenges for the translator lies in those pesky, elusive, mercurial little words that inhabit all idiomatic expressions and try to place us all in time and space. Prepositions are the tiny stumbling blocks that we translators, again and again, beat our shins against.) As for Sapinkopf's version, I admire the synergistic strength of the double meaning that inhabits "the calling of the eternal written on your face." This translation suggests that eternity is not merely the destiny awaiting us, but an active agent calling us to come. This is probably the strongest moment in Sapinkopf's translation.

All three translators more or less agree on what comes next, the summoning up of streets, places, and people who were the "witnesses of your face." But the concluding two lines present a last important challenge. The original explains that the speaker is summoning those witnesses *Para que eles te chamassem para que eles desfizessem / O tecido que a morte entrelaçava em ti*. For me the key words here are *desfizessem, tecido,* and *entrelaçava*. Here are the three translations, with the translations of those three words italicized by me:

> So they would call you so they would *unweave*
> The *tissue* that death *was binding* around you (Fainlight)

> In hopes they would call you in hopes they would *unravel*
> The *fabric* that death *was weaving* in you (Zenith)

> So they might call you back might *unweave*
> The *cloth* death *wove* in you (Sapinkopf)

"Unweave" reminds us of the three classical Fates, one of whom is the weaver. It is as if the speaker hopes that somehow the humble folk alive in the square can "unweave" the weavings of fate. Zenith has a very different solution, less melodious, but more ominous imagistically. In my own translation, I choose a verb drawn from Shakespeare's most headlong tragedy: "undo," that desperate reminder of irreversibility so central to Macbeth's fate forged by doing. For me, the translator's cultural resonances can be a source of valid inspiration not available to the original poet. Who, in the Anglophone world, can ever forget "what's done cannot be undone"? I ought to mention that *desfizessem* means simply "to unmake" or "undo."

As for *tecido*, Fainlight uses "tissue," which seems too gauzy to be much of a threat. In any case, she sees it as surrounding the victim: "the tissue that death was binding around you." Zenith chooses "fabric" and has death "weaving [it] in you." This is quite disturbing, as we see that the enemy has already penetrated the body, and is destroying it from within. Sapinkopf also places what has been woven within: "the cloth death wove in you." My own choice (see below) leans toward the Fainlight interpretation, perhaps because I imagine the fabric or tissue as rather like a spiderweb, finally cocooning the victim in death. In any case, I force upon the poem something none of my colleagues hazard, a final concluding rhyme that is not present in the original and is therefore a sign of translator's license or even self-indulgence:

> So that they could call out to you, so that they could undo
> The fabric that death was weaving around you.

I like my rhythm and rhyme, but I must admit that Zenith's and Sapinkopf's vision of an internal weaving is more disturbing and effective, especially in an era in which cancer so often truly does weave its fabric within us.

A last word of caution to the reader. Flaubert was wrong when he spoke of "*le mot juste*." The very nature of reality and language precludes such a thing. As all translators realize, we search for *le mot juste*, knowing we must settle for something that merely approaches it. Even at our luckiest, what we have is perhaps *un mot juste*, but never the Platonic *le*. Language can never be the true equivalent of the thing itself, *das Ding an sich*. As T. S. Eliot said, in another context: "For us, there is only the trying." But what a pleasure is that trying, and that constant falling short.

The Small Square

My life had taken the shape of the small square
That autumn in which your death meticulously organized itself
I grasped hold of the square because you loved
The humble and nostalgic humankind of its small shops
Where clerks roll up and unroll ribbons and cloth
I tried to become you because you were going to die
And all of life was leaving, ceasing to be mine
I tried to smile as you smiled
To the newspaperman, the tobacconist
And the woman without legs who sells violets
I asked the woman without legs to pray for you
I lit candles on all the altars
Of the churches on the corner of the square
For the moment I opened my eyes and saw, it was to read
The vocation of eternity written on your face
I called together the streets, the places, the people
Who were witnesses to your face
So that they could call out to you, so that they could undo
The fabric that death was weaving around you.

translated by Alexis Levitin (1983)

Paul Celan

(German, 1920–1970)

TRANSLATIONS BY

Michael Hamburger, John Felstiner,
Jerome Rothenberg

. . . .

COMMENTARY BY

Stephen Tapscott

ZÄHLE die Mandeln,
zähle, was bitter war und dich wachhielt,
zähl mich dazu:

Ich suchte dein Aug, als du's aufschlugst und niemand dich ansah,
ich spann jenen heimlichen Faden,
an dem der Tau, den du dachtest,
hinunterglitt zu den Krügen,
die ein Spruch, der zu niemandes Herz fand, behütet.

Dort erst tratest du ganz in den Namen, der dein ist,
schrittest du sicheren Fußes zu dir,
schwangen die Hämmer frei im Glockenstuhl deines Schweigens,
stieß das Erlauschte zu dir,
legte das Tote den Arm auch um dich,
und ihr ginget selbdritt durch den Abend.

Mache mich bitter.
Zähle mich zu den Mandeln.

Paul Celan (1952)

COUNT the almonds,
count what was bitter and kept you awake,
count me in:

I looked for your eye when you opened it, no one was looking at you,
I spun that secret thread
on which the dew you were thinking
slid down to the jugs
guarded by words that to no one's heart found their way.

Only there did you wholly enter the name that is yours,
sure-footed stepped into yourself,
freely the hammers swung in the bell frame of your silence,
the listened-for reached you,
what is dead put its arm round you also
and the three of you walked through the evening.

Make me bitter.
Count me among the almonds.

translated by Michael Hamburger (1972)

Count up the almonds,
count what was bitter and kept you waking,
count me in too:

I sought your eye when you looked out and no one saw you,
I spun that secret thread
where the dew you mused on
slid down to pitchers
tended by a word that reached no one's heart.

There you first fully entered the name that is yours,
you stepped toward yourself on steady feet,
the hammers swung free in the belfry of your silence,
things overheard thrust through to you,
what's dead put its arm around you too,
and the three of you walked through the evening.

Render me bitter.
Number me among the almonds.

translated by John Felstiner (2000)

Count the almonds,
count what was bitter and kept you awake,
count me in with them:

I searched for your eye which you opened when nobody saw you,
I spun that mysterious thread
down which the dew that you dreamed
slithered into a pitcher
kept from harm by a word found in nobody's heart.

There you first came into a name that was yours,
sure of foot you advanced on yourself,
the clappers swung free in your silence's belltower,
whatever you heard took a hold of you,
what was dead laid its hand on you too,
and threefold you moved through the evening.

Make me bitter.
Count me in with the almonds.

translated by Jerome Rothenberg (2005)

Commentary by Stephen Tapscott
Conversions

Genesis 11 tells the story of the Tower of Babel in terms of division *and* of unity. "Let us make us a name," the people propose; human aspiration leads to the construction of a tower that challenges the singular nature of God "on high." The Lord's punishment for this assertion is to "confound" them, separating human languages. From another perspective, this is also a story of unity, a pure coherence or the longing toward it—the prerogative of the mind beyond the power of separate languages.

The story serves as a paradigm of translation—the need for translation and its aspirations—from both perspectives. In David Young's apt metaphor, various versions of the poem "converse." In my experience (I read the German, and I rely gratefully on translations), a Celan poem comes into focus slowly, as a synthesis of the original and of several translations. The "pure" Celan poem exists at the intersection of its individual versions and interpretations.

———

"Paul Celan" was the name Paul Antschel gave himself after World War II. Raised in a Jewish, German-speaking, middle-class household in Czernowitz, in Romania, Antschel—a sometime medical student who wrote poems and studied languages—was out of the family home on the night, in June 1942, when his family was taken by the Gestapo. His parents, he later learned, were separated in the camps: his father assigned to work-details (he soon died of typhus), his mother, judged unfit to work, was shot. Antschel himself spent almost two years in work camps. In 1944 he returned to Czernowitz. The first poem he published under the name Paul Celan was the now-famous "Todesfuge" ("Death Fugue"), in 1945. By the late 1940s he was living in Paris, a Jewish exile writing in German.

"ZÄHLE die Mandeln" is a relatively early poem, published in 1952 as the final poem of *Mohn und Gedächtnis* (Poppy and Remembrance), a book that includes the "Todesfuge" as its centerpiece. Addressed chiefly to Celan's mother, it is a poem of reckoning and reckoning-up, of guilt, of witness and elegy and wide identification, of laying a public claim to the right to suffer and to be counted with those who have suffered. (Two people were transported to the camps; the poem envisions *selbdritt* as "three of you/ threefold.") I think it's not too far-fetched to hear in the poem some distant echoes of the story of Babel (in the scattering of people and the claims to identification with the "confounded," in the high bell tower of memory, in the downward-pouring movements, in the reclaiming of the names of the lost, in the destabilization and reclaiming of language). Celan was himself a talented translator (of Verlaine, Shakespeare, Esenin, and others during this period)[1] and a scholar of Jewish traditions, which he worked to infuse into the German of his poems. The irony of Celan's writing in German—as a Jew, an orphaned survivor, and an exile writing in a compromised mother language—also inflects the "Todesfuge." That poem assumes the actions of an "us" ("Black milk of dawn . . . we drink it"); the "Mandeln" lyric lays out the prior claim to speak *as* an "us."

"Mandeln" is thus a poem suggesting that translation—the displacement from one metaphor or person or name into another, a process of transport—is a kind of longing, or compensation. It has no title, lacking a name of its own except insofar as its opening line begins the experience. Its name is its claim; the reality of the poem precedes and exceeds its own naming, which is retrospective and compensatory—just as the speaker claims identity with those whose "names" they enter as "truly yours."

Several grammatical structures bind the poem together in German— its repetitions, for instance. The first three imperative lines insist on the action of *zählen*: "to pay," "to count." (The preposition *zu* and the preposition/ adverb *dazu* create an idiom, "to count up/among/with something/some- one.") And the last line returns to the *zählen* verb. The reiterations mat- ter because of their binding power *and* their differences: the repetitions play on different connotations of the German verb. (Lists often work this way. Whitman in "Song of Myself" breezily asserts "I am afoot with my vi- sion," but the repeated action of "seeing" changes: the import of his "vision" changes the more Whitman looks and repeats.)

ZÄHLE die Mandeln: Celan opens the poem with a familiar-form command (request?) to count—and to be counted—as a memorializing gesture, but the verb in German also objectifies, rendering units in order to *be* counted. It carries, I think, an element of rage about the humiliation in the "enumeration" of transported Jews at an assignment point. It's an act of compensation to imagine that moment, when Paul Antschel was not present; he sometimes claimed he had quarreled with his father that evening, which was why he had not been at home when they were taken.

> *Mach mich bitter.*
> *Zähle mich zu den Mandeln.*

The final repetition of the verb, in its idiomatic form (*zähle mich zu*, "count me among/count me in/reckon me with"), is a request to be identified, on the same terms as others who were brutally objectified. Among or with—whom? What *are* those "almonds"? The almond-shaped eyes of his Jewish family? The home life that had included his mother's baking almond pastries? The collective Jewish dead—or the living, in a Zionist future in a Levantine almond grove or in a future within German traditions? The eyes of survivors, or of "observant" Jews—that is, among those who bear witness through identification with the lost? The Jews of ancient and continuous history, whose tradition is replete with almonds, from Exodus onward? (Aaron's rod bears a design of flowering almonds.) A sense of witness to the stunned sense of ending, that one's self is both an ending and a beginning *because of* those endings?

The English translations of the poem propose slightly different variants among these possibilities (especially of *zählen* and almonds)—requiring less a comparison among translations than an acknowledgment of their complementarity. Different translations are helpful because the poem is various within itself, its emotions and tones "confounded."

Different translations are different interpretations, each in good faith, complementing one another toward a unity, as in the Babel story, toward a collectively "pure" linguistic experience. Translations of Celan poems may differ because of the polyvalence of the original, or of historical circumstances, or of changing critical assumptions about method or the poet's career. In the years just after the Shoah, we tended to read Celan as a voice of witness and of historical grief and survivor guilt; the poems were rendered as testimony, as voice: broken, reaching through the limits of language, trying to articulate the unspeakable. Through Theodor Adorno, readers questioned whether writing lyric poetry after Auschwitz was "barbaric" (a provocation that was taken in some circles to allude to the "Todesfuge"). Early translations of Celan began with these legitimate historical assumptions about the problems of lyricism in the face of totalitarianism, or traumatic memory, or even "reification" and survivor guilt. For me, Michael Hamburger's translation of the "Almonds" poem enacts this tension, which is essentially a moral problem.

Hamburger's version depends on an interpretation that leads him to choices favoring lucidity and moments of idiomatic clarity. From the start of the original, the German verb *zähle* ("count") both demands and requests. Connected by commas, the three apposed imperatives—or the three senses of their grammatical objects, initially the "almonds"—are implicitly made parallel. The almonds and whatever was "bitter and kept you awake" demand to be included in the "counting"—as does the speaker. Here Hamburger introduces an English-language idiom: "count what was bitter and kept you awake, / count me in." Maybe because there's a kind of general Britishness about Hamburger's translations, I think the American idiom emphasizes this "spokenness." The idiom carries a tone of enthusiasm, of willed choice ("Invitation? Count me in!"). I don't hear that buoyancy in the German, which seems a more somber demand—as if the speaker feels himself included and is requiring that his identity, or identification, be acknowledged. He is already, for better or worse, included: among the almonds, among that which made the sufferers bitter and wakeful. "To count," "to be counted," is "to be distinguished" in several senses; to be enumerated among the causes of bitterness and sleeplessness is a harsh distinction.[2] It's a small thing, Hamburger's use of the American idiom—a formal attempt to match idiom for idiom. (Hamburger calls his principle of translation "mimetic.") It's rhythmically accurate: its three-word line matches the original line's horizontal rhythm, as Celan closes the stanza crisply. It summarizes something of Hamburger's generous method, to render the Celan into a readable English poem, with formal and tonal effects matching those subtle dimensions of the original. Hamburger's "count me in" is more poignant than John Felstiner's ("count me in too"), less explanatory than Jerome Rothenberg's ("count me in with them").

Hamburger often seems to me a generous, inclusive scholar-translator—in a field that itself attracts the generous of spirit. Although he worked for decades passionately, under sometimes difficult circumstances (Celan could be personally difficult), and although he had produced his own admirable translations of early and middle Celan poems in at least two anthologies (1962 and 1976), as an editor he included and foregrounded other translators' versions of Celan poems that he himself had translated well.

––––––––

The generosity of John Felstiner is felt in his candid and welcoming sense of scholarly responsibility. Both in his rich book *Translating Neruda: The Way to Macchu Picchu* and in his textual biography of Celan, Felstiner's method is to assimilate biographical and textual data, and candidly to translate the poems from within that matrix. His translations emerge as products of that preparation. (Felstiner is brilliant, for instance, in his ability to read Celan as engaged with Hebrew textual and cultural traditions. This essay owes much of its biographical grounding—e.g., Celan's sense of almonds as a Biblical metaphor of Jewish identity—to Felstiner's mosaically careful book *Paul Celan: Poet, Survivor, Jew*.)

Felstiner frankly enfolds the footnotes of the poem into the text. In his translation he breaks the rules of consistency, choosing English synonyms in order to interpolate tonal connotations: "*Render* me bitter. / *Number* me among the almonds" (italics mine). His version sacrifices the repetition of the verb *zählen* in order to suggest connotations from the rest of the poem. (I also suspect that the slant rhyme "render/number" echoes the sense of repetition in Celan's retrieval of *zählen* at the end of the original.) Felstiner's verb "render"

makes the last lines more passive, more tragically doubled (Jewish bodies were "rendered" like animals in an abbatoir—and Celan demands to be numbered among those units/bodies/names). "Render me bitter" recalls the bitterness both of guilt and of Zyklon-B gas. Felstiner's last line abjures the eagerness of "count me in"; "number me" recalls the permanent indignity of marked tattooed bodies. Felstiner's version is both a command and a harsh request: to be enumerated among the Jews of the "almond-eyed" tradition, and to be included among those—"threefold"—with whom, for circumstantial reasons, he was not included. He changes the number by adding himself.

––––––––

Felstiner's translation marks a change in Celan's reception—from witness/survivor to historical metonymy, a world poet who interconnects traditions. (Later translators enlarge this sense of allusiveness: Nikolai Popov and Heather McHugh are brilliantly alert to Celan's use of concepts from "jurisprudence . . . geology . . . anatomy . . . neurophysiology . . . nautical and aeronautical navigations . . . heavy industry . . . manufacturing . . . biotech . . . electronics . . . cabbalistic esoterica . . .") These emphases do not, of course, diminish the force of the declarative voice of witness—but they do relocate Celan's work interpretatively. These markers of change in reception are, at best, arbitrary—and if the third phase of the translation of Celan's work inscribes him as largely "experimental" for contemporary poets, Felstiner's translations obviously overlap into that category. For instance, echoing Celan's own difficulties about the unhealing, untranslatable nature of the Shoah, Felstiner's translation of the "Todesfuge" daringly moves the poem into American avant-garde territory shadowed by Adorno. Throughout that translation, the original German slowly reabsorbs the translation ("this Death is ein Meister aus Deutschland")—until eventually the concluding lines of the Felstiner translation are the same as those in Celan's German:

dein goldenes Haar Margarete
dein aschenes Haar Shulamith

Felstiner's version suggests that translation is a problematic undertaking in the face of trauma based on totalizing power, that the historical facts may be unspeakable, even that the "original" concepts of the German idioms have infiltrated the English vernacular as concepts on their own.

––––––––––

The third version of the poem, Jerome Rothenberg's elegant translation, appears in a collection edited by the poet Pierre Joris; it summarizes much of the nature of contemporary interest in Celan. Rothenberg smooths some of the roughness of earlier versions in favor of a more accessible voice—which is not to say that the "roughness" of the surface in other translations is inaccurate. Hamburger's version has a declarative voice; Felstiner's seems written, textual; Rothenberg's is written but informal, a transcription of speech, a voicing of a poem that in the original behaves like a translation. Rothenberg's is the version that gives the Biblical-archaic "threefold" for *selbdritt*. And Rothenberg splits the difference at the end of the poem, keeping (like Hamburger) the simplicity of the "bitter" line and specifying (like Felstiner) "almonds" as the context that the speaker wants to be counted *in with*, like a brutal harvest—that is, making the context historically specific but impersonal.

> Make me bitter.
> Count me in with the almonds.

I don't know whether Rothenberg (or Pierre Joris, the editor) worked from the paradigm laid out by Jacques Derrida in his famous readings of Celan, but the interpretative/translational practices are convergent—deriving, I think, from a sense throughout Celan of the presence of death and forgetting: of loved ones, a tradition, a language. (Derrida suggests that translation is part of the "resurrection" that a poem aspires to, revisiting Walter Benjamin's famous observations about translation as part of the possible "afterlife" of a text.) For poets including Geoffrey Hill, David Young, and Heather McHugh, Celan is a structurally informing figure. Rothenberg's consistent, accessible translations, which were paradoxically some of the earlier translations of Celan, speak to this contemporary interest.

I'm interested in the honorable differences between these translations, because in their differences they reflect, in their solid merits, the polyvalence of Celan's poem. I think that is what Benjamin means, in "The Task of the Translator" (1923), when he claims that a poem in translation(s) can approach the nature of "pure language" (that Heideggerian ambition). The Celan poem emerges, for me, as the conversion, or convergence, of the original with several translations. As Michael Hamburger puts it, "It seems likely that the translation of his work will . . . have to be done in stages, patiently, for a long time to come."

Notes

1. I would like to claim that in this period Celan knew Osip Mandelstam's poems—because the Russian Jewish poet's last name translates as "almond branch" and because much of his life and work parallel Celan's. In works like "Fourth Prose" (1930) Mandelstam punningly explores similar questions about the "double nature" of the fruit/almond that is separated from its "tree." Celan subsequently translated Mandelstam. However, his serious interest in Mandelstam occurs later in the 1950s; the dates don't really match up.

2. Joachim Neugroschel, initially Celan's designated American translator, renders the first lines as Hamburger does, but softens the American idiom, as Rothenberg does: "Count me in with them." That choice—introducing a "them" both present and multiple, and also perhaps all the more demeaned by the act of counting—lends an element of justification, of personal or historical specificity to the speaker's demand to be included.

Wisława Szymborska

(Polish, 1923–2012)

TRANSLATIONS BY

Magnus J. Kryński and Robert A. Maguire,
Stanisław Barańczak and Clare Cavanagh,
Joanna Trzeciak

....

COMMENTARY BY

Alissa Valles

Tortury

Nic się nie zmieniło.
Ciało jest bolesne,
jeść musi i oddychać powietrzem i spać,
ma cienką skórę, a tuż pod nią krew,
ma spory zasób zębów i paznokci,
kości jego łamliwe, stawy rozciągliwe.
W torturach jest to wszystko brane pod uwagę.

Nic się nie zmieniło.
Ciało drży, jak drżało
przed założeniem Rzymu i po założeniu,
w dwudziestym wieku przed i po Chrystusie,
tortury są, jak były, zmalała tylko ziemia
i cokolwiek się dzieje, to tak jak za ścianą.

Nic się nie zmieniło.
Przybyło tylko ludzi,
obok starych przewinień zjawiły się nowe,
rzeczywiste, wmówione, chwilowe i żadne,
ale krzyk, jakim ciało za nie odpowiada,
był, jest i będzie krzykiem niewinności,
podług odwiecznej skali i rejestru.

Nic się nie zmieniło.
Chyba tylko maniery, ceremonie, tańce.
Ruch rąk osłaniających głowę
pozostał jednak ten sam.
Ciało się wije, szarpie i wyrywa,
ścięte z nóg pada, podkurcza kolana,
sinieje, puchnie, ślini się i broczy.

Nic się nie zmieniło.
Poza biegiem rzek,
linią lasów, wybrzeży, pustyń i lodowców.
Wśród tych pejzaży duszyczka się snuje,
znika, powraca, zbliża się, oddala,
sama dla siebie obca, nieuchwytna,
raz pewna, raz niepewna swojego istnienia,
podczas gdy ciało jest i jest i jest
i nie ma się gdzie podziać.

Wisława Szymborska (1986)

Tortures

Nothing has changed.
The body is susceptible to pain,
it must eat and breathe air and sleep,
it has thin skin and blood right underneath,
an adequate stock of teeth and nails,
its bones are breakable, its joints are stretchable.
In tortures all this is taken into account.

Nothing has changed.
The body shudders as it shuddered
before the founding of Rome and after,
in the twentieth century before and after Christ.
Tortures are as they were, it's just the earth that's grown smaller,
and whatever happens seems right on the other side of the wall.

Nothing has changed.
It's just that there are more people,
besides the old offenses new ones have appeared,
real, imaginary, temporary, and none,
but the howl with which the body responds to them,
was, is and ever will be a howl of innocence
according to the time-honored scale and tonality.

Nothing has changed.
Maybe just the manners, ceremonies, dances.
Yet the movement of the hands in protecting the head is the same.
The body writhes, jerks and tries to pull away,
its legs give out, it falls, the knees fly up,
it turns blue, swells, salivates and bleeds.

Nothing has changed.
Except for the course of boundaries,
the line of forests, coasts, deserts and glaciers.
Amid these landscapes traipses the soul,
disappears, comes back, draws nearer, moves away,
alien to itself, elusive,
at times certain, at others uncertain of its own existence,
while the body is and is and is
and has no place of its own.

translated by Magnus J. Kryński and Robert A. Maguire (1993)

Tortures

Nothing has changed.
The body is a reservoir of pain;
it has to eat and breathe the air, and sleep;
it has thin skin and the blood is just beneath it;
it has a good supply of teeth and fingernails;
its bones can be broken; its joints can be stretched.
In tortures, all of this is considered.

Nothing has changed.
The body still trembles as it trembled
before Rome was founded and after,
in the twentieth century before and after Christ.
Tortures are just what they were, only the earth has shrunk
and whatever goes on, sounds as if, it's just a room away.

Nothing has changed.
Except there are more people,
and new offenses have sprung up beside the old ones—
real, make-believe, short-lived, and nonexistent.
But the cry with which the body answers for them
was, is, and will be a cry of innocence
in keeping with the age-old scale and pitch.

Nothing has changed.
Except perhaps the manners, ceremonies, dances.
The gesture of the hands, shielding the head
has nonetheless remained the same.
The body writhes, jerks, and tugs,
falls to the ground when shoved, pulls up its knees,
bruises, swells, drools, and bleeds.

Nothing has changed.
Except for the boundaries of rivers,
the shapes of forests, shores, deserts, and glaciers.
The little soul roams among these landscapes,
disappears, returns, draws near, moves away,
evasive and a stranger to itself,
now sure, now uncertain of its own existence,
whereas the body is and is and is
and has nowhere to go.

translated by Stanisław Barańczak and Clare Cavanagh (1996)

Torture

Nothing has changed.
The body is painful,
it must eat, breathe air, and sleep,
it has thin skin, with blood right beneath,
it has a goodly supply of teeth and nails,
its bones are brittle, its joints extensible.
In torture, all this is taken into account.

Nothing has changed.
The body trembles, as it trembled
before and after the founding of Rome,
in the twentieth century before and after Christ.
Torture is, the way it's always been, only the earth has shrunk,
and whatever happens, feels like it happens next door.

Nothing has changed.
Only there are more people,
and next to old transgressions, new ones have appeared,
real, alleged, momentary, none,
but the scream, the body's answer for them—
was, is, and always will be the scream of innocence,
in accord with the age-old scale and register.

Nothing has changed.
Except maybe manners, ceremonies, dances.
Yet the gesture of arms shielding the head
has remained the same.
The body writhes, struggles, and tries to break free.
Bowled over, it falls, draws in its knees,
bruises, swells, drools, and bleeds.

Nothing has changed.
Except for the courses of rivers,
the contours of forests, seashores, deserts, and icebergs.
Among these landscapes the poor soul winds,
vanishes, returns, approaches, recedes.
A stranger to itself, evasive,
at one moment sure, the next unsure of its existence,
while the body is and is and is
and has no place to go.

translated by Joanna Trzeciak (2001)

Commentary by Alissa Valles
Szymborska: Torture(s)

Wisława Szymborska's work has traveled in style, with a whole retinue of English translators. Besides the best-known versions of her poems, by Stanisław Barańczak and Clare Cavanagh, published as *View with a Grain of Sand: Selected Poems* in Szymborska's Nobel year, 1996, and later expanded to form *Poems New and Collected*, there have been a host of translators in the UK and the United States who have tried their hand at this tricky poet. They include Adam Czerniawski, Grażyna Drabik with Austin Flint, Iwona Gleb, Regina Grol, Magnus J. Kryński with Robert A. Maguire, and of course Czeslaw Milosz, who broke the ice effectively but modestly with a version of the poem "I Am Too Near" in *Postwar Polish Poetry* (1968). More than three decades later, in 2001, Milosz wrote a foreword to a new Szymborska collection translated by Joanna Trzeciak, *Miracle Fair*. In it, he calls "Torture," from the 1986 collection *Ludzie na moście* (*People on a Bridge*), one of Szymborska's most moving poems, remarking that "particular to our century is a coming to grips with the fragility of our bodily existence." Events in the years since the poem was written—the Iraq War, Guantánamo Bay, Abu Ghraib—have given it a special charge, and it seems to me that the differing English versions only add to its power.

Translating the poem's bald title, "Tortury," already involves a big decision. The plural Polish word *tortury* evokes endless repetition, the expansive nature of torture, the seemingly infinite variety of its methods, and contrasts these with the unchanging human body. Two of the three translations examined here seek to retain the contrast by choosing "Tortures" over "Torture," but I admit to preferring the latter, which suggests not so much the variety of the thing as its universality, and the continuity with which it has been practiced. "Torture," which as a word hints at a shadow form or inversion of the word "culture," derives from the Latin word *torquere*, "to twist," also the root of the word "distortion." The plural "tortures" summons a more medieval (even scholastic) world, whereas the singular in English sounds contemporary, while preserving more than a flicker of the Inquisition. Newspapers in recent years have written of torture and more euphemistically of "enhanced interrogation techniques," but I have not often come across "tortures."

In her first line, Szymborska leaves little room for invention, but there are many ways to render the second concise declarative, *Ciało jest bolesne*. None of the three versions here conveys the hint of a palindrome in Szymborska's sequence—*lo-es-ol-es*—but the shortest translation, Joanna Trzeciak's, is the most aurally satisfying. Trzeciak also stays closest to the original in syntax and literal meaning. "The body is painful": noun, verb, adjective. It tells us the body is capable of suffering from pain, but also says the body is a painful (embarrassing, mortal) subject, and in human (not only Polish Catholic) culture often a shameful (sinful, guilty) one. Barańczak and Cavanagh's "The body is a reservoir of pain" focuses attention squarely on the body as a site, and the suggestion of a container, a collection of resources, also prepares the reader for the laundry list of attributes that follows in this stanza. Although the added metaphor may act against the poem's project of inverting the classical view of the body as a vessel for the soul, this more elaborate rendering carries an interesting ambiguity, reminding one that a reservoir can hold things besides pain, and so can the body—pain is one of its many capacities. Kryński and Maguire's "The body is susceptible to pain" is slightly ponderous, but like "reservoir," it gives us a glimpse of the body's other susceptibilities. "The body is painful" offers a more implacable view.

In her famous book *The Body in Pain*, published in the same year as Szymborska's *People on a Bridge*, Elaine Scarry describes the "structure of torture" as involving the conscious use of the body's resources against itself: it turns everything in the world (history, family, furniture, walls, time, the elements) against the body. Szymborska's poem chillingly portrays the special sadism of this systematic process: "a good supply" (Barańczak/Cavanagh) or, even better, "a goodly supply of teeth and nails" (Trzeciak) both render the way *spóry zasób* presents the body's own fine toolbox as seen from the torturer's perspective, its assets turned into liabilities; Kryński/Maguire's "adequate stock" weakens the advertising effect slightly, and why limit *paznokci* ("nails") to "fingernails," as Barańczak and Cavanagh do? In the last lines of the stanza, Trzeciak and Kryński/Maguire both stick close to the Polish syntax, respectively choosing for *łamliwe* and *rozciągliwe* the adjectives "brittle"/"breakable" and "extensible"/"stretchable," whereas Barańczak and Cavanagh prefer to use a passive constructions with "can be," which lengthens the line but has the advantage of suggesting the shadowy presence of the torturer. In the final line the sense of efficiency gone haywire finds expression in the bureaucratic and (crucially) subjectless phrase *jest to wszystko brane pod uwagę*. I think the choice by both Trzeciak and Kryński/ Maguire, "all this is taken into account," is closer to the Polish (with its passive form of the verb *brać*, "to take") and spookier than Barańczak and Cavanagh's "all of this is considered," though lexically that is also a legitimate translation and an equally passive expression. Both versions achieve the sinister note of care ascribed to the torturer (an important element of what Scarry calls torture's "fiction of power").

"Tremble" (Barańczak/Cavanagh and Trzeciak) is the most straightforward translation of the Polish verb *drzeć*, and I see no justification for ramping up the second stanza by using "shudders" (Kryński/Maguire). Because the poem dwells, especially in the following stanza, on the scale of pain, its spectrum, the intensity of the verb is not a trivial thing.

The last line of the second stanza gives rise to an interesting variety of solutions, all of which introduce a verb ("sounds as if," "feels like," "seems") absent from (and in colloquial speech unnecessary to) the Polish, which contains only the words *to* ("it"), *tak jak* ("as if"), and *za ścianą* ("behind a wall"). In translating this sense of unseen proximity, it may be logical to refer to sound, and the Barańczak/Cavanagh choice of "sounds" does refer ahead to the "cry" in the next stanza. Trzeciak's "feels like it's happening" keeps the frame of physical reference open, as it is in the original, but in this version the line also repeats the verb "to happen," which makes the line a bit too chatty (like the previous line—which is eleven words to Szymborska's seven both here and in the Barańczak/Cavanagh version, and twelve in Kryński/Maguire's). Kryński and Maguire do find a way to get Szymborska's *za ścianą* (behind a wall) into the line, which is good because walls are such a crucial feature of imprisonment and torture (cf. "walling"), and because the other expressions—"next door"/"a room away"—subtly

domesticate the image. (Although there may be an argument for doing that, too, if you think there is more power in the idea of torture in a domestic, rather than an institutional, setting.)

In the third stanza the mention of old and new "offenses"/"transgressions" is sly, because though evidently referring to the old and new crimes (both real and not) of which a prisoner can be accused, it also suggests the old and new ways torturers have found to break the law (offense) and/or violate the boundaries of the body (transgression). The stanza maintains this ambiguity, a possible elision of (or at least simultaneous reference to) the prisoner's and the torturer's crimes, in "the body's answer"/"the body answers": what is the body answering to or for, and who is the transgressor? This crucial double meaning is also part of the structure of torture, in the sense that at a certain point torture functions as punishment for *and* proof of a prisoner's guilt. There is an interesting variety in the words each translation uses to describe the new offenses or transgressions: apart from "real," which is used in all, only "none" is used in more than one (Trzeciak and Kryński/ Maguire). *Żadne* is always a difficult word to put into English; its tone is perhaps best conveyed by a phrase like "none whatsoever," and Barańczak and Cavanagh get closest to its dry humor by using "nonexistent." The same witty and streetwise diction characteristic of this translation duo is also present in "make-believe, short-lived." Trzeciak chooses the more explicitly legalistic "alleged" for *wmówione* and chooses, as she often does, a more literal word, "momentary," to translate *chwilowe* (from *chwila*, "moment").

At the end of the third stanza, I prefer the Barańczak/Cavanagh choice of "cry" for *krzyk*, and fail to understand why Kryński and Maguire would choose "howl." Polish has a clear equivalent of "howl," *wycie*, a sound associated with animals, which doesn't occur in Szymborska's poem. I understand why Trzeciak uses the rawer, less decorous "scream," but it does not work as well as "cry" would in her phrase "scream of innocence"; also, in my mind, a scream is more directly expressive of horror than of indignation or protest, and is usually expressed in Polish by the word *pisk*, *wzrask*, or indeed *wycie*.

When we arrive at stanza 4, *ruch rąk* can be a "gesture," which sounds more deliberate, or a "movement," which may be entirely automatic. The contrast in this stanza is between forms of culture and natural reactions, so Kryński/Maguire's "movement" may be more appropriate, as well as more literally faithful to the original. I prefer Trzeciak's "arms" over "hands" in Barańczak/Cavanagh and Kryński/Maguire, even if *rąk/ręce* can mean either; rehearsing the defensive action, I find myself throwing up my arms as well as my hands. *Ścięte z nóg* can be read literally as "cut" or "knocked down," or as an idiom meaning "exhausted," "dead on your feet," which makes Trzeciak's "bowled over" a strange choice, because neither its literal nor its figurative meanings fit the context. "Shoved" (Barańczak and Cavanagh), on the other hand, is too oblique, too mild, especially when moved to the other end of the clause. The Kryński/Maguire version tries to get around the problem by making "legs," not "it" (the body), the subject, and to say "its legs give out" does at least get an anatomical concreteness into the line, although at the price of sounding a bit redundant when followed by "it falls." But in the same line in Kryński/Maguire, "fly up" is too vigorous for *podkurcza*, for which either "pulls up" (Barańczak and Cavanagh) or "draws in" (Trzeciak) does the job. The relentlessly matter-of-fact last line of this stanza leaves little room for difference, though I must express a strong preference for the brutal "drools" over the clinical "salivates."

The last stanza completes the poem's inversion of the traditional view of a changeable body and changeless soul, making of the body a constant fact and of the soul an elusive, wandering rumor. The natural world, too, is fickle. Rivers change their "courses" (Trzeciak's word suggests direction, which accords with the Polish *bieg*, which means "run") or "boundaries" (Barańczak and Cavanagh steer the meaning toward a river's width rather than its path). The phrase "course of boundaries" makes no sense to me—where have the rivers gone in Kryński and Maguire? For *linią lasów* I favor the painterly "shapes" or "contours" of forests; Kryński and Maguire's direct translation "line of forests" is too literal. *Lodowców* are literally "glaciers," but can I suppose be stretched to Trzeciak's "icebergs," ordinarily *góre lodowe* in Polish. More challenging is *duszyczka*, a diminutive of *dusza* ("soul"). Kryński and Maguire ignore the eloquent diminutive altogether, whereas Barańczak/Cavanagh and Trzeciak have "little soul" and "poor soul," respectively.

"Poor soul" is a more expressive translation of *duszyczka*, a word that, like Hadrian's famous *animula*, manages to combine pity, ruefulness, scorn, and tenderness. T. S. Eliot's "simple soul" in his poem "Animula" might have been an alternate choice, though it would add an element of immaturity, while in Szymborska's poem the soul, though portrayed as small, uncertain, is no particular age.

Kryński/Maguire's "elusive" for *nieuchwytna* works better in this context than "evasive," the choice of both Barańczak/Cavanagh and Trzeciak. "Evasive" is a word laden with associations of dishonesty, and Szymborska, as far as I can tell, is not attributing any guilt to the soul for being hard to pin down; she merely ascribes to the soul an unsure, shadowy existence. I prefer Trzeciak's matching "sure"/"unsure" to the variation introduced in the other two translations, "sure"/"uncertain" and "certain"/"uncertain." Generally this poem makes great use of parallelisms, and I feel these should be preserved wherever possible.

Earlier in the stanza, the verb *snuć się* is rendered adequately by either "roams" (Barańczak/Cavanagh) or "winds" (Trzeciak), though the latter has more of the Polish sense of threading one's way and of spinning a yarn. "Traipses" (Kryński/Maguire) is too quaint. "Roams," like "wander," is more indeterminate and directionless, which is fine, unless you want a more pointed contrast in the end with the body's having "nowhere to go" (Barańczak/Cavanagh) or "no place to go" (Trzeciak). Rhythmically, I lean toward the latter, as I do in general: as poetry, Trzeciak's version ("scream" notwithstanding) satisfies me most fully, but Barańczak and Cavanagh's translation is strong and subtle and gets under one's skin. The Kryński/Maguire version seems to me the least sure-footed of the three, though even if it were the only translation in English, it would still convey Szymborska's deeply humane, elegant, and frightening argument.

Yehuda Amichai

(Hebrew, 1924–2000)

TRANSLATIONS BY
Glenda Abramson,
Benjamin and Barbara Harshav,
Robert Alter

························

COMMENTARY BY
Chana Bloch

אֵל מָלֵא רַחֲמִים

אֵל מָלֵא רַחֲמִים,
אִלְמָלֵא הָאֵל מָלֵא רַחֲמִים
הָיוּ הָרַחֲמִים בָּעוֹלָם וְלֹא רַק בּוֹ.
אֲנִי, שֶׁקָּטַפְתִּי פְּרָחִים בַּהָר
וְהִסְתַּכַּלְתִּי אֶל כָּל הָעֲמָקִים,
אֲנִי, שֶׁהֵבֵאתִי גְּוִיּוֹת מִן הַגְּבָעוֹת,
יוֹדֵעַ לְסַפֵּר שֶׁהָעוֹלָם רֵיק מֵרַחֲמִים.

אֲנִי שֶׁהָיִיתִי מֶלֶךְ הַמֶּלַח לְיַד הַיָּם,
שֶׁעָמַדְתִּי בְּלִי הַחְלָטָה מוּל חַלּוֹנִי,
שֶׁסָּפַרְתִּי צַעֲדֵי מַלְאָכִים,
שֶׁלִּבִּי הֵרִים מִשְׁקָלוֹת כְּאֵב
בַּתַּחֲרֻיּוֹת הַנּוֹרָאוֹת.

אֲנִי שֶׁמִּשְׁתַּמֵּשׁ רַק בְּחֵלֶק קָטָן
מִן הַמִּלִּים בַּמִּלּוֹן.

אֲנִי, שֶׁמֻּכְרָח לִפְתֹּר חִידוֹת בְּעַל כָּרְחִי,
יוֹדֵעַ כִּי אִלְמָלֵא הָאֵל מָלֵא רַחֲמִים
הָיוּ הָרַחֲמִים בָּעוֹלָם
וְלֹא רַק בּוֹ.

Yehuda Amichai (1958)

[A transliteration appears at the end of the commentary, on p. 160.]

O Lord Full of Mercy

O Lord full of mercy
If the Lord were not so full of mercy
There would be mercy in the world
And not only in him.
I, who have gathered flowers on the mountain,
Gazed into the valleys,
I, who have brought bodies down the hillside,
I can say that the world is empty of mercy.

I, who was salt-king on the shore,
Who stood undecided at my window,
Who counted angels' footsteps,
Whose heart lifted weights of pain
In the terrible contests,
I, who use only a small portion
Of the words in the dictionary;

I, who have to solve riddles
Unwillingly, I know
That if the Lord were not so full of mercy
There would be mercy in the world
And not only in him.

translated by Glenda Abramson (1989)

God Full of Mercy

God-Full-of-Mercy, the prayer for the dead.
If God was not full of mercy,
Mercy would have been in the world,
Not just in Him.
I, who plucked flowers in the hills
And looked down into all the valleys,
I, who brought corpses down from the hills,
Can tell you that the world is empty of mercy.

I, who was King of Salt at the seashore,
Who stood without a decision at my window,
Who counted the steps of angels,
Whose heart lifted weights of anguish
In the horrible contests.

I, who use only a small part
Of the words in the dictionary.

I, who must decipher riddles
I don't want to decipher,
Know that if not for the God-full of mercy
There would be mercy in the world,
Not just in Him.

translated by Benjamin and Barbara Harshav (1994)

God Full of Mercy

God full of mercy.
Were God not full of mercy
there would be mercy in the world, and not just in Him.
I, who plucked flowers on the mountain
and looked in all the valleys,
I, who hauled from the hills dead bodies,
can say that the world is empty of mercy.

I who was Salt King by the sea,
who stood indecisive at my window,
who counted the steps of angels,
whose heart lifted the weights of pain
in the terrible competitions,
I, who use just a small part
of the words in the dictionary.

I, who must solve riddles despite myself,
know that were God not full of mercy,
there would be mercy in the world
and not just in Him.

translated by Robert Alter (2015)

Commentary by Chana Bloch

The great Israeli poet Yehuda Amichai (1924–2000) writes in an accessible, colloquial Hebrew that fortunately survives translation into English—now, that's a statement sure to elicit a groan from anyone who has ever attempted to translate an Amichai poem! The concluding lines of stanza 2 in "O God Full of Mercy"—"I, who use only a small part / Of the words in the dictionary"— are often adduced in support of this view. But we need not take at face value what is after all a literary construct, Amichai's poetic persona: soldier, citizen, lover, man of few words; in short, an ordinary human being with his pleasures and his pains. Although Amichai writes in a colloquial register, his language is charged with the resonance of biblical, rabbinic, and liturgical Hebrew; the richer the resonance in Hebrew, the harder it can be to reproduce in English. The opening lines of "O God Full of Mercy" offer a revealing illustration of the difficulties one encounters in translating his poetry.

The force of the clash between line 1 and the lines that follow depends upon specific cultural knowledge. An informed reader would be aware that mercy is one of the attributes of God proclaimed on Mount Sinai (Exodus 34:6). A passage derived from this biblical text—beginning with *el rachum* ("a merciful God") and known as "the Thirteen Attributes of Mercy"—is familiar from the liturgy recited on holy days, on festival mornings, and in penitential prayers. The opening line of the poem quotes from the prayer for the dead, *El malé rachamim* ("O God full of mercy"), sung by a cantor at funerals, at the Yizkor service on Yom Kippur, and on other memorial occasions. Addressed to an exalted God who can be called upon to provide shelter to the dead and solace to the bereaved, this prayer begins: "O God full of mercy, who dwells on high, grant perfect rest on the wings of Your Divine Presence . . . to the soul of ——, who has gone to his eternal rest." Information of this sort may be provided in a footnote, though a note can hardly convey the plaintive, cantorial vibrato in which the prayer is traditionally delivered, considerably intensifying the pathos. One needs to hear the quaver in the cantor's voice to take the full measure of the speaker's exasperation in Amichai's poem.

Rachamim, usually translated as "mercy" or "compassion," has the same root letters (*r-ch-m*) as *Rechem* ("womb"). Throughout his oeuvre, Amichai associates this quality not with God but rather with a woman's sense of the empathic; in his last book and magnum opus, *Open Closed Open* (2000), he explicitly pairs *El malé rachamim* with *El malé rechem* ("God full of womb"). When we translated that book, Chana Kronfeld and I cast about for a way to re-create the play of sound and sense in English, but Amichai, who elsewhere had encouraged such attempts, told us: "There's no way to do it here. Just stick with the literal."

The opening of "O God Full of Mercy" resembles Midrash in quoting a sacred text and offering a commentary upon it, in this case employing the midrashic technique of paronomasia. The speaker's "commentary" hinges on a bit of serious wordplay that defies translation: *El malé* ("God full of") and *ilmalé* ("if not for/but for"). These words are spelled almost identically, with the vocalization (the diacritical marks inserted above, below, and inside the letters) differing only minimally. It is as if the shocking turn in the poem's opening salvo were inscribed in the language itself, and Amichai found it ready at hand.

The tone of the poem changes abruptly in line 2, where an epithet in praise of God is turned into a charge against him. "If God was not [so] full of mercy" (Harshav) has the ring of a contemptuous jibe: "God is full of himself." The speaker sees God as an infuriatingly puffed-up deity who has cornered the world supply of mercy. By logical inference, "the world is empty of mercy"; life on earth is a zero-sum game. The tone here is harshly accusatory, as in Amichai's well-known poem "God Has Pity on Kindergarten Children," which begins in Stephen Mitchell's translation:

> God has pity [*merachem*, a verb with the same root letters (*r-ch-m*)]
>   on kindergarten children.
> He has less pity on school children.
> And on grownups he has no pity at all.

"O God Full of Mercy" calls to mind the quarrels with God of Abraham, Job, Jeremiah, and Rabbi Nachman of Bratslav, though it goes quite a bit further. Looking back in anger, the speaker remembers himself as a young innocent gathering flowers and listening for angels. His life experience, however, has left him shaking his fist at a God he can no longer believe in—"the sweet, imaginary God of my childhood," as he writes in "Travels of the Last Benjamin of Tudela," an autobiographical poem that traces his loss of faith.

Amichai's Hebrew is richly textured, enlivened by a play of sound and sharpened by wit. The translations by Glenda Abramson, Benjamin and Barbara Harshav, and Robert Alter meet these challenges in a variety of ways. By beginning the first line with "O," Abramson makes clear that it is a direct address to God. *El* should be translated as "God"; "Lord" or "LORD" is usually reserved for YHWH (see Psalms 22:1 and 23:1). By italicizing the opening phrase, the Harshavs indicate that it is a quotation. They add "the prayer for the dead," which functions as a brief explanatory note; this kind of gloss can be a useful expedient, though here it interrupts the dramatic effect of the reversal. Abramson rightly translates "so full of mercy" in line 2 rather than the literal "full of mercy" in order to establish at once the speaker's vexation.

Amichai's wordplay is often crucial to the poem's effect, but as he himself acknowledges, sometimes there is "no way to do it" in English. In line 6, the nearly identical sound of *gviyot* ("corpses") and *gva'ot* ("hills") foregrounds these two nouns, drawing attention to the contrast between the beauty of nature and the horror of war. Abramson translates line 7 as "I, who have *brought bodies* down the hillside," and Alter as "I, who *hauled* from the *hills* dead bodies" (italics mine). They no doubt searched, as I did, for a pair of nouns related by sound before settling on an alliterating verb and noun. Another instance is the jarring twist on the implied divine title, *melekh ha-mlakhim*, "King of Kings," at the beginning of stanza 2. The Harshavs' translation, "King of Salt," a mock-heroic title equivalent to "King of Nothing," has the bite of Amichai's self-deprecating sarcasm, especially given that it suggests "King of Kings"; Alter's "Salt King" (and Abramson's "salt-king") evokes the Fisher King and a different set of associations. Both translations are literally correct, but only one points in the intended direction.

Finally, in line 4 of the second stanza, "pain" (Abramson, Alter) is much closer to Amichai's *ke'ev* than the Harshavs' "anguish." Though his poems

are full (yes, *full*) of feeling, they are never melodramatic; even when he writes about the most horrific subjects, Auschwitz included, he can summon up a mordant sense of humor, as in this passage from "After Auschwitz" (translated by Chana Bloch and Chana Knonfeld):

> After Auschwitz, no theology:
> the numbers on the forearms
> of the inmates of extermination
> are the telephone numbers of God,
> numbers that do not answer
> and now are disconnected, one by one.

In "O God Full of Mercy" he does so in the lines about God having a monopoly on mercy, the poet as King of Salt, and comparative sufferings—a Jewish pursuit—as an athletic contest.

There is no such thing as a perfect translation; each attempt brings into view different aspects of the original, providing in the best case a series of careful close readings that do not erase the distinctive features of the source text and its culture. Recognizing what we have been unable to carry across into English, Chana Kronfeld and I regard our translation, at the end of this commentary, as one more contribution to an ongoing process of interpretation.

> *O God full of mercy*—
> If only God were not so full of mercy
> There would be mercy in the world, not just in Him.
> I, who used to gather flowers on the mountain
> And gaze at all the valleys,
> I, who carried corpses down from the hills,
> Can tell you: the world is empty of mercy.
>
> I, who was King of Salt by the sea,
> Who stood undecided at my window,

Who used to count the footsteps of angels,
Whose heart lifted pain-weights
In those terrible competitions.
I, who use only a small part
Of the words in the dictionary.

I, who must solve riddles in spite of myself,
Know that if only God were not so full of mercy
There would be mercy in the world
And not just in Him.

Our primary objective was to convey the emotional complexity of the poem, its mixture of emotions—anger, irony, bitterness, sorrow. In the introduction to his translation of *Beowulf*, Seamus Heaney writes: "It is one thing to find lexical meanings for the words . . . but it is quite another thing to find the tuning fork that will give you the note and pitch for the overall music of the work." In every decision, we were seeking that note and pitch.

We added a dash at the end of line 1 to indicate that the quotation is interrupted, signaling the shift that follows. For the poet, the most telling proof that the world is empty of mercy is his experience of war. Amichai served with the British army in World War II, with the Palmach in 1948, and with the Israeli army in 1956 and 1973. In "Seven Laments for the War-Dead" he remembers "my good friend who died in my arms, in / his blood, / on the sands of Ashdod. 1948, June." That image and others like it haunt "the landscape of [his] memory," and with it the landscape of his poetry. Since *gviyot* in stanza 1 is a blunt term, we preferred "corpses" to "bodies" (Abramson) or "dead bodies" (Alter). In stanza 2 we chose "pain-weights," a darkly comic image, to suggest a punishing set of dumbbells, rather than "weights of pain" (Abramson) with its potential pathos (something Amichai studiously avoided). Finally, though Modern Hebrew does not distinguish between habitual, simple, and pluperfect past, we decided to differentiate the verbs in the past tense because we saw the poem as reflecting Amichai's progressive loss of belief, a reading supported by what we know of his work.

Familiarity with a poet's oeuvre is a major resource for a translator, one we share with the colleagues whose translations I compared. Each one has something to praise and something to quibble with, and each offers a different entry point into the text, a new avenue for interpretation. Happily for the reader, translation is not a zero-sum game.

I would like to thank Chana Kronfeld, my collaborator in translation and much else, for her astute critique of this essay; as always, her words are inextricably intertwined with my own.

Transliteration:

El Malé Rachamim

El malé rachamim,
ilmalé ha-el malé rachamim
hayu ha-rachamim ba-olam ve-lo rak bo.
Ani, she-katafti prachim ba-har
ve-histakalti el kol ha-amakim,
ani, she-heveti gviyot min ha-gva'ot,
yode'a le-saper she-ha-olam rek me-rachamim.

Ani she-hayiti melekh ha-melach le-yad ha-yam,
she-amadeti bli hachlata le-yad chaloni,
she-safarti tse'adey mal'achim,
she-libi herim mishkelot ke'ev
ba-tacharuyot ha-nora'ot.
Ani, she-mishtamesh rak be-chelek katan
min ha-milim she-ba-milon.

Ani, she-mukhrach li-ftor chidot be-al korchi
yode'a ki ilmalé ha-el malé rachamim
hayu ha-rachamim ba-olam
ve-lo rak bo.

Adonis

(Arabic, b. 1930)

TRANSLATIONS BY
Samuel Hazo,
Adnan Haydar and Michael Beard,
Khaled Mattawa

....

COMMENTARY BY
Kareem James Abu-Zeid

الصاعقة

ايتها الصاعقة الخضراء
يا زوجتي في الشمس والجنون
الصخرة انهارت على الجفون
فغيّري خريطة الأشياء

جئتك من أرض بلا سماء
ممتلئًا بالله والهاوية
مجنحًا بالريح والنسور
أقتحم الرمل على البذور
وأنحني للغيمة الآتية

فغيّري خريطة الأشياء
يا صورتي في الشمس والجنون
ايتها الصاعقة الخضراء

Adonis (1961)

[A transliteration appears at the end of the commentary, on p. 167.]

Thunderbolt

My green thunderbolt,
my spouse in the sun,
my madness,
change the face of things.
I've fallen under rocks.
I'm blinded and beseeching
in a land without a sky.

Possessed at times
by hell and gods,
I am an eagle
winged with wind.
I leaven seeds in soil.
I bend the bow
of the nearest cloud.

O my thunderbolt,
change everything,
change all the maps.
Be in a flash
my likeness in the sun,
my twin in madness.

translated by Samuel Hazo (1982)

Thunderbolt

I call on you, green thunderbolt.
I take you as my wife, in sunlight and in madness.
The rock has collapsed on my eyelids
so blast away the map of things.

I come to you from a skyless land,
I'm full of God,
that precipice inside.
From winds, from eagles, I take my wings.
I force seeds into the sand
and bow down to the approaching cloud.

And so I call on you to change the map of things.
You are my image in sunlight and in madness,
my green thunderbolt.

translated by Adnan Haydar and Michael Beard (2008)

Thunderbolt

Green thunderbolt,
my spouse in sun and madness,
stone has fallen on eyelids
and now you must redraw the map of things.

I came to you from an earth without sky
filled with God and the abyss,
winged with eagles and gales,
barraging, thrusting sand
into the caverns of seeds,
bowing to the coming clouds.

Redraw the map of things,
dear image of madness and sun,
my green thunderbolt.

translated by Khaled Mattawa (2010)

Commentary by Kareem James Abu-Zeid

Ali Ahmed Said was born in a small village in Syria in 1930. His choice of pen name—Adonis—is an indicator of the audacity of both his poetry and his writings on Arab culture and society. In 1961, this self-proclaimed Arab Nietzsche published *Songs of Mihyar the Damascene*, a complex two-hundred-page collection that many consider a turning point in modern Arabic poetry. Its impact on Arabic poetics has been no less substantial than the impact T. S. Eliot's "The Waste Land" had on English poetics. Many other Arab poets had begun experimenting with formal innovations as early as the late 1940s, slowly expanding Arabic poetry beyond a fairly rigid set of metrical and syllabic conventions. But it was Adonis who seemed to fully master these innovations, developing their potential and spearheading what critics generally refer to as the modernist wave of Arabic poetry. In his poetry, a revolution in form is tied to a call for a cultural revolution, an attempt at breaking with the bonds of what Adonis views as "traditionalist" thought, a term he often equates with the more orthodox schools of Islam. Mainstream Arab thought, he claims in his critical writings, is characterized by an overly pronounced orientation toward the past of the Koran and orthodox interpretations of it; tradition has the upper hand over innovation, and the Arab present conforms far too much to the (largely Islamic) norms of the past. Adonis labels this phenomenon "pastism," and his poetry attempts to both critique and transform this worldview. From the outset, his verse has therefore been polemical and controversial, leading both to a host of imitators and to criticism from all sides of the political spectrum.

The poem "Thunderbolt" (or "The Thunderbolt") lies in the middle of the third section of *Songs of Mihyar the Damascene*, in a section not innocuously entitled "The Dead God." Mihyar is Adonis's poetic alter ego, both a literary figure and a lyric mouthpiece, and he announces the death of God in much the same way that Nietzsche's Zarathustra does. The thunderbolt, here portrayed as Mihyar's wife (the word for "thunderbolt" is grammatically feminine in Arabic), embodies the poet's desire for cultural transformation, a will to explode traditional modes of thought and embrace more-radical views of the world. This is the "madness" the poem evokes, a new way of looking at the world that is oriented more toward the future than the past. "Revolution" is a key term for Adonis, though for him the most fundamental component of revolution is ontological—revolutions in our ways of viewing the world must precede all "political" (i.e., physical) revolutions. Here we have a poem that both announces that revolution (the storm is coming on "the approaching cloud") and demands it ("change the map of things"). Furthermore, Adonis's choice of the color green is by no means coincidental: he is reappropriating the color most intimately associated with Islam, and using it as a symbol purely of rebirth and growth (represented in this poem by the "seeds" in the second stanza), hence gutting it of its traditionally Islamic associations.

Adonis' poetry—with its rich rhymes, frequent echoes, and eagerness to exploit the polysemic nature of many Arabic words—is notoriously difficult to translate, and all three translators are forced to emphasize certain aspects of the poem at the expense of others. In general, Samuel Hazo's is by far the freest of the three. Hazo's first stanza does away with Adonis's image of the rock collapsing on the eyelids, but keeps the motif of sight while lending the stanza a tone of desperation by inserting the verse "I'm blinded and beseeching" (which is not in the original Arabic). In the second stanza, Hazo emphasizes the iconoclastic tone of the poem by choosing to translate *hawiyah* as "hell"—the word literally means "abyss," but it is often used in opposition to the heaven of monotheistic religions. The beginning of the second stanza merits a closer look, as Hazo makes several interesting choices in the lines "Possessed at times / by hell and gods." The Arabic literally reads "Filled with God and the abyss." By choosing to translate the Arabic word *allah*—the God of monotheism, and more specifically of Islam—as "gods" in the plural, he undoes some of his previous choices, and undermines the evident iconoclasm of the original poem. Choosing "possessed" instead of "filled" seems like a more logical choice, as he is adding to the tone of desperation that he established earlier (but which is not necessarily in the original)—"possessed" implies a certain passivity, a lack of control. Hazo's willingness to stray from the literal meaning of the original text takes its most interesting turn in the final stanza, where the Arabic "so change the map of things" becomes "change everything, / change all the maps." With "change all the maps," Hazo is bringing the implicit political content of this poem to the fore. He chooses, in other words, to unpack and expand the verse, and make a more explicitly political statement out of it.

The opening of Adnan Haydar and Michael Beard's translation of this poem stands in stark contrast to Samuel Hazo's. By adding two verbs to both of the first two lines (neither of which is present in the Arabic), they emphasize not desperation but rather control, power: "*I call on you*, green thunderbolt. / *I take you* as my wife, in sunlight and in madness" (my italics). They then reinforce this notion of power and add an element of violence to it by translating "so change the map of things" to "so blast away the map of things": the image they create is that of a thunderbolt striking stone. Their translation of this verse is, in a sense, even more radical than the original text, as it emphasizes destruction over change. The translators add even more forcefulness to the lyric at the beginning of the second stanza by bringing the past-tense "I came" into the present tense: "I come to you from a skyless land, / I'm full of God, / that precipice inside." Here, interestingly, they turn the inherent contrast between God and the abyss that exists in the original text into an apposition: in their translation, God *is* the "precipice inside." Although they lose the notion of hell, their choice of the word "precipice" emphasizes the notion of falling, which makes for a smooth transition to the airy heights of the remainder of the stanza ("winds," "eagles," "wings," etc.). In their translation of the final stanza, they again choose to emphasize the notion of power and action by inserting verbs that are not present in the Arabic: "And so *I call on you* to change the map of things. / *You are* my image in sunlight and madness, / my green thunderbolt" (my italics once again). On the one hand, the addition of so many new verbs makes for a much more forceful poem, and helps convey the destruction that is inherent in the figure of the thunderbolt. On the other hand, adding so many verbs compels the translators to turn this into a poem full of complete sentences—their translation has no fewer than eight periods, while the original text only has two—which takes away from the flow of the poem and gives it a more choppy feel.

Khaled Mattawa's translation hews more closely to the original than the other two, and succeeds at maintaining the concision of the Arabic text. His first three verses are virtually a word-for-word rendering of the original, but he introduces an interesting change to the fourth and final verse of the first stanza by translating the literal "change the map of things" as "and now you must redraw the map of things." By choosing "redraw" instead of "change," he brings the notion of writing or artistry more fully into the poem. But by taking away the grammatical imperative, he adds a layer of ambiguity that is not in the original: "and now you must redraw" could, of course, be read as a sort of command, but it could also indicate that the thunderbolt has no say in the matter. Either way, the choice of words is much less forceful and violent than the "blast away" of Haydar and Beard. But his translation, in general, is the most fluid of the three—it has far fewer periods, and maintains a sense of continuity by using present participles ("barraging," "thrusting," "bowing") where the other translations use conjugated verbs. Mattawa also establishes a clear rhythmic flow, particularly in the second half, with almost all of the verses hovering between six and seven syllables.

Although this concision, coupled with a relative faithfulness to the original, sets Mattawa's translation apart from the other two, it is futile to make the claim that any one is better than the other two. Each has its own merits and drawbacks, and each brings different aspects of this complex text to the fore.

Transliteration:

al-saʿiqa

ayyatuha al-saʿiqatu al-khadra'
ya zawjati fi al-shamsi wa-l-junun
al-sakhratu inharat ʿala al-jufun
fa-ghayyiri kharitata al-ashya'.

ji'tuki min ardin bila sama'
mumtali'an bi-allahi wa-l-hawiya
mujannahan bi-l-rihi wa-l-nusuur,
aqtahimu al-ramlua ʿala al-budhur
wa-anhani li-l-ghaymati al-atiya,

fa-ghayyiri kharitata al-ashya'
ya surati fi al-shams wa-l-junun
ayyatuha al-saʿiqatu al-khadra'.

Tomas Tranströmer

(Swedish, 1931–2015)

TRANSLATIONS BY

Robin Fulton,

May Swenson and Leif Sjöberg,

Robin Robertson

• •

COMMENTARY BY

Johannes Göransson

Till vänner bakom en gräns

I

Jag skrev så kargt till er. Men det jag inte fick skriva
svällde och svällde som ett gammaldags luftskepp
och gled bort till sist genom natthimlen.

II

Nu är brevet hos censorn. Han tänder sin lampa.
I skenet flyger mina ord upp som apor på ett galler
ruskar till, blir still, och visar tänderna!

III

Läs mellan raderna. Vi ska träffas om 200 år
då mikrofonerna i hotellets väggar är glömda
och äntligen får sova, bli ortoceratiter.

Tomas Tranströmer (1968)

To Friends Behind a Frontier

1

I wrote so meagerly to you. But what I couldn't write
swelled and swelled like an old-fashioned airship
and drifted away at last through the night sky.

2

The letter is now at the censor's. He lights his lamp.
In the glare my words fly up like monkeys on a grille,
rattle it, stop, and bare their teeth.

3

Read between the lines. We'll meet in 200 years
when the microphones in the hotel walls are forgotten
and can at last sleep, become trilobites.

translated by Robin Fulton (1997)

To Friends Behind a Border

I

I wrote so stingily to you. But what I didn't dare write
swelled and swelled like an old-fashioned dirigible
and finally sailed away through the night sky.

II

Now my letter is with the censor. He turns on his lamp.
In the beam my words leap like apes onto a grating,
shake it, go stiff, and bare their teeth.

III

Read between the lines. We shall meet in 200 years
when the microphones in the hotel walls, forgotten and
allowed to sleep at last, are imbedded fossils

translated by May Swenson and Leif Sjöberg (1972)

To Friends Behind a Border

I

I wrote to you so cautiously. But whatever I couldn't say
filled and grew like a hot-air balloon
and finally floated away through the night sky.

II

Now my letter is with the censor. He lights his lamp.
In its glare my words leap like monkeys at a wire mesh,
clattering it, stopping to bare their teeth.

III

Read between the lines. We will meet in two hundred years
when the microphones in the hotel walls are forgotten—
when they can sleep at last, become ammonites.

translated by Robin Robertson (2006)

Poems "Between the Lines" and "Behind Borders":
Translations of Tranströmer's Ineffable Poetics

1.

Starting with his 1954 debut, *17 Dikter* (*17 Poems*), Tomas Tranströmer rose to prominence in Swedish poetry with his brief, highly metaphorical depictions of liminal states of consciousness. Tranströmer's first few collections garnered great praise in Sweden, and he quickly became one of the leading poets of his generation. Adding to his acclaim, Robert Bly began to translate his work in the mid-1960s, generating an international reputation that few, if any, Swedish poets had ever enjoyed.

Bly used Tranströmer—together with other foreign poets like Federico García Lorca and Georg Trakl—to create an international canon of "leaping poets" as an intuitive, surrealist-influenced alternative tradition to the conservative, formalist, Anglo-American canon of the New Critical establishment. Soon other poets and translators, such as the Scottish poet Robin Fulton, started making their own versions of Tranströmer, in English as well as other languages, including German and even Chinese. Gradually Tranströmer began to gather a whole host of international awards and honors, culminating with the Nobel Prize in 2011. However, Tranströmer's path to international prominence was not without its setbacks. Some of his struggles came from the domestic literary scene. In the late 1960s, the Swedish literary climate became increasingly Marxist, and younger poets and critics demanded a "new simplicity" from its poetry—politically charged, simple and unadorned, set in the urban reality of modern Sweden. Tranströmer's use of elaborate metaphors, his almost diorama-like miniatures, and his pervasively pastoral settings (usually the Swedish countryside) made him the target of critics who felt he was a "bourgeois" poet: apolitical and escapist. In a 1967 letter to Bly, Tranströmer describes the situation like this: "The political accusation consists of the fact that I'm not directed by ideology; this year one should preferably be a card-carrying Marxist. Instead, suspect elements of old-fashioned individualism, including religiosity, have been detected."

The charges had some validity. Tranströmer's poems often have pastoral settings, and—unlike Bly's own poetry from the 1960s—they tend to steer away from overt political issues. Rather than treating such topics explicitly, Tranströmer tends to portray political issues as a kind of background noise, threatening the poem's communication of something ineffable. Often in his 1960s poetry, newspapers flutter and TVs are full of static: warnings of what may encroach upon this transformative act of communication.

However, Tranströmer maintained his standing in the Swedish poetry canon, in part no doubt due to the many translations of his work from abroad. By the time he won the Nobel Prize, there could be no doubt about his international prominence. Other poets (for example, Ann Jäderlund, Bruno K. Öijer, and several poets published by the journal *OEI*) have been far more influential in Sweden for many years, but Tranströmer has remained the most visible Swedish poet internationally, and his work seems to continually elicit new translations.

2.

"Till vänner bakom en gräns," written in 1968—at the height both of the Cold War and of the criticisms of Tranströmer's apolitical "religiosity"—is an unusual poem for Tranströmer because it focuses on politics and explicitly treats the relationship between poetry (and more generally acts of communication) and the political situation. Tranströmer wrote the poem following a trip to Estonia, Latvia, and Russia, during which he was particularly disturbed by the presence of surveillance and censorship in the Baltics.

While the poem has an explicitly political focus, it also follows Tranströmer's general tendency to see politics as interfering with the communication of poetry. The poem does not promote a political agenda—or take sides in the Cold War—but posits that poetry exists in opposition to repressive politics and their borders. The poem offers an ideal of communication—perhaps even of translation—as private and profound, in contrast to the repressive regime of politics, which leads on the one hand to censorship, and on the other to the usurping of privacy through surveillance technology.

On a simple level, it is a poem about writing a letter to friends behind a border. But it's also an epistolary poem addressed to the friends, perhaps expressing that which the speaker "couldn't" or "didn't dare" (depending on the translation; the Swedish original is ambiguous in this regard) to write in the letter. It's a poem about a letter, a poem as a letter, a poem as a stand-in for the letter, and a poem as a supplement to the letter. Perhaps the poem is the true letter. While the official letter is "meager" and (still) clashes with the censor, the poem is something ineffable that cannot be gleaned by the censor, something "between the lines."

The most political aspect of the poem might be that it imagines a future when the "frontier" of the title has become outdated, a state that Tranströmer represents by comparing no-longer-functioning surveillance microphones in the walls to orthoceras, which Tranströmer describes as "a special type of fossil, often found in Baltic limestone; they are a little like fossil microphones (from the Silurian age)." It's a brilliant metaphor since it makes symbolic sense—the equipment becomes useless, outdated—and visual sense: we can imagine an old microphone looking like a fossil. (The Stasi Museum in Berlin now exhibits old surveillance machines as if they were fossils; the poem's prediction has proved correct.)

3.

There have been many versions of Tranströmer's poetry, but the differences between them tend to be slight. Of the ones gathered here, Fulton is good at re-creating Tranströmer's austere but visceral language. The simple line *Han tänder sin lampa* is perhaps most readily translated as "He turns on his lamp" (as in the translation by May Swenson and Leif Sjöberg), but Fulton and Robertson both use the more visceral "He lights his lamp" (in the Swedish, *tänder* means both "to turn on a light" and "to light a match"), which cinematically lights up the face of the censor as he reads the letter. The translation by Swenson (a U.S. poet of Swedish descent) and Sjöberg (a Swedish poet of Tranströmer's generation) is not much different from Fulton's. They translate *apor* as "apes" instead of "monkeys," perhaps because of the proximity of the signifiers (even though *apor* means "monkeys"

in Swedish). This may not be the best solution, since apes tend to be too big, strong, and cumbersome to clamber on bars the way monkeys do in Tranströmer's metaphor.

What troubles all the translators is the final image of the *ortoceratiter*. Each tries to come up with more-common words for the fossil, suggesting that there is something unassimilably foreign about Tranströmer's word choice. But in the original poem, the word's foreignness emphasizes the signifier over the signified—word as artifice, word as useless ornament. Surprisingly, the word hardly needs to be translated, since the scientific term is based on the same Latin word in both English and Swedish.

4.

What separates Robin Robertson's from the translations by Fulton and Swenson/Sjöberg is that he frequently tries to iron out Tranströmer's often somewhat awkward or austere lines to make them more manageable, but in the process they become less evocative. In the second stanza he writes: "In its glare my words leap like monkeys at a wire mesh, / clattering it, stopping to bare their teeth." This streamlines what's actually happening in Tranströmer's original: the monkeys first rattle the grate ("mesh" is too soft), then they stop (they are tired), and then they bare their teeth. It's a spastic, jerky movement, not the smooth, single movement suggested by Robertson.

When they were published, in 2006, the Robertson translations proved controversial because Robertson openly admitted, in an October 28, 2006, article in the *Guardian*, that he did not know Swedish and was basing his translations on previous translations, invoking Robert Lowell's famous "imitations": "In my relatively free versions of some of Tranströmer's poems I have attempted to steer a middle ground between Lowell's rangy, risk-taking rewritings and the traditional, strictly literal approach." As Lawrence Venuti says, in a 2011 essay in *Translation Studies*, this followed a long line of "poet's version"s from throughout the twentieth century. However, Fulton objected that Robertson's poems were not just ignorant ("they show a cavalier disregard for Tranströmer's texts") but also too similar to his own translations ("an excessively large number of Robertson's lines are identical to mine").

As Venuti says about the many versions of Rilke, the later versions of Tranströmer take on a "stylistic elegance" and are "remarkably fluent." It appears that as Tranströmer's poetry has gone from challenging the status quo (in the United States) to acceptability, so the translations have become increasingly fluent and elegant. It is as if his increasing acceptability has to be underscored with increasingly more-acceptable versions of his poems.

5.

We may wonder why publishers and translators feel the need to continually retranslate and republish Tranströmer's poems, even as they offer very little difference from previous translations (so little that they may at times be seen as plagiarisms). Tranströmer's own poem contains one possible answer: if the true poem is "between the lines," there is in his work a sense of the authentic poem as something ineffable, something that cannot ever be fully grasped, fully translated. As a result, his poems will continually call for new translations, translations that will inevitably fail.

However, perhaps there is a simpler answer: Tranströmer is retranslated because he is the most translated Swedish poet. Translations can pose challenges to the status quo of U.S. poetry by offering alternative canons, but once a poet like Tranströmer has become part of the U.S. canon of "international poetry," it becomes an act of conservatism to continue translating him: we translate and review the translations because the poet is accepted and publishable. In so doing we perform a conservative act: we retranslate Tranströmer rather than engaging with contemporary Swedish poets; for example, poets who might challenge the status quo the way Tranströmer did in the 1960s.

Marin Sorescu

(Romanian, 1936–1996)

TRANSLATIONS BY

John F. Deane,

W. D. Snodgrass with

Dona Roşu and Luciana Costea,

David Constantine with

Joana Russell-Gebbett

· ·

COMMENTARY BY

Adam J. Sorkin

Adam

Cu toate că se afla în rai,
Adam se plimba pe alei preocupat şi trist
Pentru că nu ştia ce-i mai lipseşte.

Atunci Dumnezeu a confecţionat-o pe Eva
Dintr-o coastă a lui Adam.
Şi primului om atît de mult i-a plăcut această minune,
Încît chiar în clipa aceea
Şi-a pipăit coasta imediat următoare,
Simţindu-şi degetele frumos fulgerate
De nişte sîni tari şi coapse dulci
Ca de contururi de note muzicale.
O nouă Evă răsărise în faţa lui.
Tocmai îşi scosese oglinjoara
Şi se ruja pe buze.
„Asta e viaţa!" a oftat Adam
Şi-a mai creat încă una.

Şi tot aşa, de cîte ori Eva oficială
Se întoarce cu spatele,
Sau pleca la piaţă după aur, smirnă şi tămîie,
Adam scotea la lumină o nouă cadînă
Din haremul lui intercostal.

Dumnezeu a observat
Această creaţie deşănţată a lui Adam.
L-a chemat la el, l-a sictirit dumnezeieşte,
Şi l-a izgonit din rai
Pentru suprarealism.

Marin Sorescu (1968)

Adam

Distressed at being in Paradise
Adam, preoccupied and sad, strolled about the paths
not knowing what it was he was still missing.

Then God manufactured Eve
out of one of Adam's ribs.
This miracle pleased the first man so much
that straight away
he touched the rib next to it
feeling his fingers beautifully warmed
by firm breasts and smooth thighs
well rounded out by notes of music.
A new Eve had risen before him.
Primly she had taken out a little mirror
and was painting her lips.
"This is life!" Adam had sighed
and created yet another.
And so on and on, whenever the official Eve
turned her back
or went to the market for gold, frankincense and myrrh,
Adam brought a new odalisque to light
from his inter-rib harem.

God noticed
this immoderate creation of Adam,
called him and, divinely reproaching him,
threw him out of paradise for committing
surrealism.

translated by John F. Deane (1987)

Adam

Although in Paradise,
Adam kept on prowling the alleys, preoccupied and sad,
Since he couldn't figure out what was still missing.

Then God manufactured Eve
Out of one of Adam's ribs
And the first man was so delighted by this marvel
That he touched, instantly, his very next rib
And felt his fingers beautifully uplifted
By firm breasts and sweet thighs
Like the contours of musical phrases.
A new Eve rose before him.

She just took out a tiny mirror
And put some lipstick on her mouth.
"This is the life!" sighed Adam,
And created another one.

And over and over, each time the authorized Eve
Turned her back
Or went to shop for incense, gold and myrrh,
Adam brought to light a new odalisque
From his intercostal harem.
God took note of
Adam's dissolute creation.
He called him in, magisterially chewed him out,
Then banished him from Paradise
On a charge of surrealism.

translated by W. D. Snodgrass with Dona Roșu
and Luciana Costea (2007)

Adam

Adam in Paradise was still a sad man
Who walked with his head down
After something. Then God fleshed Eve
From one of Adam's ribs.

The miracle tickled Adam.
He wished hard and strummed a rung higher
And the curve of a girl, from the breast to the hip,
Pressed against his hand with a feeling music.

When she was separate
And he saw her tracing with her finger-tips
Her own smile Adam spent
Another Eve from his basket.

Eve Number One
God's promotion
Whenever she turned her back
Or was gone shopping for unnecessaries
Adam plucked at his cage
And a new Eve sprouted.

God got wise
And carpeted Adam. Son, he said,
Who told *you* to multiply?
Too much imagination, that's your trouble.
Off you go now, the hard earth awaits you.
Dig and delve.

(Exit Adam, strumming.)

translated by David Constantine with
Joana Russell-Gebbett (1987)

Commentary by Adam J. Sorkin

Marin Sorescu, the internationally celebrated Romanian poet and playwright, was his country's best-known and most frequently translated contemporary writer at the time of his untimely death, in 1996. Born of a peasant background in 1936 in an agricultural village in the southern Romanian region of Oltenia, Sorescu came to prominence in the mid-1960s during a period of relative cultural freedom in communist Romania, a temporary thaw during which a lyrical revival flourished. Romanian poets threw off the last of the constraints of an imposed proletarian aesthetic and drew on poetic traditions held artificially in abeyance since the 1930s, including native strains of surrealism, hermeticism, and absurdism, as well as strategies of modernistic and expressionistic poetry. Nina Cassian called the half decade or so before dictator Nicolae Ceaușescu's demagoguery revealed itself in the early 1970s a brief, limited "golden age," during which writers such as Nichita Stănescu, Mihai Ursachi, Mircea Ivănescu, Ana Blandiana, Sorescu, and Cassian herself could create major, highly individualistic work.

During this interlude of relaxed state and party control of publication and content, many of Marin Sorescu's most important poetry collections appeared in rapid succession, starting with *Poems*, 1965; *The Death of the Clock*, 1966; *The Youth of Don Quixote*, 1968, which included the poem "Adam"; *Cough*, 1970; *Soul, Good for Everything*, 1972; and *And So*, 1973. By 1972, Sorescu, who was permitted to travel abroad for festivals and other occasions, including residency fellowships at the University of Iowa International Writing Program and in West Berlin, had a first book in English, *Frames*, translated into English by Roy MacGregor-Hastie, and published in Romania. In the mid-1970s Oskar Pastior produced two volumes translated into German, which served as the basis of Michael Hamburger's 1983 Bloodaxe *Selected Poems*. Sorescu's wry poetry also attracted other notable translators, including Seamus Heaney, Ted Hughes, Paul Muldoon, D. J. Enright, Michael Longley, Stuart Friebert, and the three whose versions appear here. Sorescu remained productive throughout his career, with a bit of a hiatus when he turned to painting in the 1980s

after problems with Romanian authorities. A spate of publication activity followed the December 1989 fall of communism. His final book, *The Bridge* (1997), composed on his sickbed as he was dying of liver cancer and at a time when he knew he was his country's Nobel Prize nominee, came out in English from Bloodaxe in 2004, in my translation with Lidia Vianu.

I chose Sorescu's poem "Adam" not because it's about my Old Testament namesake but because it represents both the author's characteristic strengths and some typical translation issues. Part of Sorescu's popularity results from his approachable style, an anti-lyrical, unornamented lucidity in free verse (although he also wrote formal rhymed poems and a number of collections in village dialect); the manner he is famous for is ironically playful in method, sardonic in tone, irreverent in attitude. Sorescu's metaphysical imagination treats poems as teasing conundrums, each one a single metaphor that reaches outward with compressed meanings. "Poetry must be concise, almost algebraic," Sorescu writes in the afterword to *The Youth of Don Quixote*; the writer "is either a thinker or nothing." Elsewhere he explains, "Poetry . . . is the tongue under which we place the bitter medicines of life."

This directness of style that paradoxically gives rise to indirectness and allegory presents a translator with an initial problem, because these seemingly easy-to-translate poems too automatically fall into a literalness of equivalents, a kind of language-to-language paraphrase. Dictionary meanings can go far in conveying the gist of a Sorescu poem—the images and dramatic situation. Romanian colleagues jealous of his success in English and other European languages have complained—I myself heard this said over the years, always grudgingly—that Sorescu is a cinch to translate because he wrote in Esperanto. Paraphrase, however, is not poetry, and the quality of the original begins with Sorescu's verbal facility and naturalness of expression. Any Sorescu translation must face the dilemma of Oscar Wilde's quip, "To be natural is such a very difficult pose to keep up."

Let's look at the opening stanza of "Adam." Even "Google Translate" almost gets this; that is, if we allow for the madcap irrationality of its not adhering to the third-person singular protagonist, Adam, named in the second line, and its choice (if one can speak of choices) of "heaven" over the contextually right "paradise" or "Eden" for *rai* in line 1: "Although it [= he] is in heaven / Adam was walking on the footpath concerned and sad / Because they do [= he does] not know what's missing." This comes near enough to a rough sketch of the well-defined scene the poem starts with, but nowhere near to its charm. In contrast, a successful poetic translation has to arise from small, deft touches, not broad outlines. One can see such choices in the ways the adjectives and the verb get rendered. In David Constantine's rather free version of the poem (I'll refer to the three versions of "Adam" by their main translator, who surely would have had final authority over the English text), Adam "walked with his head down"; the translation embodies the mood in an action but treats the verb plainly—*plimba* means "walk," "stroll," or even "promenade." John F. Deane's Adam simply "strolled"; W. D. Snodgrass's first man, more vigorous if less nonchalant, "kept on prowling." Would Eden have had alleys or paths? The Romanian noun *alee* means both, and more. My own version of the poem toys with the third sense I mentioned for *plimba*: my Adam "paced the promenades." The third and final line of the opening stanza in Romanian, the line in the poem most like prose, prepares for Adam's motivation in this unfolding mini-drama. I admire Constantine's condensing many syllables into two words, "After something," although it's not the kind of radical rewording that I tend to use in my own translations. It keeps the poem moving, but so does Snodgrass's efficient "a-poetry-translation-should-be-at-least-as-well-written-as-prose" rendering (apologies to Ezra Pound). I can't help but think that Sorescu, who encouraged multiple variations of his poems (some included as paired translations in the 1987 book *The Biggest Egg in the World*), and who once offered both Neil Astley of Bloodaxe and me exclusive permission to translate one of his postcommunist books, must have relished these plural productions, too—like Adam with his bevy of Eves.

I won't trudge through all three versions belaboring line after line, but in passing I'll remark that it's second nature for translators to attend to multiple phrasings, connotations, and other nuances in these ways. Four other elements of "Adam" merit comment, however. The first is a single past-tense verb, Sorescu's *a confecționat*, to describe how God made Eve; yes, it's "manufactured" (Deane and Snodgrass) (or "made"—my three Romanian-English dictionaries agree on this pair—and I'll add "confected," its Latinate cognate), but "fleshed Eve" (Constantine) is a metaphorical extension. Probably, though, it should be "fashioned," for, in Romanian as in French, the word is associated with ready-made, off-the-rack apparel. Does the hint of "fashion" add anything to the Eves who busy themselves with their makeup and go shopping? I believe so.

The second element I'll emphasize is Sorescu's figurative language in the simile in the second stanza, after the poem moves along rather perkily to Adam's prestidigitation as imitator of his celestial creator's activity. Those breasts and thighs of successive Eves whom Adam brings forth not in sorrow but in obvious glee are "Like the contours of musical phrases," to quote Snodgrass's rendering of the line *Ca de contururi de note muzicale*. I think it's interesting that the original refers to the rounded shape of musical notes, and no version sticks to that. Translation is always an act of interpretation, interpretation an act of imagination. The simile, the only one in the poem, is strongly sensory, and the Eves' rising up has the music "round[ing] out" and the fingers "warmed" (Deane) in what I might term translator's synesthesia, perhaps from the Romanian *fulgerate*—an adjective (past participle) that derives from *fulger*, a "flash or glare or glitter, like lightning."

The third moment is to me most critical, a hinge for the entire poem. More or less in the middle of the poem, there's an embedded one-liner that encapsulates Adam's rebellious spirit, the sort of moment in which, in translating Sorescu, I'm always reminded that he was a skilled dramatist. What should Adam "sigh" in English ("sigh"? I hear it as a self-satisfied sigh) after he has conjured up yet another Eve? The line has to work as a minimalist showstopper. The Romanian idiom *Asta e viața* comes across as almost identical to that English idiom of resigned acceptance of something that can't be helped, "That's life." This is how Deane construes it, with "This is life," and so it often is in Romanian speech. There's a parallel possibility, however, for Sorescu's phrase contains the definite article embedded as the *a* (versus an *ă*) at the end of *viața*, that is, "That/this is the life." I agree with, no, I covet the way Snodgrass hits it off ("This is the life!")—so much so that once, when we happened to be together at the same festival in Romania while I was working on this poem, I told him, "I want to steal that line." He replied, "Go ahead." I didn't, and in my translation, challenged to capture the same complex emotion, I came up with "What a life!" The tone is right, but now I judge that the phrase is wrong. If I get a chance to reprint the translation, I'll make it Snodgrass's zinger, "This is the life!"—and convince myself I'm not swiping the phrase but using it in his memory.

Finally, how does one end the poem in English after the comic metaphor (combining Arabic plus Latin, no less) at the end of the penultimate stanza, *Din haremul lui intercostal*—"from his intercostal harem," a phrase that, who knows why, Constantine omits, to the poem's detriment, I'd argue. He writes, "Adam plucked at his cage," which at least extends the translation's implied stringed instrument. Deane, who notes in his introduction that he worked from English drafts—a trot, I assume, done by somebody for him—alongside German and Spanish translations, converts "intercostal" to "inter-rib." I can only guess that maybe this derives from a reluctance to accept a Latinate equivalent. Romanian is a Romance language, and translations with Latin roots sometimes spring to mind with little effort and even less thought. I constantly remind myself that Latin derivations are secondary to the Anglo-Saxon word-hoard of English. Yet occasionally the borrowings do make for more effective style, and in this instance the adjective should be odd. Similarly, at the end, Constantine (with an impulse toward simplification, or aversion to a direct cognate parallel to Deane's "inter-rib"?) omits the word "surrealism" (*suprarealism*). But surrealism, until not long before forbidden in Romania as degenerate bourgeois art, would have been a pointed reference in the 1960s. In any event, as the final stanza starts, the question I raise stems from a verb and its object: God did what? "noticed," "took note of," "got wise," or in cognate, observed. And saw what? "Too much imagination," chides Constantine's God, who morphs into a speaking character. Or the "immoderate" or "dissolute" "creation" that Deane and Snodgrass use for *creație deșănțată*.

We all know the end of this little tale: the expulsion. This is turned absurd, however: Sorescu's Adam gets thrown out of Eden alone—God ban-

ishes a third-person singular. Adam is sent off for his sin, but what was it? Or is this a case of divine envy, an Old Testament power trip by a jealous God? And was the representative man's first disobedience just a young man's escapade, or has it political implications? The poem doesn't feel political to me; it lacks the pointed evasions, the oblique storytelling, the clever camouflage I sometimes see in Sorescu. Also, it appeared before the bleak, repressive final two decades of Romanian communism, when Sorescu, whom George Szirtes praised as "the foxiest of poets," created a paradigm of duplicitous, implicitly subversive expression among censored East European literatures, a poetry full of the now-you-see-it-now-you-don't references that Romanians called "lizards": "We created codes in our struggle against censorship," Sorescu told my frequent co-translator Lidia Vianu in a 1991 interview. "These lizards are living animals. . . . knots of meaning, ambiguous messages." There was a silent compact that readers would understand every possible verbal hint as political and resistant. Nonetheless, I'm wary of taking Adam's existential insubordination too far. However we interpret it, the end of the parable of the Fall, according to Sorescu, is that God unambiguously "carpeted Adam" (Constantine), "called him in, magisterially chewed him out" (Snodgrass), or "divinely reproach[ed] him" (Deane, a weaker chastisement). My translation used "divinely gave him hell," but writing this commentary, it suddenly hit me that the phrase in English has got to be "gave him holy hell." *Shh*, don't tell a soul. I claim it for my "Adam." All these alternatives aim at the poet's wit and respect his tendency toward vernacular rather than formal diction, as well as demonstrate the intricacy of the decisions a translator has to make while keeping the poetry unforced, not to mention sharply delineated and funny where it needs to be.

One last point: the reader cannot help noticing that, while all three of these versions of Marin Sorescu's "Adam" in English are effective and praiseworthy, two of them (within a relatively narrow range of differences of synonyms and phrasing) stay close to literal, with creative touches here and there, whereas Constantine's defies Sorescu's form and takes liberties with the content of the original. His mode of translation lies within the category John Dryden defined in the seventeenth century and Robert Lowell revived in the twentieth: imitation, wherein the translator plays loose with both words and sense. In Constantine's "Adam," this goes only halfway: the lineaments of the original still are apparent. But the gap between Deane and Snodgrass on the one hand, and Constantine on the other, illustrates the range of intention in the practice of translation. I know of six English versions of the poem in print plus one posted somewhere on the Web, and David Constantine's is unique. This discrepancy raises an important question: what, finally, should one translate? The poet's words, or the inner poem? Hopefully, a good translator can be true to both. Whether with the surprise twist of "surrealism" being Adam's unpardonable sin (now, there's a devilish temptation!) or Constantine's borrowing God's final admonishment to Adam from (of all things) a nursery rhyme, "One, Two, Buckle My Shoe" ("Eleven, twelve, / Dig and delve"), these three English-language avatars of "Adam" end delightfully, with satirical comeuppance of human striving, shrewd ridicule of deceived authority, a genial, impish last line, and more—vintage Sorescu.

Constantine appends a parenthetical flourish. This farewell fillip provides a ready-made gesture of closure for the Adam who has written these comments, and so, with a wink: (Exit translator, strumming).

Félix Morisseau-Leroy

(Haitian Creole, 1912–1998)

TRANSLATIONS BY

Mary Birnbaum, David Brooks Andrews,
Molly Lynn Watt, Ruby Poltorak

....

COMMENTARY BY

Danielle Legros Georges

Mwen menm ou menm

Mwen menm ou menm li menm yo menm

Kan m di mwen se li menm

Lè m di li se ou

Yo se mwen se li se ou menm

Nou se nou menm menm

Nou tout fin vye lèd

Nou tout koupab kou inosan

Ak yon peyi sou bra n

Kou yon timoun malad.

Félix Morisseau-Leroy (1972)

Mwen menm ou menm

Mwen menm ou menm   **li menm**   **yo menm**

Me/I [myself] you [yourself]   he, him/she, her/it [himself/herself/itself] they/them [themselves]

li refers to either gender, and also to "it"

menm literally means "the same" but is used freely in Creole as an emphatic reiteration of what precedes it, e.g., *me, myself* or *the process, itself*

Kan   m   di   mwen   se   li menm

When   I   say   me/I   it is   he, him/she, her/it [himself/herself/itself]

m is an abbreviation of *mwen*

Lè   m di   li   se   ou

At the time at which/when   I   say   he, him/she, her/it   it is/are   you

Yo   se   mwen   se   li   se   ou menm

They   are/it is   me/I   are/is   he/him, she/her, it   are/is   you [yourself]

Nou   se   nou   menm   menm

We/us   are   we/us   ourselves   ourselves

Nou tout   fin   vye   lèd

We   all   have grown/ended up/   tired/beat up/old   ugly /(plural) "uglies"

Nou tout   koupab   kou   inosan

We   all (are)   culpable/guilty   as/like/   innocent(s)/the innocent

Ak   yon   peyi   sou   bra   n

With one/a   country   on top of/on/ in   arms/arm   (ours)

n is an abbreviation for *nou* we/us

Following a noun/subject, *nou* (and like pronouns) becomes possessive

Kou   yon   timoun   malad.

Like/as   one/a   child   sick/ill   Creole articles and adjectives can sometimes follow nouns.

trot by Danielle Legros Georges with Jean-Claude Martineau (2012)

I and You the Same

I—you   he—she—they—
When I say I, I mean he and she.
When I say he and she, I mean you.
We are we, all the same.
We have ended up worn-out and haggard.
We are all to blame like the innocent.
In our arms, one country—one country—
Like a weak, sick child.

translated by Mary Birnbaum (2012)

The Same

When I say it is he
I mean   he is you
they are me
they are he   they are you
we are the same   the same
grown weary and old
culpable as innocents
bearing the country
like we carry
our sick child

translated by Molly Lynn Watt (2012)

I myself, you yourself

I myself, you yourself, she herself, they themselves.

When I say I, it is she herself,
The moment when I say she, it is you.
They are me. It is she. It is you yourself.
We are us, ourselves, ourselves.
We all have grown tired, ugly.
We all are guilty as the innocent.
With one country in our arms
like a sick child.

translated by David Brooks Andrews (2012)

I, self

I, self   you, self   he and she, self   they, self
When I say me it is he and she, self
When I say he and she it is you
They are me is he is she is you, self
We is we, self, weself.
We all done got ol' an' ugly
We all guilty as innocent
Wid a country on we arm
Like a sick chil'

translated by Ruby Poltorak (2012)

The Personal and Shared Pronouns of Félix Morisseau-Leroy

Félix Morisseau-Leroy is a poet beloved by many Haitian poetry auditors and readers. The term "auditors" precedes "readers" because from the 1950s until Morisseau-Leroy died, in 1998, those who encountered his Haitian Creole poems for the first time often heard them broadcast via radio in Port-au-Prince and elsewhere in Haiti. Morisseau-Leroy also rode Haiti's diasporic airwaves, which reached across the ocean and connected Montreal and Miami, New York and Dakar, Boston and Kinshasa, Chicago and Havana, Santo Domingo and Nassau.

To write "auditors" is to emphasize the power of Haitian radio—and also to indicate a context in which print literacy and access to formal education have been a challenge for large numbers of Haitian citizens. To write "auditors" is to reveal the long arm of colonialism and its contribution to the country's poverty, achieved in part through an enduring policy of linguistic imperialism.

Haitian Creole, which emerged in the seventeenth century as an amalgam of West African languages and French, became Haiti's demotic or mother tongue. The French spoken and used by the seventeenth- and eigheenth-century European controllers of Saint-Domingue (Haiti's colonial designation), and later by a small minority, remained the only language recognized by the state through the late twentieth century. Creole, the language of almost all Haitians, was not allowed in primary and secondary schools until 1979, and didn't become widely recognized as an official state language (alongside French) until 1987.

Morisseau-Leroy's decision to use Creole as a language of literary production was a decidedly political one—one that initially met resistance in the country's influential and Francophone literary circles. As early as 1941, Morisseau-Leroy, a member of the intellectual elite (and then an emerging literary figure), tied the decision to use Creole to the quest for civic inclusion of all in the life of the nation. Arguing that Creole merited greater attention in the realms of education, culture, and literature, he began to create literary texts in the language. One of the first important Haitian writers to do so, he paved the way for his contemporaries and a following generation of Creole-language Haitian writers, creating an aesthetic space for texts that celebrated and reflected historically marginalized Haitian Creole concerns, culture, and identity.

———

"Mwen menm ou menm" is one of Morisseau-Leroy's lesser-known poems. Its nine short lines bear the title, roughly, "Me/I You," which heralds the straightforwardness of the poem's language and poetics. Morisseau-Leroy was writing deliberately for the common woman, man, and child. The title suggests a pair: a speaker and an addressee. A relationship is drawn immediately, as is the possibility of a dialogue. What the poet gives us, however, is a monologue that speaks others into being. The poem's first line ("Me/I," "you" "he/she/it," "they") consists of a simple list of pronouns. The speaker's addressee, "you," is joined by a "he" or a "she" and a "they"—with each term standing alongside the others and giving way to the next. Lines 2 and 3 ("When I say me, I mean her/him, / when I say him/her it's you") introduce and expand the important notion of interchangeability and boundarylessness in the poem.

The poem's fifth and central line finally articulates a previously tacit "we"—anchoring the concept of the collective, the condition beyond the individual. Here time and space shift, and the speaker's perspective becomes an analytic one. Functioning as a pivot, this line effects a transition toward the poem's second thesis: shared history. This history, referenced but not elaborated on, has resulted in the "old ugliness" of the community. A paradoxical statement follows, labeling the community as both culpable and innocent. To render these abstractions of guilt and goodness concrete, Morisseau-Leroy gives us the image of a sick child in "our arms"—and a powerful metaphor: the child becomes a country. "We" (the collective) then instantly become the custodians of that child, in addition to being bearers of the scars of history.

Morisseau-Leroy adopts a nationalist stance but takes care to begin his poem with the subjective, autonomous "myself" before progressing to common concerns. Privileging neither the individual nor the social being, he evokes a more durable form of social organization than the state. Moreover, while the poem falls within the *engagée* tradition, its political nature is not the poem's only consideration. Aesthetics matter, and Morisseau-Leroy's singular use of syntax, attention to structure, and use of poetic elements are apparent.

Morisseau-Leroy's leitmotifs—the connections between individuals, the weight of history, the implication of the individual in the civic, and parental and collective responsibility—find expression in a poem that is more for the ear than the mind's eye. Its formal aspects lean toward the lyrical. Less painter than sculptor, less photographer than drummer, Morisseau-Leroy engages in a rhythmic chiseling out of content, a building up of metaphysical structure through a litany of pronouns, each followed by the reflexive *menm*, or "self." Appearing ten times in the poem (including the title), *menm* also modifies, with each appearance, a different self. Here are sameness and difference simultaneously. Here are repetitions and a parallelism that allow for great nuance. Discovery and literacy are also implied. Evoked in the utterance and repetition of pronouns is early education: our first incremental lessons in declension and exposures to the architecture of language.

"Mwen menm ou menm" is built almost entirely of monosyllabic words. These reinforce the poem's feeling of simplicity. This pattern is broken in the last three lines, as the poem's language becomes more figurative. Read in Creole and scanned, the poem reveals a first line of four iambic feet, an opening incantatory rhythm that begets a heterogeneous (and wild) company of anapests, trochees, iambs, and spondees—a diverse community, as it were, of metric feet, as if to echo the community of selves the poem's content conveys.

In 2012 I taught an Introduction to Literary Translation seminar in the annual Writers' Workshop of the William Joiner Institute for the Study of War and Social Consequences (housed at the University of Massachusetts, Boston). I placed "Mwen menm ou menm" on a list of poems to be considered by students for two reasons: first, because of Morisseau-Leroy's exploration of colonial legacies, neocolonial or postcolonial challenges, and general commitment to issues of social justice, and second because it presents students with a particular semantic puzzle.

Almost every text meant for translation, I believe, contains at least one major challenge. With "Mwen menm ou menm" we were confronted with the conundrum of how to tackle the small but mighty word *li*, which appears four times in the short poem. The translation of *li* was the focus and purpose of our class exercise.

Li is the third-person-singular pronoun: "he," "she," or "it." It is gender-neutral: we have no way of knowing whether a "he," "she," or "it" is signified. (English, of course, does not contain the equivalent pronominal gender freedom.) To confound matters, *li*, in addition to serving as a subject, can also operate as an object, i.e., "her," "him," or "it." (Finally, and unrelated to this poem, *li* also means "to read." Three *li*s in a row can mean, among other things, [a] "She read it," [b] "read, read, read," or [c] "him, him, him.") What to do with a signifier with so many signifieds?

Words, of course, do not exist in isolation. Context, then, became especially important to us and to an elegant translation of *li*. I felt it was important for us to maintain fidelity to what noted literary translator Edith Grossman, in *Why Translation Matters*, calls the "the implications and echoes of the first author's tone, intention, and level of discourse." Good translations, she writes, "are good because they are faithful to this contextual significance." The social conditions in and against which Morisseau-Leroy's work was produced (articulated earlier in this essay) would be vital to our understanding and translation of *li* and of "Mwen menm ou menm" in general.

The poem's first line gives us the first *li*. The line translates roughly as "Me/I you he/she/it they"—with my underscored text representing the possibilities for *li*. Here translators had to make a choice—would *li* become the masculine pronoun "he" or "him"? Would it become the feminine "she" or "her"? Would *li* become "he and she," "her and him," or some variation of the aforementioned? Turning *li* into "it" seemed to us an ungainly choice and a removal from the realm of the human—one that no one in the class (thank goodness) made. Equally awful would have been allowing the rough gang of "he, she, it" or "him, her, it" onto the line—an error the students (many seasoned writers but new to translation) had the good sense to avoid.

Here is what happened. Mary Birnbaum and Ruby Poltorak replaced *li* with "he and she," Molly Lynn Watt chose "he," and David Brooks Andrews elected "she." The implications? The translations including both genders present us with more individuals: the speaker and at least two others. The strong notion of community embedded in the original is foregrounded as a result. Birnbaum reinforces the idea of a collective, and by extension a nation, with a repetition in her text: "In our arms, one country—one country." The Watt and Andrews texts imply a dyad and intimate space—the exchanges of a couple. The original title, roughly "Me/I You," is echoed in this choice, as is the idea of guardianship that appears at the poem's end. Watt's translation deepens the concept, explicitly articulating it as parenthood. The original's last two lines, roughly "with a country in our arms / like a sick child," beautifully become, in her translation, "bearing the country / like we carry / our sick child." Morisseau-Leroy's original simile is actualized and rendered immediate within the context of a made family. Both sets of choices—whether highlighting the civic or the private sphere, the communal or the familial—mirror the *spirit* of the original.

An interesting side note: Andrews, a man, makes *li* feminine—and Watts renders her *li* masculine. I am presuming a (perhaps unconscious) heteronormativity as an informing impulse in their decisions. If this is the case, does the lack of gender in the "we" of Birnbaum and Poltorak, both women, represent a gesture of inclusivity, a choice to privilege the collective, as I have suggested above?

Despite possible differences in approach, each of the translators finds a way to reflect the closeness, borderlessness, and reflexivity in the original, its impulse toward unification. The means by which we consider ourselves attached, and how this finds expression, emerge in the different translations. They serve to illustrate that we bring our whole selves to any literary encounter, which calls to mind translator David Bellos's principle of the "variability of translations [as] incontrovertible evidence of the limitless flexibility of human minds." "Give a hundred competent translators a page to translate," he notes, "and the chances of any two versions being identical are close to zero."

As regards the title, Birnbaum takes a liberty, calling her English translation "I and You the Same." While reflecting the original's dyad, she underscores the sense of sameness and equity the poem is exploring. "The Same" does not appear in the original title, but the poem relies on the idea.

Morisseau-Leroy's strategy is slippage, one pronoun morphing into the next. This slippage is reinforced in Birnbaum's first line through the use of dashes that connect and at the same time render discrete each pronoun.

Andrews's title "I myself, you yourself," remains closer to the original, taking into account each of its words, including the reflexive *menm*. While not necessary, "myself" and "yourself" operate as echoes, expansions of the self. Furthermore, "I" and "you" are each given a similar suffix—each carries or is followed by some sort of "self."

Watt takes the greatest leap in interpreting Morisseau-Leroy's title. She gives us "The Same." This title serves as summary more than translation—which, of course, raises the question of what a translation ought to do. Here the overarching meaning or the spirit of the text takes over. A second surprise: Watt does not include the poem's first line and goes straight to the original's second line. Compression, naturally, is the result—and this economy and tightness are seen through to the end. Watt's universe privileges the nuclear family; hers is a private, small world. A simplicity seems to guide her approach—and the poem stays true to this simplicity. Her intimate tone is reinforced with the non-capitalization of the beginnings of all but the first two lines, reminiscent of the poems of Lucille Clifton, poems that are, like Morisseau-Leroy's poem, often both intensely personal and political.

Poltorak's title, "I, self," keeps the original's speaker, but disappears its addressee. While her title is befuddling, her choice of an interpretative framework is unusual and daring: she translates Morisseau-Leroy's Haitian Creole into an English Creole. The Creole Morisseau-Leroy was using existed in a context in which one could not avoid the power of French. In the same way, the English Creole used by Poltorak sets itself against standard English, and in an inchoate way shares and underscores the original's sense of political and linguistic context. We readers of Poltorak's translation know we are reading an English different from the sort that appears in textbooks and other formal texts—and understand that there is meaning in this choice. Initially this translation felt to me like a strange simulation, but the more I read it, the more her choices make sense to me—and I suspect Félix Morisseau-Leroy might appreciate it, too, looking at us, as some Haitians might say, from "the other side of the water."

Acknowledgments

The editors wish to thank the University of Houston for a project completion grant that helped support the production of this book. We would also like to thank Jeff Shotts, Katie Dublinski, and the rest of the Graywolf staff for their support of this book. Martha Collins would also like to thank Marc Levy and Rick Hilles, whose comments prompted consideration of the project long before it became viable. And thanks as well to Rosanna Warren, Eliot Weinberger, Marcia Karp, and Jessica Cohen for their suggestions and help, and to Jia-xiu Pan for her calligraphy of "Returning to Fields and Gardens" by Tao Qian.

Thanks as well to the *Massachusetts Review* for publishing Danielle Legros Georges's contribution.

Adonis, "Thunderbolt" in the original Arabic language version is reprinted here by permission of Dar Al Saqi. All rights remain with the original Arabic rights holder.

Adonis, "Thunderbolt" from *Mihyar of Damascus: His Songs*, translated by Adnan Haydar and Michael Beard. Translation copyright © 2008 by Adnan Haydar and Michael Beard. Reprinted with the permission of BOA Editions, Ltd., www.boaeditions.org.

Adonis, "Thunderbolt": translated by Samuel Hazo. Originally published in *Transformations of the Lover*, Byblos Editions VII, 1982. Reprinted by permission of Samuel Hazo. All rights reserved.

Adonis, "Thunderbolt": translated by Khaled Mattawa. Originally published in English in *Selected Poems*, Yale University Press, 2010. Reprinted by permission of Yale University Press.

Anna Akhmatova, "Last Meeting," translated by Stephen Berg: from *With Akhmatova at the Black Gates: Variations*. Copyright 1981 by Stephen Berg. Used with permission of the University of Illinois Press.

Anna Akhmatova's "Song of the final meeting": translated by Andrey Kneller. Copyright 2008 by Andrey Kneller. Reprinted by permission of Andrey Kneller.

Anna Akhmatova, "Song of the Last Meeting," translated by Gerard Shelley first appeared in *Modern Poems from Russia*, Allen & Unwin, 1942. Reprinted by permission of The Taylor & Francis Group. All rights reserved.

Yehuda Amichai's "רחמים מלא אל" reprinted by permission of Schocken Publishing House, Ltd.

Yehuda Amichai's "O Lord Full of Mercy," translated by Glenda Abramson, first appeared in *The Writing of Yehuda Amichai: A Thematic Approach* (State University of New York Press, 1989) and is reprinted here by permission of The State University of New York Press.

Yehuda Amichai's "God Full of Mercy": translated by Robert Alter. Originally published in English in *The Poetry of Yehuda Amichai*, Farrar, Straus and Giroux, 2015. Reprinted by permission of Farrar, Straus and Giroux.

Yehuda Amichai's "God Full of Mercy": translated by Benjamin and Barbara Harshav. Originally published in English in *Yehuda Amichai: A Life in Poetry*, HarperCollins, 1994. Reprinted by permission of Hana Amichai.

Matsuo Bashō's untitled haiku, translated by Nobuyuki Yuasa: from *The Narrow Road to the Deep North and Other Travel Sketches* by Matsuo Bashō, translated with an introduction by Nobuyuki Yuasa (Penguin Classics, 1966). Copyright © Nobuyuki Yuasa, 1966.

Charles Baudelaire's "A Prankster": translated by Rosemary Lloyd. Originally published in English in *The Prose Poems and La Fanfarlo*, Oxford University Press, 2001. Reprinted by permission of Oxford University Press.

Charles Baudelaire's "A Wag": translated by Louise Varèse, from *Paris Spleen*, copyright © 1947 by New Directions Publishing Corp. Reprinted by permission of New Directions Publishing Corp.

About the Contributors

Kareem James Abu-Zeid's most recent translations include Najwan Darwish's *Nothing More to Lose*, Dunya Mikhail's *The Iraqi Nights*, and Rabee Jaber's *Confessions*. His distinctions include residencies from the Lannan Foundation and the Banff Centre, a Fulbright Fellowship, and *Poetry* magazine's 2014 translation prize. He holds a PhD and an MA in comparative literature from UC Berkeley and a BA from Princeton University. He also translates from French and German.

Distinguished professor of comparative literature at Indiana University, Guggenheim fellow, and nominee for four Pulitzer prizes, **Willis Barnstone** authored *The Poetics of Translation: History, Theory, Practice, The Gnostic Bible, Border of a Dream: Selected Poems, Mexico in My Heart: New and Selected Poems, The Restored New Testament, The Poems of Jesus Christ, Poets of the Bible: From Solomon's Song of Songs to John's Revelation*, and many other books.

Chana Bloch's *Swimming in the Rain: New and Selected Poems, 1980–2015* includes work from *The Secrets of the Tribe, The Past Keeps Changing, Mrs. Dumpty*, and *Blood Honey*. The former director of creative writing at Mills College and the first poetry editor of *Persimmon Tree*, Bloch co-translated the biblical Song of Songs and Israeli poets Yehuda Amichai and Dahlia Ravikovitch. New poems of hers have appeared in the *New Yorker, The Best American Poetry 2015*, and *Pushcart Prize XL*.

Karen Emmerich is a translator from modern Greek and an assistant professor of comparative literature at Princeton University. Her monograph *Literary Translation and the Making of Originals* is forthcoming. Her translations have received honors and awards from the National Endowment for the Arts, PEN America, and the Modern Greek Studies Association.

Danielle Legros Georges is the author of two volumes of poetry, *The Dear Remote Nearness of You* and *Maroon*. She is translating from the French the early twentieth-century poems of Ida Faubert, now considered a Haitian literary foremother. She is a professor in the Creative Arts in Learning Division of Lesley University and poet laureate of the city of Boston.

Johannes Göransson is the author of six books of poetry (most recently *The Sugar Book*) and the essay "Transgressive Circulation," about translation. He is the translator of several volumes of poetry, including books by the Swedish poets Aase Berg, Henry Parland, and Ann Jäderlund, and the Korean poet Kim Yideum. He is an editor at Action Books and teaches in the University of Notre Dame MFA program.

Joanna Trzeciak Huss is associate professor of translation studies at Kent State University. Her translations have appeared in the *New York Times*, the *New Yorker, TLS, Harper's Magazine*, the *Atlantic*, and the *Paris Review*. *Miracle Fair: Selected Poems of Wisława Szymborska* was awarded the Heldt Prize. *Sobbing Superpower: Selected Poems of Tadeusz Różewicz*, shortlisted for the Griffin Poetry Prize, received the Found in Translation Award and the AATSEEL Award for Best Literary Translation into English. She has been the recipient of IREX, NEH, and Fulbright fellowships.

George Kalogeris is the author of *Dialogos: Paired Poems in Translation*, and of a book of poems based on the notebooks of Albert Camus, *Camus: Carnets*. His poems and translations are anthologized in *Joining Music with Reason: 34 Poets, British and American*, edited by Christopher Ricks. He teaches English literature and classics in translation at Suffolk University.

J. Kates has been awarded three National Endowment for the Arts Translation Fellowships, a New Hampshire State Council on the Arts Fellowship in poetry, and the Cliff Becker Book Prize. His books include three chapbooks and one full book of poems. His translations include books by Tatiana Shcherbina, Mikhail Aizenberg, Jean-Pierre Rosnay, Regina Derieva, Aleksey Porvin, Nikolai Baitov, Genrikh Sapgir, Sergey Stratanovsky, and two anthologies of Russian poetry. A former president of the American Literary Translators Association, he is also a co-translator of Latin American poetry.

Alexis Levitin translates works from Portugal, Brazil, and Ecuador. His forty books of translation include Clarice Lispector's *Soulstorm* and Eugenio de Andrade's *Forbidden Words*. In 2010, he edited *Brazil: A Traveler's Literary Companion*. His other books include *Blood of the Sun* and *Tiger Fur*, both by Brazilian poet Salgado Maranhão. One of his most recent translations is Sophia de Mello Breyner Andresen's *Exemplary Tales*.

Bonnie S. McDougall is honorary associate in Chinese Studies at the University of Sydney and professor emeritus at the University of Edinburgh. She has written extensively on modern Chinese literature, and has translated poetry, fiction, drama, letters, essays, and film scripts by Bei Dao, Gu Cheng, Ah Cheng, Chen Kaige, Lu Xun, Mao Zedong, Wang Anyi, Yu Dafu, Leung Ping-kwan, Dung Kai-cheung, and many others.

Jennifer Moxley is the author of six books of poetry, a book of essays, and a memoir. Her 2014 book, *The Open Secret*, won the William Carlos Williams Award and was a finalist for the Kingsley Tufts Poetry Award. She has translated three books from the French: Jacqueline Risset's *Sleep's Powers* and *The Translation Begins*, and Anne Portugal's *Absolute Bob*. In 2013 she served as a panelist for the National Endowment for the Arts Translation Fellowships.

Carl Phillips's most recent book of poems, *Reconnaissance*, won the Lambda Literary Award and the PEN Center USA's Poetry Award. He has translated Sophocles's *Philoctetes* and written two books of prose, most recently *The Art of Daring: Risk, Restlessness, Imagination*. Phillips is a professor of English at Washington University in St. Louis, Missouri.

Hiroaki Sato has published three dozen translations of Japanese poems. *From the Country of Eight Islands: An Anthology of Japanese Poetry*, co-translated with Burton Watson, won the PEN Translation Prize. *Persona: A Biography of Yukio Mishima*, is his greatly expanded adaptation in English of Naoki Inose's book about the same author. He writes a monthly column for the *Japan Times*, "The View from New York."

Cindy Schuster's translations of Latin American writers, including Rodolfo Walsh, José Emilio Pacheco, Ena Lucía Portela, and Mario Bellatin, have appeared in numerous journals and anthologies. She is co-translator, with Dick Cluster, of *Cubana: Contemporary Fiction by Cuban Women*. She was awarded a Translation Fellowship from the National Endowment for the Arts and was a winner of the Loft Mentor Series in Poetry and Creative Prose. She holds a Ph.D. in Spanish from the University of California, Irvine.

Rebecca Seiferle has translated César Vallejo's *The Black Heralds*, and her translation of Vallejo's *Trilce* was a finalist for the PEN/West Translation Award. Her translations of various poets are included in *The Whole Island: Six Decades of Cuban Poetry* and *Reversible Monuments: Contemporary Mexican Poetry*. Seiferle is the author of the poetry collection *Wild Tongue*, which won the Grub Street National Book Prize in Poetry, and *Bitters*, which won the Western States Book Award.

Adam J. Sorkin has published more than fifty books of Romanian translations and has won numerous awards, including the Poetry Society (U.K.) Translation Prize for Marin Sorescu's *The Bridge*, the Kenneth Rexroth Memorial Translation Prize, the Ioan Flora Translation Prize, and the Poesis Translation Prize. His most recent book is *The Hunchbacks' Bus* by Nora Iuga, translated with Diana Manole; forthcoming are *Syllables of Flesh* by Floarea Țuțuianu, translated with Irma Giannetti, and *Eclogue* by Ioana Ieronim, translated with the author.

Susan Stewart's six books of poems include *Columbarium*, winner of the National Book Critics Circle Award, *Red Rover*, and *Cinder: New and Selected Poems*. Her translations and co-translations include Euripides's *Andromache*, Alda Merini's *Love Lessons*, Laudomia Bonanni's *The Reprisal*, and Milo De Angelis's *Theme of Farewell and After-Poems*, which was shortlisted for the American Literary Translators Association National Translation Award. She is the Avalon Foundation University Professor in the Humanities at Princeton University and a MacArthur Fellow and member of the American Academy of Arts and Sciences.

Cole Swensen is the author of seventeen collections of poetry; her work has won the Iowa Poetry Prize, the New American Writing Award, and an award from the National Poetry Series. Also a translator, she won the 2004 PEN Center USA Literary Award for Translation and has been a finalist three times for the Best Translated Book Award and once for the National Translation Award. She divides her time between Paris and Providence, Rhode Island.

Arthur Sze has published nine books of poetry, including *Compass Rose*, *The Ginkgo Light*, *Quipu*, *The Redshifting Web: Poems 1970–1998*, and *Archipelago*. His honors include the Jackson Poetry Prize, a Lannan Literary Award, a Lila Wallace–Reader's Digest Writers' Award, a Guggenheim Fellowship, two National Endowment for the Arts Fellowships, and an American Book Award. His book of translations, *The Silk Dragon: Translations from the Chinese*, received a Western States Book Award.

Stephen Tapscott is the author of four books of poems and a book of criticism, the editor of *Twentieth-Century Latin American Poetry: A Bilingual Anthology*, and the translator of works by Pablo Neruda and Gabriela Mistral (Spanish), Marina Tsvetaeva (Russian), Max Kratochwill and Georg Trakl (German), and others. He works at MIT in Cambridge, Massachusetts.

Alissa Valles is the author of the poetry collections *Orphan Fire* and *Anastylosis*. She edited and co-translated Zbigniew Herbert's *Collected Poems 1956–1998* and *Collected Prose 1948–1998*. Her translation of Ryszard Krynicki's *Our Life Grows* is forthcoming in 2017.

Sidney Wade's sixth collection of poems, *Straits and Narrows*, was published in April 2013. Her seventh, *Bird Book*, is forthcoming in late 2017. She has served as president of the Association of Writers and Writing Programs and secretary/treasurer of the American Literary Translators Association and has taught workshops in poetry and translation at the University of Florida's MFA@FLA program for twenty-three years. Her translation, with Efe Murad, of the selected poems of Melih Cevdet Anday won the Meral Divitçi Prize and will be published in 2017.

Poet and translator **Ellen Doré Watson** directs the Poetry Center at Smith College and has translated a dozen books from Brazilian Portuguese, notably poetry by Adélia Prado, the most recent of which, *The Mystical Rose*, was shortlisted for the Popescu European Poetry Translation Prize. A recipient of a National Endowment for the Arts Translation Fellowship and the author of five books of poems, she is an editor at the *Massachusetts Review* and teaches at the Drew University MFA in Poetry Program.

David Young is the author of eleven poetry collections, most recently *Field of Light and Shadow: Selected and New Poems*. His translations include Rainer Maria Rilke, Günter Eich, and Celan from German; Miroslav Holub from Czech; Petrarch and Eugenie Montale from Italian; Pablo Neruda from Spanish; Du Fu, Du Mu, Yu Xuanji, and others from classical Chinese; and Bashō from Japanese. He has also authored literary criticism on Shakespeare, Yeats, and modernist poetry. He is coeditor of *FIELD* magazine and of Oberlin College Press.

About the Editors

Martha Collins is the author of eight books of poetry, including *Admit One: An American Scrapbook*, *Day Unto Day*, *White Papers*, and *Blue Front*. She has also published four collections of co-translated Vietnamese poems, most recently *Black Stars: Poems by Ngo Tu Lap*, as well as translations from Spanish, German, Italian, and French. She has taught both undergraduate and graduate translation workshops, and has published essays on the art of literary translation. She is editor-at-large for *FIELD* magazine, and one of the translation editors for Oberlin College Press.

Kevin Prufer is the author of six collections of poems, most recently *Churches*, *In a Beautiful Country*, and *National Anthem*. He has also served as coeditor of numerous volumes, including *New European Poets* and *Literary Publishing in the Twenty-First Century*. Cocurator of the Unsung Masters Series (which brings great, out-of-print authors to new readers), Prufer teaches in the Creative Writing Program at the University of Houston and at Lesley University's Low-Residency MFA Program.

The text of *Into English* is set in Arno Pro.
Book design by Rachel Holscher.
Composition by Bookmobile Design and
Digital Publisher Services, Minneapolis, Minnesota.
Manufactured by Versa Press on acid-free,
30 percent postconsumer wastepaper.